# Critical Features of Piaget's Theory of the Development of Thought

Edited by
Frank B. Murray
University of Delaware

MSS Information Corporation
655 Madison Avenue, New York, N.Y. 10021

This is a custom-made book of readings prepared for the courses taught by the editor, as well as for related courses and for college and university libraries. For information about our program, please write to:

MSS INFORMATION CORPORATION
655 Madison Avenue
New York, New York 10021

MSS wishes to express its appreciation to the authors of the articles in this collection for their cooperation in making their work available in this format.

**Library of Congress Cataloging in Publication Data**

Murray, Frank B comp.
Critical features of Piaget's theory of the development of thought.

1. Cognition (Child psychology) 2. Piaget, Jean, 1896- I. Title.
BF723.C5M87 153.4'13 72-6359
ISBN 0-8422-5046-8
ISBN 0-8422-0244-7 (pbk.)

# CONTENTS

# PART I: OVERVIEW AND INTRODUCTION

# Piaget Rediscovered

Eleanor Duckworth

Everybody in education realizes that Piaget is saying something that is relevant to the teaching of children. For the most part he is understood to be underestimating the value of teaching. He is understood to be saying something like this: Children go through certain stages of intellectual development from birth through adolescence. These stages materialize, fully constructed, when their time has come, and there is little we can do to advance them. What we must do in education is to realize the limits of children's understanding at certain ages, and plan our teaching so it falls within these limits.

In two recent conferences, one at Cornell, one at Berkeley, Piaget made clear that the implications of his psychology for education are a good deal more fecund than this. In fact, the only one of these statements that he would support is that children go through certain stages of intellectual development. Contrary to the view most often attributed to him, he maintains that good pedagogy *can* have an effect on this development.

I will start with the essentials of Piaget's theory of intellectual development, as presented at these conferences, and then go on to some implications for education.

Development of intellectual capacity goes through a number of stages whose order is constant, but whose time of appearance may vary both with the individual and with the society. Each new level of development is a new coherence, a new structuring of elements which until that time have not been systematically related to each other.

Piaget discussed four factors contributing to this development: nervous maturation, encounters with experience, social transmission, and equilibration or auto-regulation. While the first three do indeed play a role, Piaget finds each of them insufficient in itself. His findings lead him to conclude that an individual's intellectual development is a process of equilibration, where the individual himself is the active motor and coordinator of his own development.

What the first three factors have in common is that the individual is passive. Something is done *to* him; his physiological system matures, or he is presented with physical or linguistic material to absorb. But intellectual development is not this passive. Piaget finds it necessary to call upon the factor of the individual's own activity. An individual learns to see the world as coherent, as structured, to the extent that he acts upon the world, transforms it, and succeeds in coordinating these actions and transformations.

Development proceeds as partial understandings are revised, broadened, and related to one another. Piaget's model for this is one of auto-regulation to attain even broader and more stable equilibrium in the individual's dealing with his world.

As far as education is concerned, the chief

JOURNAL OF RESEARCH IN SCIENCE TEACHING, 1964, Vol. 2, pp. 172-175.

outcome of this theory of intellectual development is a plea that children be allowed to do their own learning. Piaget is not saying that intellectual development proceeds at its own pace no matter what you try to do. He is saying that what schools usually try to do is ineffectual. You cannot further understanding in a child simply by talking to him. Good pedagogy must involve presenting the child with situations in which he himself experiments in the broadest sense of that term—trying things out to see what happens, manipulating things, manipulating symbols, posing questions and seeking his own answers, reconciling what he finds at one time with what he finds at another, and comparing his findings with those of other children.

Beyond this general implication, Piaget does not claim to be an educator. During the course of the two conferences he made no single discourse on pedagogy. But he made a number of points which I have gathered together here. Most of them are not new ideas, but it seems to me that it is of importance, somehow, to realize that this is what he is saying.

I shall start with comments on one or two teaching practices often associated with Piaget's name because of some relationships to his research. One is the head-on attack on a specific notion in a precise and limited way. This is the type of attack engaged in by psychological experimenters, in trying to teach four- and five-year-olds, for example, that the amount of liquid stays the same when poured into a glass of a different shape. (In Piaget's own research, when a child asserts that the same amount of liquid is conserved, this is taken as an indication of a certain structure of mental operations. For this reason, performance on this task is an important indicator of intellectual level.)

Piaget sees little sense in intensive specific training on tasks like this one. His feeling is that no learning of significance will take place. Even if the child does manage to learn something about this situation, the learning is not likely to have a general effect on his level of understanding.

But notice that he is *not* thereby saying that a young child's mental structure cannot be touched. He is only saying that this type of specific attack is rather trivial. Modifying a child's effective set of mental operations depends on a much wider, longer-lasting, and fundamental approach which involves all of the child's activity.

Piaget amplified this point about the importance of investigative activity in general in reply to a question on cross-cultural comparisons. Montreal psychologists, using Piaget's material as tests, found children in Martinique to be delayed several years compared to children in Montreal. Similarly, there is a significant delay of children in Iranian villages over children in Iranian cities. Piaget was asked what factors in the adult societies might account for these differences.

In reply, he first pointed out that the schools in Martinique follow the same curriculum as the schools in France, so that scholastic preparation was not likely to account for the difference. Then he quoted the psychologist who had done the research in Martinique, who pointed out that the climate is fine, agriculture flourishes, and living poses few problems. There seems to be little call for questioning and struggling for solutions in general, little call for either physical or intellectual activity. Piaget speculated that this could be the significant factor.

Another pedagogical approach often associated with Piaget's name has to do with teaching the "structure" of a subject matter area. This has been associated with him because of the importance that mental structures play in his psychological theory. The word "structure" is seized upon as the link.

The pedagogical idea is that children should be taught the unifying themes of a subject matter area, after which they will be able to relate individual items to this general structure. (This seems to be what Bruner often means by 'teaching the structure' in *The Process of Education*.) Commenting on this procedure, Piaget made the following statement:

> The question comes up whether to teach the structure, or to present the child with situations where he is active and creates the structures himself. . . . The goal in education is not to increase the amount of knowledge, but to create the possibilities for a child to invent and discover. When we teach too fast, we keep the child from inventing and discovering himself. . . . Teaching means creating situations where structures can be discovered; it does not mean transmitting structures which may be assimilated at nothing other than a verbal level.

Piaget addressed two remarks to problems of teacher training. The first is that adults, as well as children, can learn better by doing things than by being told about them. He was talking about teachers in training, when he said, "If they read about it, it will be deformed, as is all learning that is not the results of the subject's own activity."

The second is that prospective teachers ought to spend some time questioning children in a one-to-one situation, in order to realize how hard it is to understand what children mean, and even more, how hard it is to make oneself understood by children. Each prospective teacher should work on an original investigation to find out what children think about some problem, and thus be forced to phrase the problem and establish communication with a number of different children. Facing the difficulties of this type of research will have a sobering effect on a teacher who thinks he is talking successfully to a whole class of children at once.

Permit me one other point of psychological theory as context for another of Piaget's remarks. Piaget sees the process of equilibration as a process of balance between assimilation and accommodation in a biological sense. An individual assimilates the world which comes down to saying he sees it in his own way. But sometimes something presents itself in such a way that he cannot assimilate it into his view of things, so he must change his view; he must accommodate if he wants to incorporate this new item.

The question arose in this conference as to whether school situations could lead a child to accommodate wrongly, that is, to change his ideas on the wrong basis. Piaget replied:

> This is a very interesting question. This is a big danger of school—false accommodation which satisfies a child because it agrees with a verbal formula he has been given. This is a false equilibrium which satisfies a child by accommodating to words—to authority and not to objects as they present themselves to him. . . . A teacher would do better not to correct a child's schemas, but to provide situations so he will correct them himself.

Here are a few other remarks at random:

> Experience is always necessary for intellectual development. . . . But I fear that we may fall into the illusion that being submitted to an experience (a demonstration) is sufficient for a subject to disengage the structure involved. But more than this is required. The subject must be active, must transform things, and find the structure of his own actions on the objects.

> When I say "active," I mean it in two senses. One is acting on material things. But the other means doing things in social collaboration, in a group effort. This leads to a critical frame of mind, where children must communicate with each other. This is an essential factor in intellectual development. Cooperation is indeed co-operation.
>
> (The role of social interaction is important in Piaget's theory of development. A characteristic phenomenon in intellectual difficulties of pre-school children is that they have difficulty conceiving of any point of view other than their own. Coming to an awareness that another child sees something differently from the way he sees it plays an important role in bringing a child to accommodate, to rebuild his point of view, and to come closer to a coherent operational structure.)

> The best idea I have heard from a pedagog at the International Bureau of Education in Geneva was made by a Canadian. He said that in his province they had just decided every class should have two classrooms—one where the teacher is, and one where the teacher isn't.

> The teacher must provide the instruments which the children can use to decide things by themselves. Children themselves must verify, experimentally in physics, deductively in mathematics. A ready-made truth is only a half-truth.

One participant asked what Piaget thought of having children of different ages in a class together. He replied that it might be helpful especially for the older ones. They could be given some responsibility of teaching younger ones. "Nobody knows better than a professor that the best way to learn something is to teach it."

Yes, the element of surprise is an essential motor in education and in scientific research in general. What distinguishes a good scientist is that he is amazed by things which seem natural to others. Surprise plays an important role; we might well try to develop an aptitude for surprise.

Words are probably not a short-cut to a better understanding. . . .The level of understanding seems to modify the language that is used, rather than vice versa. . .Mainly, language serves to translate what is already understood; or else language may even present a danger if it is used to introduce an idea which is not yet accessible.

The principle goal of education is to create men who are capable of doing new things, not simply repeating what other generations have done—men who are creators, inventors, and discoverers. The second goal of education is to form minds which can be critical, can verify, and do not accept everything they are offered. The great danger today is from slogans, collective opinions, ready-made trends of thought. We have to be able to resist individually, to criticize, to distinguish between what is proven and what is not. So we need pupils who are active, who learn early to find out by themselves, partly by their own spontaneous activity and partly through material we set up for them; who learn early to tell what is verifiable and what is simply the first idea to come to them.

# JEAN PIAGET AND THE WORLD OF THE CHILD [1]

READ D. TUDDENHAM [2]

*University of California, Berkeley*

WE have gathered today to honor the University of Geneva on its four hundredth anniversary. As a citizen of a nation not yet 200 years old—and as a member of a University which has not quite rounded out its first century of service, I feel considerable awe at a city state which measures its age in millenia, and at a University which has endured 4 centuries—a University so venerable that in comparison our oldest American university is young. I am sure I speak not only for myself, but for generations of foreign students at Geneva, in expressing gratitude for the intellectual stimulation and opportunity for growth which Geneva has for so long offered to so many.

For many visitors, the central symbol of Geneva is the Palais des Nations—home of the League and now of the United Nations, impressive both as a building and as the objectification of an ideal. But when we think of Geneva's international importance, we sometimes forget that its selection by world organizations—the UN, the Red Cross, and the rest—was not the cause, but the consequence of Geneva's identification with peace, with the rule of law, and with the hope of international friendship.

A better symbol is the University, which stands in the Rue de Candolle, serene and dignified despite bursting throngs of students and the encroaching noise and traffic of the modern city; for the University best exemplifies the spirit of Geneva—a spirit of independence forged by the stubborn Calvinists of the Reformation, when Geneva was a beleaguered island of dissent fighting for survival against a surrounding sea of orthodoxy. That spirit, strengthened and liberalized by philosophers as diverse as Rousseau and Voltaire who both found refuge there in later ages, evolved ultimately into a spirit of freedom, and of hospitality to new ideas. It is this spirit we salute, in honoring the University of Geneva.

This spirit, nurtured through 400 years, has fostered the assemblage at Geneva of a university faculty which though not large, is not easily matched in distinction. Among the most renowned is Jean Piaget, who has been for more than 40 years engaged with his associates in a prodigious program of research and theory building which will have, I am sure, a lasting influence upon American psychology.

It is difficult to characterize Piaget's work, for it is both deep and broad in scope. He has been in turn a biologist, psychologist, philosopher, and logician, and in all four fields he has made major contributions. He is currently Professor of Psychology at the University of Geneva and at the Sorbonne. He is coeditor of the *Archives de Psychologie* and of the *Revue Suisse de Psychologie*. He is Director of the Institut des Sciences de l'Éducation (successor to the Institut Jean Jacques Rousseau), founder of the Centre d'Epistemologie Génétique, and Director of the Bureau International de l'Éducation, an affiliate of the United Nations Educational, Scientific, and Cultural Organization, which entitles him to the black passport of diplomatic status. Widely traveled, he has been honored by many foreign universities and governments. He is a member of the French Légion d'Honneur and holds honorary doctorates from the Sorbonne, from Brussels, Brandeis, Harvard, and other universities.

Since his book, the *Language and Thought of the Child*, appeared in 1923, Piaget and his collaborators have published more than 20 full-length books and largely filled 30 bulky annual volumes of the *Archives de Psychologie;* in all, over 180 major studies covering thousands of pages, of which the barest fraction has been translated into English. I am acquainted with only a small part of this fantastic productivity, and considering the brief time

[1] Public lecture given at Berkeley on May 23, 1964, as a part of the University of California fete celebrating the four hundredth anniversary of the founding of the University of Geneva.

[2] The author wishes to acknowledge his indebtedness to earlier writers on Piaget, not all of whom could be mentioned in the lecture. However, special acknowledgment is owing to Flavell (1962) in connection with the biographical account, and to Wolff (1960) for portions of the summary of theory.

AMERICAN PSYCHOLOGIST, 1966, Vol. 21, No. 3, pp. 207-217.

at my disposal, it may be just as well that my knowledge of it is not encyclopedic. In any case you will understand why this morning's talk is scarcely a preface to an introduction to Piaget.

Now in spite of his stature in the field, there is nothing remotely pretentious about Piaget. As many of you know, he paid a brief visit to Berkeley in March (1964). If you were fortunate enough to attend his evening lecture, I need not tell you of his personal charm and wit which withstood the rigors of translation from one language to another. For those who did not attend, a word of description may not be amiss.

Imagine a man approaching 70, a man of average build, of clear and ruddy complexion, and with snow-white hair worn long over his collar. He moves deliberately, but his blue eyes sparkle with youth, good humor, and zest. Benevolent enough, but not heavy enough, to look like Santa Claus, he reminds one faintly of the pictures of Franz Liszt that have come down to us. A man of great vigor, he still bicycles the several miles from his home to his office in the Palais Wilson and back again each day; and despite a man-killing schedule of conferences and meetings here in Berkeley, he wore out relays of us who tried to entertain him, and had energy left to spare for private hikes in Strawberry Canyon.

It was my privilege to introduce him to San Francisco on a Sunday of perfect temperature and brilliant sunshine. He found San Francisco "formidable," but astonished me by saying that what he particularly wanted to do, was drive the Lombard Street hill, "the one that curves back and forth like a snake." I had never driven it and did not much want to, so I took him up to Coit Tower in the hope he would settle for seeing the street in the distance. He enjoyed the view from Telegraph Hill and appreciated not only the tower itself but also its name. (Parenthetically, there has been some question about the influence of Freud upon Piaget. There is not much evidence of influence, but I assure anyone who doubts it, that he is familiar with psychoanalytic symbolism and loves a pun.)—But then he said, "Now let's go drive down the twisting street."—So there was no help for it. We went, and a child on a roller coaster could not have enjoyed the steep climb and abrupt descent any more than he did.

Later he admired Sausalito and Muir Woods, but although a passionate botanist by avocation, his real affection is reserved not for redwoods, but for succulents—especially sedums. If there are present today any residents of Mill Valley, you may have seen us stopping before several gardens containing sedums, while Piaget got out and took a promising cutting to carry back to Geneva. If a policeman had stopped us, I would probably have just kept still and left it to Piaget's warm smile and eloquent French to keep us out of jail.

Now Piaget's botanical interests represent, to a degree, a change from his earliest interest, which was in zoology. Born in Neuchâtel in 1896, he published his first paper when he was 10 years old on an albino sparrow he found hopping in the public garden. His interest soon turned to molluscs. Before he was 21, he had published 20 papers on molluscs and related topics, and had been offered sight unseen the curatorship of molluscs at Geneva while still in secondary school. He took his baccalaureate at Neuchâtel in 1915 followed by his doctorate in 1918.

Throughout these early years he read widely in other fields—religion, philosophy, and psychology. He came thus to the view that biology should contribute to the solution of classical problems in epistemology, but realized that something was needed to bridge the two. In later years, his developmental psychology came to provide the link, culminating in his three-volume work of 1950 on genetic epistemology, unfortunately still untranslated.

After receiving his doctorate, his interests shifted more explicitly to psychology, and he left Neuchâtel to visit and study at various other centers, including Bleuler's psychiatric clinic and the Sorbonne. Binet had died in 1911, but in Paris, Piaget was given the opportunity by Simon, Binet's collaborator in the Simon-Binet tests, to work in Binet's old laboratory at a Paris grade school. The problem suggested was a standardization of Burt's reasoning tests on Paris school children. Although Piaget was not much interested in the psychometric aspects of the problem, he found himself fascinated by the processes whereby the child achieved his answers—and wrong answers were often more enlightening than right ones.

The psychiatric examining procedures learned at Bleuler's clinic were pressed into service to elucidate the child's reasoning, and came ultimately to constitute the *méthode clinique* by which much of Piaget's data have been collected. This method of intensive interrogation is common enough among psychiatrists, but it is likely to scandalize the American psychologist trained in the canons of objectivity and standardization of procedure, because it risks leading the child and putting words in his mouth. Yet in skillful hands, it yields subtle insights which our "measurement" approach precludes.

In view of his work in Binet's laboratory, it is interesting to trace Piaget's relation to the great French psychologist who had died when Piaget was in adolescence. Certainly Piaget has relatively little in common with the Binet of the famous intelligence tests, because Piaget has never been much interested in mental testing or in individual differences. But he has much in common with the Binet of earlier years, whose interests, like Piaget's, ranged over much of science. More specifically, he seems the direct heir of the Binet who wrote the famous volume, *The Psychology of Reasoning*, a book which anticipates Piaget in its concern with the subtle qualitative aspects of thought, and further anticipates him in the employment of the psychologist's own children as experimental subjects—a procedure which might be impractical in this country where statistically adequate samples of 40 or 50 are a desideratum for the simplest investigation!

In 1921 Piaget published four papers describing the results of his work with Burt's tests and other such problems. On the strength of them, Claparède, who was then the Professor of Psychology at Geneva, invited Piaget to the post of Director of Studies at the Institut Jean Jacques Rousseau, and Piaget accepted. Although at first he divided his time between Geneva and Neuchâtel, and until fairly recently spent part of each week at the Sorbonne, his work for the last 40 years has been largely identified with the University of Geneva.

In all the vast corpus of Piaget's work are there unifying trends or concerns which can serve to orient us in this brief survey? Apart from his zoological studies and a few mathematical papers on logic as such, the central preoccupation has been with epistemology—the fundamental problem of how we come to know our world. But this problem is approached, not via traditional philosophical speculation, but rather via scientific observation and experimentation, although sometimes of an unconventional kind. The subjects are infants, children, and adolescents, and the emphasis is always developmental.

Some of this work is on perception, and is concerned with discovering the laws of perceptual development and the differences between perceptual and cognitive functions. To this end, the Geneva workers have shown a persistent interest in optical illusions. For example, they have systematically altered various aspects of the stimulus configuration and measured the magnitude and direction of the observer's errors as a function of his age. These perception studies, over 40 in number, are more rigorous and quantitative than the studies on cognitive development, and substitute for the *méthode clinique* the traditional experimental approach.

In summary, Piaget finds a general tendency, though by no means a linear one, nor one found in all instances, whereby perceptual judgments grow more accurate with age. However, he regards perceptual development as essentially continuous, and he does not consider that the developmental stages, which are so important in his cognitive theory, exist in the perceptual domain. Indeed, he has repeatedly contrasted the perceptual versus the conceptual or inferential process even in the young child, and emphasized that the two functions follow very different paths in development. Wohlwill (1962) has suggested that Piaget's denial of stages in perception while affirming them for cognition stems not from the finding that ontogenetic change in perception is necessarily more gradual, but rather because the differences between successive perceptual achievements are only quantitative, whereas one can find structural criteria—that is to say the presence or absence of particular logical operations—to differentiate the stages of conceptual development.

Time precludes further discussion of the Geneva work on perception, though it constitutes a large and important body of data and interpretation for the perception psychologist. Let us turn instead to the more familiar studies concerned with reasoning and inference.

To throw Piaget's contributions into sharper focus, let us digress briefly to consider the epistemological problem, one of the great imponderables which have engaged men's attention at least since the golden age of Greek philosophy. Now philosophers often ask questions in ways which admit of no final answer. They thus get a great deal of mileage out of them, and the same controversies keep recurring, century after century. For our purpose we need go no further back than the views of the British associationists of the seventeenth and eighteenth centuries.

The epistemological problem has to do with the nature of reality and of our knowledge of it. It probably never occurs to the naive man in the street to question the objective reality and existence of the things of the physical world—tables, chairs, people, books, etc.—which we see all about us. So uncritical an attitude does not characterize philosophers, though different ones have taken opposite sides of the question, sides to which we give the general labels "empiricism" and "idealism."

John Locke (1947) was an empiricist. Writing near the end of the seventeenth century, he rejected the idealist doctrine offered by Descartes and tracing back through the scholastics to Plato, that the mind comes furnished a priori, with a considerable array of innate ideas. Instead he sponsored the view, then much less familiar than it is now, that *all* knowledge is derived from experience. In Book II of his great *Essay Concerning Human Understanding*, he writes,

> Let us then suppose the mind to be, as we say, white paper, void of all characters, without any ideas; how comes it to be furnished? Whence comes it by that vast store, which the busy and boundless fancy of man has painted on it with an almost endless variety? Whence has it all the materials of reason and knowledge? To this I answer one word, from experience: in that all our knowledge is founded, and from that ultimately derives itself [p. 26].

And again in Book IV,

> Since the mind in all its thoughts and reasonings hath no other immediate object but its own ideas, which it alone does or can contemplate, it is evident that our knowledge is only conversant about them [p. 252].

From this it would seem to follow that we cannot know of the existence of other people, or of the physical world; for these, if they exist, are not merely ideas. Each one of us, so far as knowledge is concerned, is shut up in himself and cut off from contact with the world.

Now Locke usually shrank back from drawing the implications of his theories when they seemed to run counter to his own common sense. George Berkeley, Bishop of Cloyne, is best known in California for our city of Berkeley which was named for him, although he might not recognize his own name as we pronounce it. In philosophy, he was an immediate successor of Locke and set out to resolve Locke's inconsistencies. Boldly pushing Locke's views to their logical consequence, he found himself in the position of denying the very existence of matter, i.e., the external world, and affirming that only the mind is ultimately real. He asserted that material objects exist only through being perceived. Bertrand Russell (1945) puts the matter very clearly.

> To the objection that, for example, a tree would cease to exist if no one was looking at it, he replied that God always perceives everything; if there were no God, what we take to be material objects would have a jerky life, suddenly leaping into being when we look at them; but as it is, owing to God's perceptions, trees, rocks, and stones have an existence as continuous as common sense supposes. This, in Berkeley's opinion, is a weighty argument for the existence of God [p. 647].

Berkeley's idealist view seems intuitively false to at least some philosophers, and to most people who are not philosophers, but it is hard to refute. Berkeley's finding himself in the idealist camp by merely seeking to embrace the implications of the empiricist position shows how slippery some of the central questions of philosophy can become when phrased in traditional forms. Obviously such questions as, "Is there an external reality?" or even merely, "What is knowledge?" can lead only to speculative controversy. If the epistemological problem is formulated in more restricted terms of *how* is knowledge acquired, rather than *what* is knowledge, it may become susceptible of scientific experimental attack.

Returning to Piaget, it is clear that his genius has lain in his resourcefulness in investigating the more manageable question, "How does knowledge develop and change?" As you can see, Piaget's epistemology is at once empirical—even experimental—and developmental in orientation. Leaving aside the question of whether the world is real, he has observed and recorded the activities of the child from earliest infancy to adolescence in acquiring the strategies for coping with it.

On the traditional epistemological issue, Piaget is hard to classify. Some have considered him an idealist, some an empiricist, and both sides can marshal quotations in support. Bärbel Inhelder (1962, p. 20) writes amusingly about this. It seems that after considerable contact in a seminar,

Konrad Lorenz remarked, "All along I have thought that Piaget was one of those tiresome empiricists, and only now after studying his work on the genesis of the categories of thought, have I come to realize that he is not so far removed from Kant." On the other hand, some Russian colleagues who believed Piaget to be an idealist because he did not admit that knowledge of the external world is simply a reflection of the objects in it, posed to him the following leading question: "Do you think an object exists prior to any knowledge of it?" Piaget replied, "As a psychologist, I have no idea; I only know an object to the extent that I act upon it; I can affirm nothing about it prior to such an action." Then one of the Russians said, "For us an object is part of the world. Can *the external world* exist independently of and prior to our knowledge of it?" To this, Piaget replied, "The instruments of our knowledge form part of our organism, which in turn forms part of the external world." Later, Piaget overheard them talking and agreeing, "Piaget is *not* an idealist."

Perhaps the difficulty of locating Piaget unequivocally on the empiricist-idealist continuum illustrates a central problem for the student of his work. His ideas are highly original. The terms he has coined for his central theoretical constructs are not merely unfamiliar. They seem vigorously to resist translation into other people's conceptual categories. There is no help for it, if one would understand his theories, but to try to assimilate Piaget in his own terms.

I shall try in the next few minutes to communicate a little of his theory of cognitive development which you may or may not choose to accept. In either case, his empirical findings are an enormously important body of data for students of very different theoretical positions.

Let us turn first to Piaget's theory of cognitive development. Here a confusing situation arises for the English-speaking student. Piaget's five important books of the early 1920s were translated fairly promptly into English in the first flurry of interest in his work. These volumes—*Language and Thought of the Child, Judgment and Reasoning in the Child, The Child's Conception of Physical Causality,* and *The Moral Judgment of the Child*—are widely available. It is their contents—the famous inquiries about what makes clouds move, the origins of dreams, the basis of rules for games, and a host of other such topics—which come to mind for many people when Piaget is mentioned.

Now these works were gradually superseded in Piaget's theoretical formulations, but the point has not been sufficiently appreciated. In this country, there was a decline of interest in Piaget during what Koch (1959) has called the "Age of Theory" in American psychology—roughly from the early '30s to the end of the war—a tough-minded period dominated by the rules of "hypothetico-deduction" and "operational definition" and animated by belief in the imminence of a precisely quantitative behavior theory. Piaget's work was not easily reconciled with the fashions of the period, and little was translated. Now the tide has turned, and at least a portion of Piaget's recent work is available in English, not to mention several excellent "explanations" of him by Wolff (1960), Wohlwill (1960), Hunt (1961), and especially Flavell's comprehensive volume of 1963. However, the essential continuity of development of Piaget's ideas is obscured by the discontinuity of translation. So different are the recent works from the old ones, that to read them one must master a new vocabulary and a new theoretical formulation, and this time the task is made more difficult by the heavy emphasis upon propositions of symbolic logic to explicate the developmental stages of reasoning.

To the early Piaget belonged the painstaking compilation of the forms of verbal expression according to age level from 3 years to 10 years: the demonstration that children's "explanations" of phenomena pass through *stages,* from early animistic, through magical and artificialist forms, to rational thought, and that at each level, the child constructs a systematic "cosmology" according to the modes of reasoning available to him at that stage. The empirical bases for these findings were the children's verbalizations as elicited by the *méthode clinique,* with its inherent risks of misinterpretation of what the child is trying to express. Piaget was severely and perhaps unjustly criticized on this account, for he was sharply aware of the problem. As he put it (1929),

> It is so hard not to talk too much when questioning a child, especially for a pedagogue! It is so hard not to suggest! And above all, it is so hard to find the middle course between systematization due to preconceived ideas, and incoherence due to the absence of any directing hypothesis! . . . In short, it is no simple task, and the material it yields needs to be subjected to the strictest criticism [p. 8].

In retrospect, Piaget (1952a) recognizes that his method in those years was much too exclusively verbal.

I well knew that thought proceeds from action, but believed then that language directly reflects the act, and that to understand the logic of the child one has to look for it in the domain of verbal interactions. It was only by studying the patterns of intelligent behavior of *the first two years* that I learned that for a complete understanding of the genesis of intellectual operations, manipulation and experience with objects had first to be considered [p. 247].

As Piaget notes, the shift from reliance on verbalization to observation and experiment is most important for genetic epistemology because it permits one to study infants as well as the later stages of growth, and by more or less comparable methods.

The cognitive theory starts from the central postulate that motor action is the source from which mental operations emerge. The *action* of the organism is central to the acquisitions of the operations (i.e., ideas, or strategies), which we acquire for coping with the world. In the Hegelian dialectical form which his lectures often assume, Piaget contrasts his emphasis upon the active interplay of organism and environment, both with the environmentalist view in which experience or conditioning is impressed upon a passive organism, and with the nativist view that intellectual capabilities exist preformed and merely unfold in the course of development.

Motor action is *adaptive,* and so are the cognitive activities which more and more replace overt motor behavior. Piaget's biological orientation is seen in his assertion that intelligence is an adaptation, and only one aspect of biological adaptation. Intelligence is an organizing activity which extends the biological organization. With respect to intelligence, a subject to which Piaget has given much attention, it should be noted that his interest is in the typical, not in the range of variation. For him, the word "intelligence" lacks the mental-testing connotations with which it is usually invested in English, and corresponds rather to "intellect" or to intellectual activity or adaptation.

Life is a continuous creation of increasingly complex forms, and a progressive balancing of these forms with the environment [Piaget, 1952b, p. 3].

Intellectual adaptation is the progressive differentiation and integration of inborn reflex mechanisms under the impact of experience. The differentiation of inborn reflex structures and their functions give rise to the mental operations by which man conceives of objects, space, time, and causality, and of the logical relationships which constitute the basis of scientific thought [Wolff, 1960, p. 9].

Another central postulate is that intellectual operations acquired by interaction between organism and environment are acquired in a *lawful sequence.* It should be emphasized again that Piaget's concern is with elucidating the sequence, *not* with establishing exact age norms for its stages. It should also be noted that Piaget has set out to write the ontogenetic history of cognition—*not* a complete account of personality development. What lies outside the cognitive domain is rigorously excluded.

The innate equipment consists of reflexes present at birth. A few reflexes, e.g., yawning or sneezing, are relatively fixed and unmodifiable by experience, though some, like the Babinski, change with maturation. The majority of reflexes, for example, grasping, *require* stimulation for their stabilization, are modified as a result of experience, and constitute the basic behavioral units from which more complex forms of behavior emerge. Most important, the feedback from the activation of a reflex alters all subsequent performance of that reflex. Thus, behavior is simultaneously determined by: first, the inborn structure; second, past activations, i.e., experience; and third, the particular present situation.

Now corresponding to each innate reflex there is assumed to exist in the mind a reflex *schema,* which will not become a stable structure unless repeatedly activated by external stimulation. The concept of schema is difficult. It is described as a flexible mental structure, the primary unit of mental organization. It is too invested with motor connotations to translate as "idea"; and being initially innate, it can hardly be a memory trace. Yet it covers both, and when fully developed bears some resemblance to Tolman's sign Gestalt.

When a reflex responds to a suitable external stimulus, the total sensory perception *and* motor activity are incorporated into the schema of that reflex, and change it; so that when the reflex is again stimulated, the schema has been modified. The stimulus is never again experienced in quite the same way, nor is the response quite the same. Thus the schema is invoked to account for the modification of response, *and* for the alteration of perception in the course of learning. In other words, the organism experiences and reacts to the environment always in terms of an existing organization. All experiences of a particular kind are molded into the already present schema, and in turn alter it according to the reality conditions. Hence, experiences are not recorded as isolated stimulus-response connections, or engrams impressed on a passive brain field, but are integrated into a constantly changing structure.

For the dual aspects of learning, Piaget has used the terms *assimilation* and *accommodation*. He points out first that there exists a fundamental coordination or tuning of the organism to its environment. We have eyes and skin receptors preadapted for the photic and thermal radiation found on earth, ears for sensing rapid waves of pressure in earth's atmosphere, and so forth. There exists, moreover, a fundamental tendency of organisms to take in substances and stimulations for which there already exist the appropriate internal structures and organization. This taking in is called *assimilation*. At a biological level, it refers to the physical incorporation of suitable nutrients into organic structure. At a primitive psychological level, it refers to the incorporation of the sensory and motor components of a behavioral act into the reflex schema they have activated. At more complex levels, assimilation refers to the tendency of the mental apparatus to incorporate ideas into a complex system of thought schemata.

Parallel to assimilation is the function of *accommodation*, i.e., the process by which a schema *changes* so as to adapt better to the assimilated reality. At the biological level, accommodation refers to modification of the organism in response to stimulation, e.g., skin tanning in response to sunlight, or muscle growth in response to exercise. At the lowest psychological level, it refers to the gradual adaptation of the reflexes to new stimulus conditions—what others have called conditioning or stimulus generalization. At higher levels it refers to the coordination of thought patterns to one another and to external reality.

While assimilation and accommodation seem not too far from conventional learning theory, the concept of *aliment* is more unfamiliar. Whatever can be assimilated to a schema is aliment for that schema. Now the aliment is not the *object* which seems from the point of view of the observer to activate behavior, but rather those properties of the object which are assimilated and accommodated to. For example, a nursing bottle filled with milk may be organic aliment for the metabolism, sucking aliment for the reflex sucking schema, and visual aliment for the visual schema. And if the idea strikes you as bizarre that a reflex requires to be fed, as it were, by appropriate stimulation, consider Riesen's (1947) report on the degeneration of the visual apparatus in chimpanzees reared in the dark—or the more familiar degeneration of unstimulated muscles when polio destroys the motor pathways.

Why the careful distinction between an object and its properties? Because for the infant the object does not exist! The idea of an object grows gradually out of the coordination of several schemata—that which is perceived by several sensorial avenues *becomes* the object. At first, the infant has not even awareness of the boundaries of his own body. Objects in the perceptual field—including his own hands and feet—are responded to according to the infant's limited reflexive repertoire. He sucks in response to oral stimulation, grasps in response to palmar stimulation, but makes no attempt to grasp the nursing bottle which he competently sucks, or to follow visually the bottle he can clutch if placed in his hand. Only gradually, by a process called generalizing assimilation, do stimuli which were initially specific aliment for one schema become aliment for other schemata. In parallel accommodation, a schema becomes attuned to more complex inputs, and tends to become coordinated with other schemata which are simultaneously activated. When this happens, things previously known tactilely by being grasped can be recognized by sight alone. Similarly, grasping attempts of increasing accuracy can be directed toward sources of visual stimulation. In such a fashion does the baby come to populate the world with objects, one of which is his own body, which supplies him at once with visual, tactile and kinesthetic stimuli—and when he cries, with auditory ones.

However, the infant still does not attach the concept of permanence to objects. "Out of sight" is quite literally "out of mind." One of Piaget's most interesting experiments—and one which can be repeated by any parent of an infant—concerns the growth of the idea of permanent objects. If you catch a young baby's attention with a small toy, and then hide it, he will make little response. When somewhat older, he will show diffuse motor behavior. If now he once happens to touch it, he will gradually learn to search more efficiently where the object is hidden. However, if the object is hidden in a different place, in full sight of the baby, he will search not where he saw it hidden, but where previously he had touched it. It is an intellectual achievement of some magnitude when the very young child learns to coordinate the space of things seen with the space of things touched, and seeks to touch an object where hitherto he has only seen it.

We can conclude our rapid survey of Piaget's basic concepts with a brief reference to *equilibrium*. Bruner (1959), otherwise most sympathetic, regards the notion of equilibrium as excess baggage, contributing to Piaget a comforting sense of continuity with biology, but offering little else. Perhaps the idea of disequilibrium is more easily described. A schema is in disequilibrium if adaptation (i.e., assimilation and accommodation) to the stimulus is incomplete.

It seems to me that the ideas of equilibrium and disequilibrium constitute most of Piaget's theory of motivation, which is a rather underelaborated part of his psychological system. The organism has a basic need to continue contact with an object as long as adaptation to it is incomplete—or, as Piaget would say, as long as the corresponding schema is in disequilibrium. The need for commerce with an object persists until the child's behavior has been wholly adapted to whatever novelty it presents, that is to say, it persists until the child has acquired mastery. Once accommodation is complete and assimilation is total, the schema is said to be "in equilibrium," and there is no further adaptation. There is, in short, no learning without a problem.

Further, two *schemata* are in disequilibrium until they have mutually accommodated and assimilated, and thereby been integrated into a new superordinate mental structure. This tendency to integrate schemata into more and more complex wholes is assumed by Piaget to be a native propensity of the mind, and as fundamental as the tendency toward equilibrium in physical systems. To put the matter in less cosmic terms, the person strives continually for more and more comprehensive mastery of his world. At each *stage*, however, he is concerned with those things which lie just beyond his intellectual grasp—far enough away to present a novelty to be assimilated, but not so far but what accommodation is possible. Phenomena too simple—i.e., already in equilibrium—and phenomena too complex for present adaptation are ignored in favor of those in the critical range. Anyone who has ever watched the persistence, and resistance to satiation, of a baby intent on mastering a developmental task—for example, learning to walk—will agree with Piaget as to the strength of the motivation, whether or not he accepts Piaget's thermodynamic metaphor.

What then are the general *stages* of intellectual development, and how may they be characterized? Piaget's stages are one of the best known aspects of his work, but he has not been altogether consistent either in the number of them or in the names assigned. Moreover, the stages are linked to particular chronological ages only rather loosely, and Piaget has himself offered data to show that the age at which a particular stage is reached differs for different content domains. For example, conservation (i.e., invariance under transformation) of a plastic object, such as a lump of clay, is acquired first with respect to mass, a year or so later with respect to weight, and a couple of years after that with respect to volume. Moreover, the Geneva group are concerned to demonstrate the invariance of the *sequence* of stages, not the age at which a given stage is achieved. In Martinique the children are 4 years retarded compared to those in Montreal (Laurendeau & Pinard, 1963), and certain Brazilian Indians appear never to achieve the last stage—but the sequence is everywhere the same.

When Piaget visited Berkeley, he deplored the preoccupation of American psychologists with accelerating a child's progress through the successive stages, and commented on recent work of Gruber, who found that kittens achieve awareness of the permanence of objects in 3 months, the human baby only in 9 months; but the important fact is that the cat never acquires the power to think in terms of formal logic, and the human being may!

The more recent books from Geneva usually divide development into four stages: the sensorimotor, from birth to 2 or 3 years; the preoperational stage, from around 2 to around 7 years; the stage of concrete operations, from roughly 7 years to 11 or 12; and finally the stage of formal operations. Each stage in turn has substages—no less than six for the sensorimotor period alone—which we shall not have time to describe today.

The sensorimotor period as a whole (i.e., from birth up to age 2) carries the child from inborn reflexes to acquired behavior patterns. It leads the child from a body-centered (i.e., self-centered) world to an object-centered one. During this period the various sensory spaces, of vision, touch, and the rest, are coordinated into a single space and objects evolve from their separate sensory properties into *things* with multiple properties, permanence, and spatial relationships to other objects. Altogether this stage comprises a most important set of intellectual achievements.

The preoperational stage (2 years to around 7 years) covers the important period when language is acquired. This permits the child to deal symbolically with the world instead of directly through motor activity, though his problem solving tends to be "action ridden." The child is himself still the focus of his own world, and space and time are centered on him. Time is only "before now," "now," and "not yet"; and space moves as the child moves. When he is taken for an evening walk, the moon follows *him*. Traces of this attitude are present even in adults, who often locate places and things in terms of distance and direction from themselves, rather than in terms of objective spatial relationships. By a process of "decentering," the child during this stage learns gradually to conceive of a time scale and of a spatial world which exist independent of himself. In dealing with physical objects and quantities, the child pays attention to one aspect to the neglect of other aspects. He concludes, for example, that there is more water in a glass graduate than in a beaker—though he has just seen it poured from the one vessel into the other—because in the graduate the column of water is taller, and the child neglects the reduction in diameter.

The stage of concrete operations has its beginnings as early as age 6 or 7. Now the child grows less dependent upon his own perceptions and motor actions and shows a capacity for reasoning, though still at a very concrete level. Among his "logical" acquisitions are classifying, ordering in series, and numbering. Asked to put a handful of sticks in order by length, he need no longer make all the pair comparisons but can pick out the longest, then the longest one left, and so forth, until the series is complete. When shown that Stick A is longer than Stick B, and Stick B is longer than Stick C, he can infer without actual demonstration that A is longer than C.

Here at Berkeley, my students and I have been developing test materials based on Piaget experiments, and intended to measure the abilities of children in the primary grades. i.e., at the transition point from the perceptual attitude of the preoperational stage to the reasoning attitude of the stage of concrete operations. Thus far, fifteen tests have been developed and administered to more than 300 school children. Although we abandoned the *méthode clinique* for a strictly standardized psychometric approach, we have observed precisely the same types of behavior which Piaget had previously reported.

The last of Piaget's major stages of intellectual development begins usually somewhere around 11 or 12 years and matures a couple of years later. He calls it the stage of formal operations. Now the child can deal with abstract relationships instead of with things, with the form of an argument while ignoring its content. For the first time he can intellectually manipulate the merely hypothetical, and systematically evaluate a lengthy set of alternatives. He learns to handle the logical relationships of Identity (I), Negation (N), Reciprocity (R), and Correlation (C), which permit him to deal with problems of proportionality, probability, permutations, and combinations.

I have just referred to the INRC logical group whose acquisition marks the last stage of intellectual growth. In Piaget's writings over the years, the characteristics of each stage and the differences between them have increasingly been formulated in the notation of symbolic logic—a circumstance which does not increase the comprehensibility of his latest books for nonmathematicians.

Nevertheless, this transition to the language of formal logic is of profound importance for Piaget's theory because it provides a set of explicit, mathematical models for cognitive structure, and serves as a vehicle to describe in a unified way the findings of experiments very different in content. The unity and economy of the logical theory as contrasted with his earlier multiplicity of explanatory terms—egocentrism, syncretism, animism, realism, etc.—is obvious. However, Piaget's critics have sometimes found the mathematical formulation strained. and have accused Piaget of distorting intellectual development to force it into the categories of formal logic.

Piaget's point of view may have been misunderstood. As he phrases it (1957),

> The aim is . . . to study the application of logical techniques to the psychological facts themselves. . . . The question whether the structures and operations of logic correspond to anything in our actual thought, and whether the latter conforms to logical laws, is still an open one. . . . On the other hand, the algebra of logic can help us to specify psychological structures, and put into calculus form those operations and structures central to our thought processes. . . . The psychologist welcomes the qualitative character of logic since it facilitates the analyses of the actual structures underlying intellectual operations, as contrasted with the quantitative treatment of their behavioral outcome. Most "tests" of intelligence measure the latter, but our real problem is to discover the actual operational mechanisms which govern such behavior, and not simply to measure it [pp. xvii–xviii].

Many psychologists who acknowledge the brilliant originality of many of Piaget's experiments, and the enormous importance of his empirical contribution taken as a whole, continue nevertheless to reject the formal, mathematical theory which lies closest to Piaget's heart. Yet one of the most impressive parts of Piaget's discussions here in Berkeley concerned the isomorphism between his stages and the most basic structure of mathematics itself.

Piaget points out that if one considers not the content, but the architecture, as it were, of the various branches of mathematics, one discovers first a level where the prototype structure is the group and the type of reversibility is inversion or negation. Next comes a level where structures of order, such as the lattice, are typical, and reversibility is not inversion but reciprocity. Last comes the level of topology with key concepts of neighborhood, boundary, etc. Now the first of these three levels is the oldest, one part of it, Euclidean geometry, going back to the Greeks. The second level, typified by projective geometry, dates from the late seventeenth century; and the last, or topological, level is a product only of the nineteenth century. Taken in sequence, each level is more general, i.e., involves *fewer* axioms than the preceding, and the entire sequence might theoretically be expected to have developed in the opposite order. Now the curious part, is that the sequence of acquisition of mental operations by children follows not the historical sequence, but the theoretical sequence. Small children of 3 years of age, who for example are quite unable even to copy a simple geometrical figure such as a square, have no difficulty differentiating between a closed figure like a circle and an open one like a cross, and they can easily follow instructions in putting a second circle, however imperfectly drawn, inside, or outside, or even half in and half out of the experimenter's circle. Further evidence of young children's grasp of topological principles is seen in their sure knowledge of the forms into which a sphere, such as a balloon, can be deformed—i.e., sausagelike, flat sided, or dimpled figures, etc.—and those forms such as the torus or doughnut, which cannot be obtained by deformation of a sphere. Later, with the shift from the preoperational stage to the stage of concrete operations at age 6 or 7, the child learns to handle relations of order—seriation, transitivity, reciprocal relationships, and the rest to which I have already referred. Only with the approach of adolescence does he spontaneously utilize the propositional algebraic structures which are the oldest development in the history of mathematics.

What finally are the implications of Piaget's work for fields other than psychology and mathematics? Certainly they have a major bearing upon education.

If Piaget is correct—and much work now substantiates his empirical findings at least in broad outline—methods of education will be most effective when they are attuned to the patterns of thought which are natural to a child of the age concerned. It may not be true that you can teach a child *anything* if your approach is correct, but it does look as if you can teach him a great deal more than anyone might have guessed. Of course, teachers long before Piaget recognized intuitively that a child learned better when problems were approached at a concrete rather than at an abstract level. But there is more to it than that. Bruner, at Harvard, and others in this country are attempting to find ways to introduce children to some of the abstract ideas of mathematics—for example, the algebraic concept of squaring a number—by concrete, geometric models. They hope thus possibly to accelerate a child's progress—a goal which Piaget has his reservations about. Perhaps the most dramatic evidence of a revolution which owes a great deal of its impetus to Piaget is the new elementary school mathematics, in which children even in the lower grades are being taught, and learning, and actually enjoying learning basic arithmetical and geometrical ideas introduced via set theory, which most of their parents have never heard of.

I could not better conclude this appreciation of Piaget than by quoting from William James (1890) who wrote 75 years ago in his famous *Principles of Psychology* as follows: "To the infant, sounds, sights, touches and pains form probably one unanalyzed bloom of confusion [p. 496]." We can now go beyond the philosopher's speculations and describe in some detail how the unanalyzed "bloom of confusion" of the infant becomes the world of the child—in which not only objects, but time, space, causality and the rest acquire a coherent organization. And we owe this achievement in large measure to the analyses of Jean Piaget.

## REFERENCES


BRUNER, J. S. Inhelder and Piaget's *The growth of logical thinking.* I. A psychologist's viewpoint. *British Journal of Psychology,* 1959, 50, 363-370.

FLAVELL, J. H. Historical and bibliographic note. In W. Kessen & Clementina Kuhlman (Eds.), Thought in the young child. *Monographs of the Society for Research in Child Development,* 1962, 27(2, Whole No. 83).

FLAVELL, J. H. *The developmental psychology of Jean Piaget.* Princeton, N. J.: Van Nostrand, 1963.

HUNT, J. McV. *Intelligence and experience.* New York: Ronald Press, 1961.

INHELDER, BARBEL. Some aspects of Piaget's genetic approach to cognition. In W. Kessen & Clementina Kuhlman (Eds.), Thought in the young child. *Monographs of the Society for Research in Child Development,* 1962, 27(2, Whole No. 83).

JAMES, W. *The principles of psychology.* New York: Holt, 1890.

KOCH, S. (Ed.) *Psychology: A study of a science.* Vol. 3. *Formulations of the person and the social context.* New York: McGraw-Hill, 1959.

LAURENDEAU, MONIQUE, & PINARD, A. *Causal thinking in the child, a genetic and experimental approach.* New York: International Universities Press, 1963.

LOCKE, J. *An essay concerning human understanding.* London: Dent, 1947.

PIAGET, J. *The child's conception of the world.* New York: Harcourt, Brace, 1929.

PIAGET, J. Autobiography. In E. G. Boring (Ed.), *A history of psychology in autobiography.* Vol. 4. Worcester, Mass.: Clark Univer. Press, 1952. (a)

PIAGET, J. *The origins of intelligence in children.* (2nd ed.) New York: International Universities Press, 1952. (b)

PIAGET, J. *Logic and psychology.* New York: Basic Books, 1957.

RIESEN, A. H. The development of visual perception in man and chimpanzee. *Science,* 1947, 106, 107-108.

RUSSELL, B. *A history of western philosophy.* New York: Simon & Schuster, 1945.

WOHLWILL, J. F. Developmental studies of perception. *Psychological Bulletin,* 1960, 57, 249-288.

WOHLWILL, J. F. From perception to inference: A dimension of cognitive development. In W. Kessen and Clementina Kuhlman (Eds.), Thought in the young child. *Monographs of the Society for Research in Child Development,* 1962, 27(2, Whole No. 83).

WOLFF, P. H. The developmental psychologies of Jean Piaget and psychoanalysis. *Psychological Issues,* 1960, 2(1, Whole No. 5).

# JEAN PIAGET: NOTES ON LEARNING

By FRANK G. JENNINGS

THE MAN behind the ideas of many of the plans and programs to improve the curricula in the schools is not an educator. Jean Piaget is the seventy-one-year-old French-speaking Swiss director of the Jean Jacques Rousseau Institute in Geneva, the founding director of the International Center for Genetic Epistemology, director of the International Bureau of Education, and professor of child psychology and of the history of scientific thought at the University of Geneva. Some psychologists are convinced that his work might become as influential as Freud's. Some educators are fearful that this may be true.

In March, Piaget came to this country to deliver three lectures on the nature and nurture of intelligence and on related matters in science, psychology, and education. He spoke at New York University and addressed the convention of the American Orthopsychiatric Association in Washington.

It has been said of Piaget that he is by vocation a sociologist, by avocation an epistemologist, and by method a logician. He tells his listeners and readers that he is not an educator, that he is a psychologist with an interdisciplinary bent, that he is an investigator using the tools of the related fields of biology, psychology, and logic to explore the genesis of intelligence in the human young. All his long life he has drawn upon these three fields to conduct research and to build his theories of the development of intelligence in children.

For Piaget, the crucial question in the study of the growing child is how he adjusts himself to the world in which he lives. And for Piaget there is nothing pejorative in the word *adjustment*. It involves backing and filling, winning and losing, understanding and gaining knowledge. As he expresses it:

> Knowledge is not a copy of reality. To know an object, to know an event, is not simply to look at it and make a

SATURDAY REVIEW, May, 1967, pp. 81-83.

mental copy, or image, of it. To know an object is to act on it. To know is to modify, to transform the object, and to understand the process of this transformation, and as a consequence to understand the way the object is constructed. An operation is thus the essence of knowledge; it is an interiorized action which modifies the object of knowledge.

This is the voice of the epistemologist, but it speaks from the soul of the teacher. Piaget's techniques for observing, recording, and understanding the way a child thinks is quite literally to get inside of the child's mind and see the world through the child's eyes. One of his notable experiments, for example, was to join in a child's game as an equal. He would "learn how to make a good shot at marbles, how to make bad ones, and even how to cheat.

Rules and standards for three-year-olds, he found, are almost nonexistent. Ask a three-year-old who won and you get the answer, "I won, you won, and we all won." The five-year-old sees and sometimes respects rules. For the seven-year-old they are sacred and immutable. When the Geneva boys were told that the game was played differently in Lucerne, they shouted, "But those kids over there never understood marbles, anyway."

Piaget found that ten-year-olds can get together and modify rules to meet new conditions, and with the onset of puberty, adjustments are freely made to meet unusual cases. In a ball game, the short-sighted child is allowed to stand nearer the pitcher, a cripple will be allowed a runner. Thus there is a logic of operations that is fitted to a logic of social relations. There is continuous observable growth in the way the child learns and adjusts his understanding to the requirements of the world around him.

Piaget sees four major stages of growth through childhood; the first is the *sensory-motor* stage, which lasts from birth to about two years. Here the child learns his muscles and senses and develops certain habits for dealing with external objects and events. Language begins to gain form. He can deal with and know that things exist even when they are beyond his sight or touch. He begins to "symbolize," to represent things by word or gesture.

The second stage is the *preoperational* or *representational* stage. It begins with the beginning of organized language and continues to about the age of six. This is the period of greatest language growth and through the use of words and other symbols the child can represent the outside world and his own inner world of feeling. It is a period when magical explanations make sense, when "God pushes the sun around" and stars must go to bed when he does. The child begins to gain a sense of symmetry, depends on trial and error adjustments, and manages things by a kind of intuitive regulation.

The third stage, between seven and eleven years, is one in which the child acquires the ability to carry out what Piaget calls *concrete operations*. He can move things around, make them fit properly. He acquires fine motor skills and can organize what he has and knows how to solve physical problems.

The fourth stage is one of *formal operations* and prepares the way for adult thinking. It usually begins between twelve and fifteen years and involves the development of "hypothetical reasoning based upon a logic of all possible combinations and to perform controlled experimentation."

In successive studies Piaget and his associates have explored the growth of intelligence, the development of moral awareness, the child's concept of physical reality, and the elaboration of appropriate logic to deal with complex nonrepresentational problems.

Although *The Language and Thought of the Child* was published in English in 1926, it was not until the early 1950s that Piaget's ideas made any significant impact in the United States. Professor Jerome S. Bruner of Harvard is probably responsible for the current public awareness, which can be traced to his important little book *The Process of Education* (1960), and his most recent book, *Toward a Theory of Instruction* (1966). Bruner describes Piaget as "unquestionably, the most impressive figure in the field of cognitive development." Piaget, he says "is often interpreted in the wrong way by those who think that his principal mission is psychological. It is not. . .What he has done is to write the implicit logical theory on which the child proceeds in dealing with intellectual tasks."

Some American psychologists and educators make precisely this "wrong" interpretation. They see Piaget as "cold-blooded," not interested in motivational problems, not responsive to curricular concerns. They criticize him for being intellectually seductive. They object to his children, who seem to have a fair view of the world, who appear to be distressingly happy with their existence. Put this down, perhaps, to a tough-minded myopia of those who must work in the slums, or to the necessary sentiment of those who give primacy to "feeling" and "socialization." It is not that Piaget overlooks the affective domain, but rather that he appears convinced that the world is manageable only to the degree that orderly intelligence can be brought to bear upon the inescapable transactions each human being must make with it and with his fellows.

One critic recently complained that Piaget's children ". . . react as if they trusted the world, as if the environment were waiting to welcome them." Indeed, they sometimes do, for they are engaged in explorations of the greater world and of the closer environment with patient, resourceful, interested, and perhaps even loving adults who seem to believe that sovereign reason has not yet been dethroned. The great strength of reason, Piaget seems to say, is in its very tentativeness before an uncertain and sometimes disorderly universe. Patience is required, and time to grow, time to take in the outside world, to assimilate it, to understand it, and to use it generously.

# PART II: THE THEORY

# GENETIC PSYCHOLOGY

# AND EPISTEMOLOGY

By JEAN PIAGET

Specialists in genetic psychology, and especially in child psychology, do not always suspect what diverse and fruitful relationships are possible between their own subject and other more general kinds of research, such as the theory of knowledge or epistemology. And the converse is even more true, if that is possible: that child psychology has for long been regarded as a collection of case histories of infants. The necessity has not always been recognised, even in the field of general psychology, of considering all problems from the standpoint of development, and it is still true, in certain countries, that 'child psychologists' are a group apart, having no contact with the main currents of experimental psychology. Even less, as a rule, do students of the theory of knowledge suspect that, within reach as it were, in the field of psychogenetic experience, they can sometimes find solutions to the most general questions on the formation of ideas or on the analysis of intellectual activity. Yet they have been known to show inexhaustible patience when trying to reconstruct some unknown passage from the history of science for the sake of its epistemological significance.

But there is a chapter in the history of science which for a long time past should have served as an analogy to facilitate the closer connection which we are advocating: the relationship which embryology has gradually been called upon to establish first with comparative anatomy and then with the theory of evolution as a whole. Such a comparison deserves much attention, for there is no doubt that child psychology constitutes a kind of mental embryology, in that it describes the stages of the individual development, and particularly in that it studies the mechanism itself of this development. Psychogenesis represents, moreover, an integral part of embryogenesis (which does not end with birth but rather with the final stage of equilibrium which is the adult status). The intervention of social factors and elements of individual experience in no way detracts from the accuracy of this statement, for organic embryogenesis is itself also partly a function of the environment. On the other hand, it is clear that epistemology, if it is not to be restricted to pure speculation, will devote itself more

DIOGENES, 1953, Vol. 1, pp. 49-63.

and more to such purposes as the analysis of the 'stages' of scientific thought and the explanation of the intellectual mechanisms used by science in its various forms to conquer reality. The theory of knowledge is then essentially a theory of the adaptation of thought to reality, even if this adaptation in the end discloses, as after all it must, an unavoidable interaction between subject and objects. To consider epistemology, then, as a comparative anatomy of the function of thought and as a theory of intellectual evolution or of the adaptation of the mind to reality, is not to belittle the magnitude of its tasks. Above all, this is not to prejudge the solutions which it will be led to adopt, nor to advocate beforehand the necessity of a certain realism. If, in Lamarckism, the relationship between the organism and its environment showed the same simplicity as that of the mind and objects in classical empiricism, this same relationship in the field of biology has become complicated in direct proportion to our knowledge of the internal variations of the organism, until there is to-day a kind of isomorphic relationship between the different evolutionary and anti-evolutionary hypotheses on the one hand and, on the other, the varying explanations of intellectual adaptation given by epistemologists.

Once we admit comparisons of this kind, the history of the relations between embryology and other biological studies throws considerable light on the possible and, to a certain extent, the actual relationship between child psychology and epistemology. Indeed it is well known how embryology has shown the way to the solution of a number of problems which remained unsolved by comparative anatomy because of the lack of information about the structure of certain organs or even of whole organisms. Thus for a long time barnacles were classified as belonging to the Mollusca until the study of their larvae showed them to be genuine Crustacea, passing through certain stages common to all members of this group. In the same way, the division of tissues, as specified in embryology, into ectodermal, mesodermal, and endodermal has enabled us to confirm our conclusions concerning a great number of organs and has provided very valuable information about the significance of certain organic systems. (We have only to think, for instance, of the ectodermal origin of the nervous system, which could serve as the basis of an entire philosophy!) As for theories of evolution, even if the parallel between ontogenesis and phylogenesis has been exaggerated (it is still far from being precisely detailed) there is no doubt that embryology has revived the prospects of evolutionism and that its contribution, considered from an adequately critical standpoint, is of great help in the study of a problem to which after all no definitive solution has yet been found.

Although science became concerned with the development of intelligence in children, from infancy through adolescence, much later than with the embryonic phases of a variety of animals the most alien to man's rational nature, genetic psychology, as yet a young science, has nevertheless made contributions to the solution of the classical problems of epistemology which may be compared, *mutatis mutandis*, with those we have been discussing. To see this more clearly, however, we must first dispel a possible misunderstanding. Genetic psychology is a science whose methods are more and more closely related to those of biology. Epistemology, on the contrary, is usually regarded as a philosophical subject, necessarily connected with all the other aspects of philosophy and justifying, accordingly, a metaphysical position. In these circumstances, the link between the two subjects would have to be considered either as illegitimate or, on the contrary, as no less natural than the transition from any scientific study to whatever form of philosophical thought, less by way of inference than by inspiration and involving, moreover, the addition to the latter of subject considerations beyond its scope.

But apart from the fact that contemporary epistemology is increasingly the work of scientists themselves who tend to connect the problems of 'fundamentals' with the practice of their own branches of learning, it is possible to dissociate epistemology from metaphysics by methodically limiting its subject matter. Instead of asking what knowledge is in general or how scientific knowledge (similarly taken as a whole) is possible, which naturally presupposes a complete philosophic system, we can make a habit of confining our questions to the following 'positive' problems: How do different forms of knowledge, rather than knowledge itself, develop? By what process does a science pass from one determinate form subsequently held to be inadequate, to another determinate form afterwards held to be superior by the common agreement of the experts on this subject? All the epistemological problems are again encountered, but now in an historical and critical rather than an immediately philosophical perspective. It is of this genetic or scientific epistemology[1] that we shall speak here to illustrate to what extent it may look to child psychology for a helpful contribution to its problems, a contribution which may perhaps prove far from negligible.

## I.

Let us begin at once with a very important problem: Can a comparison be drawn between mathematics and physics, or are they two irreducible types of thought and understanding? It is well known that both points of view have been, and continue to be, defended. The logistic school in general favours the theory of duality, and the logical positivists of Vienna have even introduced a radical distinction between two kinds of truths: the truth of 'tautological' propositions, characteristic of logic and mathematics, whose contradictions are 'propositions without meaning', for this first type of truth depends upon an equation; and the truth of empirical propositions, characteristic of physics (or biology, etc.), whose contradictions are false propositions, but which carry a meaning (for instance: water does not freeze at 0° centigrade). On the other hand, some authors, such as Brunschvicg earlier and Gonseth to-day, consider that mathematical truth can be assimilated to physical truth because it exhibits a similar blend of deductive principles and empirical statements.

Such an argument depends partly on genetic psychology, for everyone will agree that the development of mathematics has been preceded by certain kinds of arithmetical knowledge (as, for instance, the idea of the

[1] cf. Piaget, *Introduction à l'epistémologie génétique*, Paris: Presses Universitaires de France, 1949–50.

integer, etc.) and that part of our knowledge of physics is similarly due to a pre-scientific common sense. But when mathematicians, physicists, or philosophers appeal to common sense and try to imagine how its ideas are developed, they are usually satisfied with an arbitrary reconstruction of its workings (what might be called colloquially a 'slick' reconstruction) and admit by implication that, as common sense is universal, everyone is competent to know how it works. Even if we agree that every man is a psychologist, we must, nevertheless, take certain precautions when the question is one of origins or genesis. Moreover, without in any way neglecting ethnographical and sociological research, it is a good thing to consider in this connection how the bases of arithmetical and physical knowledge are in fact constituted in the mind of the young child.

Such an analysis will allow us at the outset to dispose of a fundamental misunderstanding, which has certainly contributed to the obscuration of our topic. There is no doubt that all knowledge presupposes an element of experience, and it seems undeniable that without first handling objects the child could not establish the correspondence between one unit and another which enables him to work out an idea of the integer nor discover that the sum of certain objects is always the same, in whatever order they are counted, and so on. Even such a truth as $2+2=4$, and particularly the inverse operation, $4-2=2$, depends upon an appeal to experience; and this is true also of the elementary logical argument exemplified in the transitive relations: $A=B$; $B=C$; therefore $A=C$, which is in no sense grasped as obligatory before the age of six or seven in the case of space measurements, nor even before the age of nine in the case of weights. We have often seen children of eight or nine admit, for instance, that a brass bar $A$ weighs exactly the same as a brass bar $B$ of the same dimensions and then, despite their contrary expectation, discover by weighing them that bar $B$ weighs the same as a ball of lead $C$. When finally, the question was raised whether bar $A$ weighed as much as ball $C$, it being understood (and this was insisted upon) that $A=B$ and $B=C$, they calmly replied: 'No, this time the lead will be heavier, because lead is always heavier.'

In short, we can grant the exponents of experience that even the simplest and most general arithmetical and logical truths depend upon empirical support before giving rise to a purely deductive operation. But what sort of experience is in question, and is it possible on this basis alone to assimilate logico-mathematical experience at pre-operational levels to physical experience at the same or subsequent levels?

The examination of the child's behaviour towards the objects shows that there are two kinds of experience and two kinds of abstraction, according to whether the experience is concerned with the things themselves and allows the discovery of certain of their properties, or whether it is concerned with relationships not inherent in the things but introduced by the action, making use of the objects for its own purposes.

In the first case (we say 'first' because this is what is currently understood by the term 'experience', not because it represents a genetically anterior type of experience) we have experience of the object leading to an abstraction from the object: this is the type of physical experience which is properly a discovery of the properties of things. Moreover, this discovery always presupposes some sort of action; but a particular action, with reference to a certain quality of the object, and not, or not merely, the general relations implicit in the action. For instance, when a child discovers the unexpected fact that a ball of lead can weigh the same as a brass bar, he submits to a physical experience and abstracts the information from the objects themselves while making use at the same time of the particular action of weighing, etc.

On the other hand, the child who counts ten pebbles and discovers that there are always ten even when the order is changed, is making an experiment of quite a different kind: he is not really experimenting with pebbles, which merely serve him as instruments, but with his own activities of arranging and enumerating. But these activities exhibit two characteristics which are quite distinct from the act of weighing. First, they are activities which confer properties on the object which it did not itself possess, for the collection of pebbles comprised neither order nor number independently of the agent: it is he, then, who abstracts the information from his own activities, and not from the objects as such. Second, they are general activities, or, more precisely, they are co-ordinations of actions: indeed, whenever we act, we introduce a certain order into our activities (we 'classify the problems to be solved') whereas 'weighing' is a much more particular action. Furthermore, these general acts of co-ordination quickly become transformed, after the age of seven or eight, into purely mental operations so that, at the next stage, the child no longer needs to experiment in order to know that ten will always remain ten, independently of a given order; he deduces it logically whereas he cannot deduce the weights of objects without adequate previous data.

In the same way, to discover that $A=C$ if $A=B$ and $B=C$, is an experience concerned with the general co-ordination of actions. It can be applied to weights as to anything else, but it does not amount to abstracting the transitivity from the objects as such, even if in general the objects confirm this law, which depends on action before becoming a law of thought. It is true that the child does not consider this transitivity as necessarily applicable except in fields where he already has some previous ideas of continuity: simple quantities (length, etc.) towards the age of seven or eight, weights about the age of nine to ten, and so on. But this does not mean that the transitivity of objects is derived from physical experimentation; we shall soon see that ideas of continuity are, on the contrary, the result of logical construction.

We may conclude in the meantime that child psychology throws at least some light on our first epistemological problem. It is not because our first approach to mathematics is experimental that mathematical knowledge can be assimilated to the knowledge of physics. Instead of abstracting its content from the object itself, it contrives from the outset to endow the object with relations which are originally the subject's. Before becoming laws of thought, these relations derive from the general co-ordinations of action; but neither this active character nor the fact that the subject must undergo a certain type of experience before he can understand the operation of deduction, detracts from the validity of the statement that these relations are the expression of the subject's constructive ability rather than that of the physical properties of the object.

## II

Let us consider, as a second example, the ideas we hold on the concept of continuity. We know how Emile Meyerson, an unusually vigorous and scholarly thinker, has demonstrated the complex character of the principles of continuity. From an empirical point of view, i.e., where the content of what is continuous is provided by a physical experimentation which, however, is insufficient to impose the concept of the necessity of continuity, it may be called 'plausible'; but insofar as it is exacted by thought, it must be ascribed to the power of 'identifying' which, according to him, is characteristic of rational deduction alone. We should like to limit ourselves here to a consideration of the problem of knowing whether the contribution of the mind to the formation of our ideas of continuity is no more than this power of identification, or whether it is not equally a characteristic of thought to understand change. In other words, we should like to be able to decide whether what is 'different' is always irrational or whether reason is capable of activities other than identification pure and simple.

Let us begin again by observing the rather simple character of our ideas of continuity. If we had to wait for modern physics to discover the continuity of uniform, rectilinear movement (inertia) and the conservation of energy, etc., the Pre-Socratics certainly admitted the permanence of matter; and Meyerson himself examines the *schema* of the persistent character of objects when, as the first principle of continuity, it stands out from the field of perception. He even goes so far as to attribute awareness of this principle to animals (to a dog in pursuit of a hare) and to all forms of thought. The information provided by child psychology in this respect may thus have some significance.

This information is twofold. It concerns, first, the levels of development at which ideas of continuity are formed and, second, their precise mode of formation.

Regarding the stages at which ideas appear, we must beware of thinking that the idea of constants is formed as early as has been asserted. We must, moreover, distinguish two different cases: on the one hand, the sensory motor constants, such as the *schema* of the persistent character of objects, and the observed constants of size, shape, and colour; and, on the other hand, the constants derived from thought itself, such as the persistence of patterns, spatial measurements, physical quantities, etc. Although we do not yet know enough about the ages when observed constants are first grasped (according to Brunschvicg and Cruikshank constant size is not understood before the age of six months or thereabout) we know, on the other hand, that the persistent character of objects is grasped only during the second half of the first year (looking for an object which has completely disappeared behind a screen). The baby begins by showing no reaction at all to the vanished object. Then, during an intermediate phase, it looks for it but without allowing for its successive changes of position.

Thus the idea of the persistence of the object in nearby space, which is a kind of group constant, is developed only in connexion with the idea of a series of observed changes of position, i.e., with the organisation of space as an integral whole. As for representative constants, dependent on thought itself, the formation of such concepts comes very much later and is not found earlier than the first logical operations with respect to classes and relations (towards the age of seven to eight).

Let us take as an example the continuity of a group of objects, such as a collection of ten to twenty beads in a small glass. The child is asked to put an equal number of blue beads in a glass *A* and of red beads in a glass *B* of the same shape and size. In order not to have to count the objects, he can put a blue bead in *A* with one hand while putting a red bead in *B* with the other. As soon as the two equal sets have been completed, the child is asked to empty the contents of glass *B* into a receptacle *C* with a different shape (a glass which is taller and narrower or shorter and wider, etc.). The child now should decide whether the number of beads in *A* still remains the same as the number in *C* (or, subsequently, in *D*, etc., varying the observed shapes). Now small children deny this group continuity or, at any rate, consider it in no way obligatory. For them, there are more beads in *C* than in *A* because they reach a higher level; or else there are fewer because the glass is narrower, etc. On the other hand, towards the age of six to seven, the collection begins to be thought of as a constant whatever the observed shape of the receptacle.

Let us now consider the reasons put forward in favour of the idea of continuity at the time when it is first formed. There are three types of argument, and they recur invariably, whatever problem of continuity we may think of (conservation of quantities of matter, such as the weight or volume of balls of modelling clay whose shapes can be altered in different ways; maintenance of lengths or surfaces, despite changes in the position of the elements, etc.). The first reason seems to confirm Meyerson's theory and to relate solely to the operation of identification: the child argues that, since nothing has been taken away or added, the number of beads must still be the same. There remains the question of why this idea of identity appears so late. In fact, small children also know quite well that nothing has been removed or added, and when they are asked where the beads which they think are in *C* come from when they have not been taken from *B*, or where the beads which are missing in *C* have gone if they are not to be found in *B*, they simply dodge the question. They merely insist on the statement that the final collection *C* seems to them larger or smaller than *B* was in the first place, though accepting the evidence that no beads were introduced from outside during the course of the operation nor taken away when a new glass was used. Why, then, are small children unable to realise this identification while bigger children can base their reasoning upon it? It is because the identity of the collections *B* and *C* is only the end or result of the child's reasoning, and not the starting point.

The second reason put forward, on the other hand, throws some light on the mechanism itself of the nascent sense of reasoning: it is the concept of simple reversibility. The collection has been emptied from *B* into *C*, says the child, but it is easy to transpose collection *C* back into *B*, and it will be seen that nothing has been changed.

The third reason, finally, is reversibility applied to the relations in question, i.e., the compensation resulting from the respective changes. The collection put into *C* reaches a higher level than in *B*; but *C* is narrower than *B*; one of the modifications thus compensates for the other, therefore the relative result is the same.

The grasp of this reversibility, the first signs of which are quite general at the age of seven to eight, in fact expresses the transformation of actions into mental operations. Elementary action is a one-way process, directed towards a single end; and the whole of the small child's thought, which is no more than the mental representation of actions in images, remains irreversible precisely in as much as it is subordinate to the immediate action. Mental operations, on the other hand, are actions co-ordinated in reversible systems in such a way that each operation corresponds to a possible reversed operation by which it would be cancelled. But such an idea of reversibility is to be found only late in the development of thinking, because it presupposes a reversal of the natural course of actions, if not of the natural course of events themselves, both external and internal (the stream of consciousness, which has been described as reflecting 'immediate' facts, is the pattern of all irreversible flux).

The absence of constants, so characteristic of the thinking of small children, thus is merely the consequence of the initial irreversibility of thought; the formation of the earliest ideas of continuity, on the other hand, is due to the grasp of reversibility which characterises the first concrete mental operations. From this point of view, identity is to be considered as a conclusion—the result of putting together direct and inverse operations—and not as a starting point. It is the group of changes as such (or any other reversible system analogous to a group) which is the origin of the principle of continuity, and identity (or more precisely the 'operation of identifying') is only one aspect of the pattern in question, an aspect inseparable from the changes themselves.

Thus we perceive at once the analogy between this way of forming elementary constants and that which is found in physics itself. The elaboration of every principle of continuity has been linked with the development of an operative system of unity and, granted such a system, it is particularly difficult to dissociate change from identity, as if the latter alone could be attributed to reason and every change necessarily involved an irrational factor. In fact, change and identity must always be associated, and it is the possibility of harmonising them which constitutes the proper task of reason. The genetic study of intelligence proves a decisive argument in this respect. Neither identification nor even comparison of resemblances precedes the comprehension of change or difference, and the mental operations capable of co-ordinating both sets of ideas are developed in conjunction with one another.

III

A third example will give us an idea of the diversity of the problems which can be considered genetically by epistemology with the help of child psychology: this is the problem of the logical character or intuition *sui generis* of the integer. We know indeed that certain mathematicians—the most famous among them being Poincaré and Brouwer—are of the opinion that the integer cannot be reduced to any logical construction but that it is the object of a direct and independent rational intuition. The logistic school, on the other hand, since Frege and Russell, claim to derive integers simply from the construction of logical classes and relations. The cardinal number would thus constitute a class of equivalent classes, the members of which corresponded term to term. For instance, the logical classes formed by Napoleon's marshals, the signs of the zodiac, the Apostles, etc., can all be classified under one head, if the members of one of the classes are arranged to correspond with those of the others; then the class of these classes forms the number 12, since the sole property common to the constitutive classes in this case is that of constituting the particular whole designated by the figure 12. Similarly, the ordinal number can be formed simply from the correspondence between asymmetrical transitive relations or serial relations. Thus the construction of the integer would depend exclusively on logical forms.

The problem we have before us, then, is to know whether the integer as the product of effective thought (i.e., of thought as mental activity and independently of its relations with formal deductive theories) verifies one or the other of these solutions. Doubtless, it will be objected that this 'natural' number is not that of mathematics, which means that, even if in 'reality' the mind spontaneously proceeds in a certain manner, formal theories can explain number in their own way. But, here again, it is clear that the idea of number preceded the construction of scientific arithmetic and that, if there is either an elementary intuition of number or an essential connexion between number and logical classes and relations, the question must first be verified in this pre-scientific field.

Once again, genetic psychology contributes a partial answer to this question, an answer, again, which could not have been anticipated without the evidence of direct experience. In reality, the conception of the idea of number depends neither on an extralogical method such as the intuition which Poincaré and Brouwer advocate, nor on pure logic in the sense in which Frege and Russell use it. It depends instead on an operative synthesis of both: the elements are completely logical, but the operations which result from their co-ordination do not enter into the sphere of classes and relations. The solution suggested by psychogenetic research is not to be found in either of the theses we have been considering, but rather midway between the two.

The psychological difficulty of the thesis which supports a simple intuition of number is that the series of numbers characterised by the operation $n+1$ can be discovered only in conjunction with the logical construction of classes and relations. At the pre-operative level (before the age of six to seven) at which the child does not succeed in forming the constants necessary to reasoning because of the lack of the idea of reversibility, he is quite capable of forming ideas of the first numbers—which may be called figures because they correspond to simple, defined spatial dispositions—from 1 to 5 or 6, without the zero, just as he reasons by means of preconceptions corresponding to intuitive collective ideas. But even where groups of five or six objects are concerned, he is not assured of their continuity. When, for instance, a child aged from four to five is asked to put on a table as many red counters as there are in a spaced-out row of six blue counters, he begins by making a row of the same length, independently of the correspondence between each term in the series; then he makes a row which exactly corresponds, but continues to rely on an exclusively perceptual criterion. He confidently places one red counter for each blue one; but if the component parts of one of the two rows are spread out or closed up a little, he no longer believes in the continuity of the numerical equivalence and supposes that the longer row contains more counters. It is only towards the age of 6½ or 7, i.e., in connexion with the formation of the other ideas of continuity, that he comes to admit the invariability of the total number independently of their spatial position. Thus it is difficult to speak of an intuition of the integer before this later stage of development; and it is clear that an intuition which is derivative is no longer an intuition.

How, then, do we form the idea of an equivalence between two groups and of the continuity of this equivalence? Operations of a logical character must intervene at this point, which seems to support Russell's thesis. It is, indeed, remarkable that the concept of a series of integers is formed at precisely the intellectual level (six to seven years old) which also gives rise to the two principal constructions of the qualitative logic of classes and relations: first, the system of subordination by inclusion, which is the basis of classification (classes $A$ and $A^1$ are included in $B$: classes $B$ and $B^1$ in $C$, etc.); and, second, the concatenation or seriation of asymmetrical transitive relations ($A$ smaller than $B$, smaller than $C$, etc.). The first of these two constructions, in fact, necessarily comes into play in the perception of the continuity of wholes; for the continuity of a whole presupposes a set of graduated inclusions which links to this whole all the parts of which it is formed. As for seriation, it comes into play in the order of numbering the elements and, psychologically, is one of the conditions for the perception of their correspondence. Could we not, then, say that genetic psychology corroborates Russell's thesis of the logical character of number, since each of its component parts is definitively based upon a purely logical construction?

In one sense, yes. But the matter becomes complicated when it comes to determining the character of this operation of establishing a correspondence which guarantees the equivalence of the classes. There are, in reality, two ways of perceiving correspondence: one 'qualitative' and based on identity of the quality of the elements in correspondence; the other 'undefined' in which these qualities are abstracted. When a child draws a man from a model, he arranges the parts of his drawing to correspond with those of the model: head corresponds with head, left hand with left hand, and none of these parts are interchangeable. There is thus a qualitative correspondence, and each element is characterised by definite qualities and cannot be considered as a 'unit' whatsoever. On the other hand, when the same child arranges six red counters to correspond with six blue ones, any unit of the second group can correspond with any of the first providing there is a correspondence of unit with unit. Thus the correspondence has become 'undefined', since the qualities have been abstracted, and the elements, thus deprived of their distinctive characters, become transformed into interchangeable units.

Consequently, when a logician tells us that the class of Napoleon's marshals is equivalent to that of the signs of the zodiac and of the Apostles of Christ, the class of all these classes being the 'class of equivalent classes' which constitutes the number 12: are we dealing here with 'qualitative' correspondence or with 'undefined' correspondence? It goes without saying that it is 'undefined'. Marshal Ney, the Apostle Peter, and the sign of Cancer have no qualities in common; the members of each class correspond to those of the other classes insofar as they are interchangeable units and after their qualities have been abstracted.

Psychologically the explanation of the cardinal number in terms of the logical operation of classification depends on a vicious circle. We speak of a class of equivalent classes as if their equivalence depended on their being classes, when at the outset the 'qualitative' correspondence (which alone derives directly from the character of logical classes) has been jettisoned in favour of an 'undefined' correspondence, without being aware that this latter method itself first changes the individually characterised members of the class into numerical units. The class then has certainly been changed into number, but by the introduction of number from outside by means of an 'undefined' correspondence.

In reality the integer is certainly the result of logical operations (and it is only up to this point that child psychology confirms Russell's thesis); but it represents a combination of these operations in an original manner, which cannot be reduced to pure logic. We must therefore attempt a third solution going beyond those put forward both by Poincaré and Russell.

It is a very simple solution. Let us assume a whole made up of elements *A*, *B*, *C*, etc. If the child considers only the quality of these elements, he can begin by classifying them in different ways, i.e., he can arrange them according to their resemblances (or differences) but apart from any order (if *A* is equivalent to *B*, the one neither precedes nor succeeds the other). Or else he can order them according to their relative size or position, etc., and ignore their resemblances. In the first case the units are assembled insofar as they are equivalent. In the second case, insofar as they are different. But elementary logical operation does not allow us to link together two objects simultaneously in terms of equivalence (class) and difference (relation of order). The transformation of these logical operations into numerical operations consists, on the contrary, in abstracting the qualities and, consequently, treating any two members of the class as being at the same time equivalent in everything ($1=1$) and yet distinct—distinct, because, whatever the order chosen, their enumeration always presupposes, failing all other distinctive criteria, that one of them should be indicated either before or after another. The integer is then psychologically a synthesis of class and asymmetric transitive relation, i.e., a synthesis of logical operations; but co-ordinated in a new way, through the elimination of distinctive qualities. This is why, finally, every integer simultaneously implies a cardinal and an ordinal aspect.

These few examples help us to see how the genetic analysis of a set of ideas or operations sooner or later gives rise to epistemological problems. The importance of such problems can naturally be under-estimated insofar as we forget that fully developed thought is the result of a long process. 'We are no longer children', replied a mathematician, after hearing an exposition of the confusion of the two kinds of correspondence operations which allows Russell to pass from qualitative resemblance to numerical equivalence. But if, with the biologists, we remember that the embryonic differentiation of the tissues governs the whole of adult anatomy, we shall no longer regard the larval state of knowledge as a situation devoid of theoretical significance, and we shall make use of the new method of analysis offered by genetic psychology as a supplementary source of epistemological information. We must agree, certainly, that it is a method without relevance to a considerable number of special questions, but it is an indispensable instrument in dealing with the most general questions: for these are concerned with the most primitive concepts, i.e., just those which are most accessible to genetic research.

# RECENT DEVELOPMENTS IN PIAGET'S WORK

By D. E. BERLYNE

## I.—Introduction.

Piaget is known to English-speaking psychologists mainly for his early writings, with their thought-provoking but, according to some critics, disputable accounts of the quaint notions of young children. Doubts have been expressed about the validity of the method of interrogation used for these studies and about the generality of the findings. Repetitions with other populations have not always produced the results that Piaget's works would lead one to expect. At least one writer was moved to dismiss his 'subjective approaches to the analysis of child behaviour' as 'little removed from ordinary literary speculation.'†

Since the 1930s, however, Piaget's researches have been undergoing some gradual but profound changes. He has been turning to more exact and behaviouristic methods of collecting data: close observation of infants, setting older children practical tasks or putting precise questions to them about events enacted in front of them, and psychophysical experiments with both child and adult subjects. His theory has become more detailed and more ambitious in scope, drawing on his knowledge of biology, logic and history of science, all of them fields to which he has contributed. These developments can be summed up by saying that he has changed from one of the most celebrated *developmental* psychologists into one of the most important of contemporary *general* psychologists. But this does not mean that his work has lost any of its importance for those faced with the practical problems of childhood in their everyday work.

Like most contemporary psychologists, Piaget starts from the biological concept of 'adaptation.' He sees adaptation as an interplay of two complementary processes, which he calls '*assimilation*' and '*accommodation*.' Assimilation occurs when an organism uses something in its environment for some activity which is already part of its repertoire. At the physiological level, it is exemplified by the ingestion of food, and, at the psychological level, it embraces a variety of phenomena. Piaget sees assimilation at work, for example, whenever a situation evokes a particular pattern of behaviour because it resembles situations that have evoked it in the past, whenever something new is perceived or conceived in terms of something familiar, whenever anything is invested with value or emotional importance. Accommodation, on the other hand, means the addition of new activities to an organism's repertoire or the modification of old activities in response to the impact of environmental events.

Psychologists accustomed to other conceptual schemes may wonder whether it really helps to group together such multifarious processes under the

† Pratt, K. C.: The Neonate, in Murchison, C. (ed.). *A Handbook of Child Psychology*. Worcester, Mass.: Clark Univ. Press. 1933.

BRITISH JOURNAL OF EDUCATIONAL PSYCHOLOGY, 1957, Vol. 27, pp. 1-12.

same rubrics. Is the role played by a cow which a child confuses with a horse really analogous to that played by a cow appearing as roast beef on the child's dinner plate? Although Piaget discusses assimilation and accommodation at great length, some readers may feel that the concepts need to be analyzed more minutely before they can yield unequivocal predictions rather than describing facts already discovered. At all events, assimilation seems to include what learning theorists call 'generalization' and 'discrimination,' processes determining which response a particular stimulus will elicit, while accommodation covers 'differentiation of responses' and the learning of new responses.

As the child's development proceeds, a more and more complete balance and synthesis between assimilation and accommodation is achieved. The child is able to take account of stimuli more and more remote from him in space and time, and to resort to more and more composite and indirect methods of solving problems.

Piaget agrees with many other theorists in distinguishing 'affective' and 'cognitive' factors. The former release energy, while the latter determine how the energy will be applied. Piaget's writings have concentrated on the 'cognitive' aspect of behaviour rather than on motivation and emotion, but he insists that neither aspect must be overlooked. The child does not undergo separate intellectual and emotional developments. The most dispassionate pursuit of knowledge must be driven by some motive, and the directions in which drives and emotions impel behaviour must depend on the structures made available by the growth of intelligence.

## II.—The period of sensori-motor intelligence (birth to two years.)*

During his first two years, the child gradually advances towards the highest degree of intelligence that is possible without language and other symbolic functions. He begins life with innate reflexes, but these are, from the start, modified and made more effective by learning. New responses are soon acquired, and then complex solutions to problems are achieved by piecing together familiar responses in novel combinations. By the end of the second year, the first signs of the human capacity for symbolization appear: he invents new patterns of behaviour which show him to be representing the results of his actions to himself before they occur. In short, the sensori-motor period sees attainments comparable to the highest found in sub-human animals.

This growing ingenuity in the face of practical problems goes hand in hand with the formation of a less 'egocentric' and more 'objective' conception of the world. For some weeks after birth, the world must consist of a succession of visual patterns, sounds and other sensations. The infant comes naturally to pay attention to those external events which are associated with satisfactions or which are brought about by his own actions. Gradually, he builds up a view of the world as a collection of objects continuing to exist even when they are out of his sight and generally preserving the same sizes and shapes, despite the changes in their appearance that come with changes in position. Whereas no distinction between himself and what is outside him can have any meaning for him at first, he comes to conceive of himself as one object among the many that people the world, most of them unaffected by his activities.

The concept of an *object* is bound up with objective notions of *space, time* and *causality*, which the child does not possess as part of his native endowment but has to build up gradually through interaction with the world. After learning

* Cf. Bibilography, items 3, 4 and 6 (Ch. IV).

to select appropriate spatial directions and temporal successions for his actions, he comes to respond to the positions and times of occurrence of events outside himself, using his own body and his own actions as reference-points. Finally, he conceives of a space and a time in which both he himself and external objects are located. He learns, for example, to distinguish occasions when objects are moving independently of him from occasions when they merely appear to be changing positions because he is moving among them. Similarly, he progresses from an understanding of the relationship between his responses and their consequences to an understanding of the causal influence inanimate objects can exert on one another and even on him.

### III.—The origin of symbolic processes.*

Anything the child has achieved during the sensori-motor period is dwarfed by the prospects introduced by signs and symbols, particularly words and images. They expose him to a world of real and imaginary entities extending far beyond his momentary range of vision or even his life-span. It is a stable and consistent world, whereas the objects he perceives come and go.

Piaget deprecates the long-established belief that images are mere reactivations of traces of past experiences, passively registered by the nervous system. He insists that imagery is an extremely complex and active process, as can be seen from the time it takes to appear after birth. It grows out of the child's imitative capacities and is, in fact, 'internalized imitation.' The gradual extension of imitation during the sensori-motor period proceeds from a tendency to reproduce sounds and visual effects which have just been produced by the infant himself or by somebody else to an ability to copy an increasing range of new responses from an increasing range of models. It reaches its climax and the point at which it can perform symbolic functions with 'deferred imitation,' the imitation of the behaviour of an absent person of whom the child is 'reminded.'

Inanimate objects also can evoke imitation, as, for example, when a child opens his mouth on finding it difficult to open a match-box. Imagery consists of just such symbolic imitation 'internalized' i.e., so reduced in scale that only the subject himself is aware of it. It consists, in other words, of what behaviourists call 'implicit' or 'fractional' responses. When the first indications of imagery emerge about the middle of the second year, the child is beginning, significantly enough, to turn from 'practice' games, in which pleasure is derived from exercising simple activities, to 'symbolic games,' which involve make-believe or role-playing. The child understands, however, the nature of the relation between a symbol and what it signifies; he knows that the doll is not really a baby or that he is not really a cowboy.

Having learned to use actions and images as symbols and having by now acquired a sufficient vocabulary, he finds himself using words in a similar way. But words, more than images, are responsible for the progressive socialization of thought. Words and the concepts corresponding to them are taken over from the social group. They are, therefore, bound to edge the child's thoughts into line with those of other persons. He can influence and be influenced by, benefit from or suffer from, the beliefs and values of other members of his group and so arrive at an equilibrium and harmony with his social as well as his physical environment.

* Bibliography, items 5, 6 (Ch. V) and 16.

## IV.—Relations between perception and thought.*

In recent years, Piaget has been spending a great deal of time, together with Lambercier and other collaborators, on the painstaking investigation of visual illusions and related phenomena. This area of research, a time-honoured preserve of the more prosaic type of experimental psychology, may seem remote from the work for which he is best known. It has, nevertheless, given rise to some of his most original and comprehensive ideas, forming the kernel of his whole theory of intellectual functions. Whereas writers influenced by Gestalt psychology or by certain trends in American social psychology have tended to lump all 'cognitive' processes together, Piaget finds the differences between perceptual and conceptual processes illuminating.

There are two obvious ways in which perception contrasts with thought. One arises from the fact, emphasized by the Gestalt school, that the perceived properties of a stimulus vary according to the pattern of which it is a component. The concepts participating in thought do not share this instability. The essential nature of a number does not change, no matter what the structure into which a mathematician fits it. A journey between two towns may seem longer or shorter in different circumstances, but the distance separating the towns according to our knowledge or our calculations does not fluctuate.

Secondly, perceptions are notoriously variable from person to person and from moment to moment. If we take 1,000 subjects, show them a line three inches long and another two inches long, and ask them to select a third line equal in length to the two combined, we shall expect a distribution of results with a high variance. We shall even expect each subject's response to vary from trial to trial, especially if the two lines are shown in different arrangements. On the other hand, if we take the same 1,000 subjects, show them the figure 2 and the figure 3, and ask them to select a third figure, equal to the sum of the two, the uniformity of the responses will be remarkable.

These differences can be traced back to two related factors which inevitably distort all perception. First, perception is always 'centred' (*centré*). Sense-organs have to be oriented in one direction at once, and the optical apparatus in particular is so constructed that the centre of the visual field is seen more clearly and in more detail than other parts. As some of Piaget's psychophysical experiments show, the size of a fixated object is over-estimated in comparison with the sizes of peripheral objects. The various parts of the visual field expand and shrink in turn as the gaze wanders from one point to another. The second source of error is the fact that larger portions of a figure are likely to catch the eye more often than others, with the result that the distortions that arise when they are the centre of attention play a disproportionately large part in the net impression of the figure. What we have is, in fact, a biased sample of all possible fixations. From these assumptions, Piaget has derived a formula predicting the direction and extent of 'primary' visual illusions, i.e., those which are found in infants and lower animals as much as, if not more than, in adult human beings and which can be ascribed to the inherently 'probabilistic' nature of perception.

Perception is analogous to certain processes in physics, notably in statistical mechanics, which are likewise governed by probability. These processes are irreversible, since they always lead from a less probable to a more probable state. For example, when a hot body is brought into contact with a cool body, heat is transmitted from the former to the latter and not *vice versa*. A spoonful of sugar diffuses evenly through a cupful of tea, but particles of sugar in a mixture do not forgather at one spot. Similarly, the distortions to which perceived

* Bibliography, items 6 (Ch. III) and 14.

figures are subject work predominantly in one direction. They cannot be relied on to balance out.

Thinking can escape from these limitations, because it is comparable with physical systems of a different type, namely those possessing *reversibility*. An example is a balance with equal weights in the two pans. The depression of one pan is followed by an upward swing which restores the original situation. Such systems are in stable equilibrium precisely because a change can be cancelled by an equal change in the opposite direction. A balance, however, is inflexible in the sense that there is one state to which it invariably reverts. Thought processes require structures which permit of more mobility without threatening disequilibrium. They must be free to flit rapidly from one idea to another and to arrange ideas in new combinations. But systems of concepts must preserve their organization, despite this mobility, if thoughts are to be consistent and if they are to produce a stable conception of the world. The 'dynamic equilibrium' which Piaget attributes to thought can perhaps best be compared with that of a lift and its counterweight. The lift can move freely up and down, and the system remains intact and in equilibrium, no matter what floor is reached. This is because of its reversibility: any movement of the lift is compensated by an equal and opposite movement of the counterweight, and it can also be nullified by an equal and opposite movement of the lift.

The reversibility of logical thought is acclaimed by Piaget as the acme in which the growth of intelligence culminates. The spoken word and the performed action can never be recalled. The influence of something which has been perceived and then disappears from view lingers to infect subsequent perceptions. But a thought can be entertained and then unthought, and everything is as if it had never occurred. We are consequently able to conceive possible solutions for problems which it would be costly, dangerous or impossible to test by action. And no matter how extravagant an idea is considered and then rejected, the coherence of conceptual systems is not threatened. The world represented by thought, unlike that presented by perception, is relatively free from 'centring' (*centration*). It does not change with the location of the thinker or the direction of his attention.

These contrary characteristics are found in a pure form only in the naive perception of the infant on the one hand and in the rigorous thought of the scientist, mathematician or logician on the other. The principal merit of this part of Piaget's work, as far as child psychology is concerned, is the light it sheds on certain processes forming compromises between perception and thought. As we shall see when we return to the chronological sequence, the first attempts at thinking are still contaminated with the short-comings of perception. And perception, after the first months of life, is usually accompanied by 'perceptual activities,' which mitigate its imperfections. There is no way of removing distortion completely from perception, but one distortion can be set against another. The focus of attention can be systematically varied, so that information from a succession of fixations is compared and collated to yield something approaching an objective impression. What appears from one point of view can be related to the perseveration or anticipation of what has been or will be seen from a different angle. 'Perceptual activities' thus contribute to the 'decentring' (*decentration*) of perception and the achievement of 'semi-reversibility,' so called because errors are not corrected exactly but merely tend to cancel out in the long run. Although these activities generally enhance accuracy of perception, they can on occasion lead to 'secondary illusions,' which are less pronounced in younger than in older children. An example is the 'size-weight illusion,' which makes a small object seem heavier than a larger one of equal weight.

V.—The period of pre-conceptual thought (two to four years).*

Before his use of symbolic processes can reach fruition, the child has to re-learn on a conceptual level some of the lessons he has already mastered on the sensori-motor level. For instance, he may have learned to recognize transient stimulus-patterns as shifting appearances assumed by enduring objects. But this does not immediately make him at home with the *concept* of an object. Adults are familiar with the concept of a particular *object* (' *this table*,' ' *Socrates*'), with the concept of a *class* (' *all four-legged tables*,' ' *all men* ') and with the relation of *class-membership* which joins them (' *This is a four-legged table*,' ' *Socrates is a man*.'). These underlie our deductive reasoning, since having, for example, placed Socrates in the class of men, we can infer that Socrates has all the properties characteristic of this class.

The three-year-old child still lacks this equipment and has to use something midway between the concept of an object and that of a class, which Piaget calls the ' pre-concept.' On a walk through the woods, for example, he does not know whether he sees a succession of different snails or whether the same snail keeps on re-appearing. The distinction, in fact, means nothing to him ; to him they are all ' snail.' Similar phenomena are, in some hazy way, identified, so that a shadow under a lamp in a room has something to do with the shadows under the trees in the garden. Contrariwise, a person in new clothes may be thought to require a new name.

Unlike adults, who reason either *de*ductively from the general to the particular or *in*ductively from the particular to the general, the child at the pre-conceptual stage reasons *trans*ductively from the particular to the particular. It is a form of argument by analogy : ' A is like B in one respect, therefore A must be like B in other respects.' Transduction may often lead to valid conclusions, e.g., that if Daddy is getting hot water he must be going to shave, since he shaved after getting hot water yesterday. But it will at other times lead the child into errors of a sort said to be common in psychotics but certainly not unknown in intellectual circles.

VI.—The period of intuitive thought (four to seven years).†

When the child's reasoning has overcome these deficiences, other limitations remain, mainly because thought has not yet freed itself from perception and become ' decentred.' Intuitive thought can best be understood from an experiment Piaget is fond of quoting. The child sees some beads being poured out of one glass into a taller and thinner glass. It is made clear to him that all the beads that were in the first glass are now in the second ; none has been added or removed. He is asked whether there are now more or fewer beads in the second glass than there were in the first. The usual answer at this stage is either that there are more (because the level has risen) or that there are fewer (because the second glass is narrower).

To explain such errors, it may be worth asking why we, as adults, are able to avoid them. The first reason is that we are told by our thought processes that the number of objects in a set, if nothing is added or subtracted, must necessarily remain the same. We usually regard our thought processes as more trustworthy than our perceptions whenever the two conflict. At a conjurer's performance, for example, we do not really believe that the rabbit has been created *ex nihilo* or the lady has been sawn in half. The child at the intuitive stage is, on the other hand, still dominated by his perceptions. His conclusions

*** Bibliography, items 5 and 6 (Ch. V).**
**† Bibliography, items 5 and 6 (Ch. V).**

are still at the mercy of the changes resulting from successive 'centrings.' The second reason is that we take into account several aspects of the situation at once or in turn. We can see that the height of the column of beads has increased and that the width has decreased just enough to compensate for the increase in height. But the child focusses on one aspect and overlooks others. In his reasoning as in his perception, 'centring' causes one element to be over-emphasized and others to be relatively ignored. The instructiveness of such examples for adults, who might smile at the child's mistakes in the bead experiment but be liable to precisely the same sort of misjudgment in relation to, say, political or social problems, needs hardly be laboured.

### VII.—The period of concrete operations (seven to eleven years).*

We come at last to the first reasoning processes that would satisfy logicians. Logical (or, as Piaget calls it, 'operational') thought emerges when a certain basic stock of concepts has been acquired and when these concepts have been organized into coherent systems. The concepts which figure in operational thought are called 'operations' because they are *internalized responses.* They grow out of certain overt actions in exactly the same way as images grow out of imitation. Three sorts in particular are of importance :

(1) *Classes.*—The concept of a 'class' or the operation of 'classification' is an internalized version of the action of grouping together objects recognized as similar. Having learned to pick out all the yellow counters in a heap and *place* them together in one spot, the child acquired the ability to *think of* all yellow objects together and thus form the concept of the 'class of all yellow objects.' This means that some part of what happens in the nervous system and musculature when yellow objects are manually gathered together occurs whenever yellow objects are grouped together in thought. Once formed, classes can be joined to form more inclusive classes, so that elaborate systems of classification are built up, the one used by biologists being the clearest illustration.

(2) *Relations.*—Asymmetrical relations, such as 'a is longer than b' or 'x is the father of y,' derive by internalization from *ordering* activities, e.g., from placing objects in a row in order of increasing size. The best example of the complex systems which ordering relations can form is the family tree.

(3) *Numbers.*—The number system is the joint product of classification and ordering. The number 17, for instance, depends on the operation of grouping 17 objects together to form a class and that of placing 17 between 16 and 18 in the sequence of natural numbers.

Systems of operations are called 'groupings' (*groupements*), and their stability depends on their having five properties. Unless these properties are present, the relations between the elements of a grouping will change as attention is directed to different parts of them, as happens with perceptual patterns, and thought will not be immune from inconsistency. The five properties are as follows :

(1) *Closure.*—Any two operations can be combined to form a third operation (e.g., $2+3=5$ ; *all men and all women=all human adults* ; *A is* 2 *miles north of B and B is* 1 *mile north of C=A is* 3 *miles north of C.*

(2) *Reversibility.*—For any operation there is an opposite operation which cancels it (e.g., $2+3=5$ but $5-3=2$ ; *all men and all women=all human adults*, but *all human adults except women=all men* ; *A is* 2 *miles north of B and B is* 1 *mile north of C=A is* 3 *miles north of C*, but *A is* 3 *miles north of C and C is* 1 *mile south of B=A is* 2 *miles north of B*).

* Bibliography, items 6 (Ch. II and Ch. V), 7, 11 and 16.

(3) *Associativity.*—When three operations are to be combined, it does not matter which two are combined first. This is equivalent to the possibility of arriving at the same point by different routes (e.g., $(2+3)+4=2+(3+4)$ ; *all vertebrates and all invertebrates=all human beings and all sub-human animals* ; *a is the uncle of b and b is the father of c=a is the brother of d and d is the grandfather of c*).

(4) *Identity.*—There is a ' null operation ' formed when any operation is combined with its opposite (e.g., $2-2=0$ ; *all men except those who are men=nobody* ; *I travel* 100 *miles to the north and I travel* 100 *miles to the south=I find myself back where I started*).

(5) The fifth property has two versions, one for classes and relations and the other for numbers :

(*a*) *Tautology.*—A classification or relation which is repeated is not changed. This represents the fact, recognized by logicians but not always by conversationalists, that saying something over and over again does not convey any more information than saying it once (e.g., *all men and all men = all men* ; *a is longer than b and a is longer than b=a is longer than b*).

(*b*) *Iteration.*—A number combined with itself produces a new number (e.g., $3+3=6$ ; $3\times3=9$).*

VIII.—The period of formal operations (eleven to fifteen years).†

The eleven-year-old can apply ' operational ' thinking to practical problems and concrete situations. The adolescent takes the final steps towards complete ' decentring ' and ' reversibility ' by acquiring a capacity for abstract thought. He can be guided by the *form* of an argument or a situation and ignore its *content*. He need no longer confine his attention to what is real. He can consider hypotheses which may or may not be true and work out what would follow if they were true. Not only are the hypothetico-deductive procedures of science, mathematics and logic open to him in consequence but also the role of would-be social reformer. The adolescent's taste for theorizing and criticizing arises from his ability to see the way the world is run as only one out of many possible ways it could be run and to conceive of alternative ways that might be better.

Quite a variety of new intellectual techniques become available at the same time. The most important new equipment of all is the *calculus of propositions*. At the concrete-operations stage, he was able to use the branches of logic known as the *algebra of classes* and the *algebra of relations*. Now he can supplement these with forms of reasoning bearing on the relations between propositions or sentences. Propositional calculus uses ' second-order operations ' or operations on operations. An example would be ' *either sentence p is true or sentence q is true*.' Another would be ' *if sentence r is true, then sentence s must be true* ' or, in the parlance favoured by logicians, ' *r implies s*.'

A large part of Piaget's information on this period comes from Inhelder's ingenious experiments, in which children were invited to discover elementary laws of physics for themselves with the help of simple apparatus. Children at the intuitive-thought stage vary conditions haphazardly and observe what happens in particular cases without deriving any general principles. At the concrete-operations stage, one factor at a time is varied, and its effects are duly noted.

* Readers with mathematical interests will notice that, in so far as these properties refer to numbers, they are equivalent to the defining characteristics of a *group*. Groupings of classes and relations, on the other hand, are almost, but not quite, *groups* and almost, but not quite, *lattices*.

† Bibliography, items 7, 9, 10, 11, 15, 17.

Not before the formal-operations stage does the child plan truly scientific investigations, varying the factors in all possible combinations and in a systematic order. The pedagogical implications of Inhelder's work are unmistakeable. Children with no previous instruction appear to be capable of learning scientific laws in this way, with, presumably, more motivation and more understanding than are produced by traditional teaching methods. But, according to Piaget and Inhelder, they are not capable of the sort of thinking that makes use of such laws before the advances of the formal-operations stage have been completed.

Piaget asks why so many new ways of thinking become available about the same time, despite their superficial dissimilarity. It is, he concludes, because they all require systems of operations with similar structures, and the child is not able to organize his thinking in accordance with such structures before adolescence. He has recently been much impressed with the possibilities of modern symbolic logic and certain non-numerical branches of mathematics as means of describing the structures common to apparently different intellectual processes. This is not one of the ways in which logic has usually been used by psychologists in the past ; Piaget is interested in using ' logical models ' for much the same purpose as other psychologists have begun to use ' mathematical models.'

One new acquisition is the ability to use systems of operations in which each operation has two distinct opposites. A class (e.g., ' *all vertebrate animals* ') has the sort of opposite called an *inverse* (' *all invertebrate animals* '). A relation (e.g., ' *a is twice as heavy as b* ') has a *reciprocal* (' *b is twice as heavy as a* '). But ' *p implies q* ' has both an inverse (' *q does not imply p* ') and a reciprocal (' *q implies p* '). Likewise, when the adolescent experiments with a balance, he discovers that the effects of one operation (e.g., increasing the weight in the right-hand pan) can be cancelled either by the inverse operation (reducing the weight in the right-hand pan to its original value) or by the reciprocal operation (increasing the weight in the left-hand pan by the same amount.) Such systems with two opposites have a structure known to mathematicians as the '*four group*.'

The four group can be shown to provide the operations necessary for dealing with *proportionality*. It is no accident that the laws governing equilibrium between weights in the pans of a balance are understood at about the same age as the laws governing the sizes of shadows. In one of Inhelder's experiments, the subject is given two vertical rings of different diameters and has to place the rings between a candle and a screen in such a way that their shadows will coincide. Adolescents discover that the problem is solved when the ratio between the distances of the two rings from the candle is the same as the ratio between their diameters. Understanding proportionality opens the way to understanding *probability*, since, when we speak of the probability of a six in a game of dice, we mean the proportion of throws that will produce sixes in the long run.

*Combinatorial analysis*, depending on the structures mathematicians call ' *lattices*,' is another equally fruitful new attainment. Suppose that we have two ways of dividing up animals—into ' vertebrates (*V*) ' and ' invertebrates (*v*) ' and into ' flying (*F*) ' and ' non-flying (*f*).' A child at the concrete-operations stage is capable of allotting a particular animal to one of the four possible classes, (*V.F.*), (*V.f.*), (*v.F.*) and (*v.f.*). An adolescent at the formal-operations stage is capable of going further and considering all the sorts of animals that there are in the world or the sorts there conceivably could be. There are now *sixteen* possibilities : there might be no animals at all, there might be animals of all four classes, there might be (*v.F.*) only, there might be (*V.F.*), (*V.f.*) and (*v.f.*) animals but no (*v.F.*), etc. Now each of these sixteen combinations corresponds to one of the sixteen relations between two propositions recognized by modern logic. For example, '*if an animal can fly, it must be a vertebrate*' would correspond to (*V.F.*) *or* (*V.f.*) *or* (*v.f.*), i.e., the (*v.F.*) possibility is excluded. We can understand, therefore, why permutations and combinations and complex logical relations are mastered more or less simultaneously.

The mastery of logical relations between propositions is well illustrated in Inhelder's experiments. All attempts to study the relations between the phenomena of nature, whether in the laboratory or in practical life, must use them : '*If I put the kettle on the stove and light the gas, the water will boil*'; '*It will rain or snow tomorrow unless the forecast was wrong or unless I read a description of today's weather and thought it was the forecast for tomorrow,*' etc. The ability to think in terms of all possible combinations, which appears together with the ability to use complex statements like these, is clearly revealed when adolescents are set one of Inhelder's most instructive problems. Five vessels, all containing colourless liquids, are provided ; A, B and C, when mixed, will turn pink, D will remove the colour, and E will have no effect. The properties of the liquids can be discovered only by systematically examining mixtures of every possible pair, every possible trio, etc., in turn.

## IX.—Affective development.*

The child's physiological constitution makes him liable, right from birth, to emotional and drive states. These pleasant and unpleasant states come to be aroused, through some sort of conditioning, by the external stimulus patterns which regularly accompany them, and, when he had learned to perceive in terms of objects, he comes to like or dislike these. Human beings are naturally more important sources of satisfaction and distress than other objects, and so their actions and they themselves will have especially strong positive and negative values attached to them.

The social influences to which the appearance of language and other symbols makes the child amenable are manifested particularly clearly in the formation of 'inter-individual feelings.' The ability to picture how the world looks from another person's point of view includes the power to represent to oneself the feelings aroused in him by one's own actions. The child takes over other people's evaluations of his own behaviour and builds up an attitude to himself derived from his estimates of their attitudes to him. The stage is then set, during the pre-conceptual and intuitive periods, for the first moral feelings. These take the form of a belief in absolute prohibitions and prescriptions, derived from parental orders but somehow enjoying an existence and validity in their own right. Acts are felt to deserve punishment according to how far they depart from what is permitted, without reference to intentions or other mitigating circumstances.

When he reaches the period of concrete operations, the child can form groupings of values, as of other classifications and orderings. He can systematize his values according to their relative priorities and their mutual affinities, so that his evaluations and his motives may be consistent with one another. He can subordinate his actions to future needs, thereby achieving that 'decentring' from the present which we call *will*. His addiction to 'games with rules,' which replace 'symbolic games' about this time, shows him to have arrived at a less primitive conception of moral rules. He now sees them as conventions, accepted by a social group for the benefit of all, capable of being changed by common consent, and arising out of mutual respect between equals.

*** Bibliography, items 6 (Ch. VI) and 13.**

By the end of the formal-operations stage, feelings become 'decentred' still further, as they are released from the domination of what is known to be actually true. Motivation and evaluation now depend on *ideals*, and everything tends to be judged by how far it approximates to or falls short of the theoretical states of affairs that would fulfil these ideals. The adolescent views his own activities and plans as part of the total activity of the social group. He begins to think of himself as a fully fledged member of society, free to imitate or criticise adults. With the 'decentring' which implants the individual in the community and subordinates his activities to collective goals, the formation of the personality is complete.

## X.—Conclusions.

It is evident that Piaget's latest work will not silence his critics altogether. He still does not pay much attention to questions of sampling. Some projects, e.g., Inhelder's on adolescents, seem to have used a large part of the school population of Geneva. The data on the sensori-motor period, on the other hand, come mainly from observation of Piaget's own three children, hardly the children of the Average Man! But Piaget might well retort, like Kinsey, that such bodies of data, however imperfect, are all we have of comparable density.

Except for some means and mean deviations in his reports of perceptual experiments, he provides few statistics. There are generally no measures of variance, which one suspects must be considerable, no tests of significance, just a categorical statement that at such and such an age children do such and such, with a few specific illustrations. He is not much affected by the growing vogue for rigorous theories, with precise statement of assumptions, derivation of predictions and operational definition of concepts.

Be that as it may, Piaget is, without any doubt, one of the outstanding figures in contemporary psychology, and his contributions will eventually have to be reckoned with much more than they are both in the management of children and in many areas which may not seem directly connected with child psychology. His ideas are closely tied to observation of behaviour, and this makes them the sort of psychology which moves science forward because it is testable by reference to the facts of behaviour. At the same time, it goes beyond the facts just sufficiently to open up new lines of research and to attempt the sort of synthesis which is one of the chief aims of science.

Not the least reason for paying attention to Piaget's work is the relation it bears to trends followed by English-speaking psychologists. At times, his conclusions parallel those reached independently by other investigators; at other times, they serve to correct or supplement what psychologists with other approaches have to say. Like those influenced by Gestalt psychology, Piaget affirms that perceptions and thoughts cannot be understood without reference to the wholes in which they are organized. He disagrees with them in denying that wholes are unanalyzable into component relations and in insisting that the wholes figuring in thought are radically different from those figuring in perception. There are, throughout his writings, many reminders of psycho-analytic concepts—the 'omnipotence' and 'oceanic feeling' of infancy, 'functional pleasure,' the formation of the ego and the super-ego, the advance from the pleasure principle to the reality principle. But he makes many detailed criticisms of psycho-analytic theories, and the child as described by him certainly seems tranquil and studious by comparison with the passion-torn 'polymorphous pervert' that emerges from Freudian writings.

But Piaget's closest affinities are undoubtedly with the neo-behaviourists. He does not hold with early attempts to explain everything by 'conditioned reflexes ' or ' association.' But many of his observations and many aspects of his theory harmonize extremely well with conceptions of learning based on studies of what has come to be called ' instrumental ' or ' operant conditioning.' The sequence of more and more complex behaviour patterns which he depicts as outgrowths of simple reflexes and habits parallels Hull's list of progressively more intricate ' adaptive behaviour mechanisms,' found in animals.* And Piaget's view of images and thought operations as ' internalized ' overt responses approximates very closely to the view prevalent among stimulus-response learning theorists.

One body of work which has grown up in Great Britain and the U.S.A. and which Piaget is eagerly endeavouring to bring into relation with his own findings is that centering on cybernetics, information theory and game theory.† But it is to be hoped that other common ground between his psychology and others with different starting-points will be explored. It is certainly high time that the national self-sufficiences which disfigure psychology in contradistinction to other branches of science were left behind.

## XI.—Selected bibliography.


A.—In English.

1 Mays, W. (1955). How we form conceps. *Sci. News*, 35, 11-23.
2 Mays, W. (1954). Professor Piaget's épistémologie génétique. *Proc. II. Int. Cong. Phil. Sci.*, 5, 94-99.
3 Piaget, J. (1953). *The Origin of Intelligence in the Child.* London : Routledge and Kegan Paul.
4 Piaget, J. (1955). *The Child's Construction of Reality.* London : Routledge and Kegan Paul.
5 Piaget, J. (1951). *Play, Dreams and Imitation in Childhood.* London : Heinemann.
6 Piaget, J. (1950). *The Psychology of Intelligence.* London : Routledge and Kegan Paul.
7 Piaget, J. (1953). *Logic and Psychology.* Manchester : Univ. Press.
8 Piaget, J. (1952). Genetic psychology and epistemology. *Diogenes*, 1, 49-63.

B.—In French.

9 Inhelder, B. (1954). Les attitudes expérimentales de l'enfant et de l'adolescent. *Bull. de Psychol.*, 7, 272-282.
10 Inhelder, B., and Piaget, J. (1955). *De la logique de l'enfant à la logique de l'adolescent.* Paris : Presses Universitaires de France.
11 Piaget, J. (1949). *Traité de logique.* Paris : Colin.
12 Piaget, J. (1950). *Introduction à l'épistémologie génétique.* Tome I : *La pensée mathématique,* Tome II : *La pensée physique,* Tome III : *La pensée biologique, La pensée psychologique, La pensée sociologique.* Paris : Presses Universitaires de France.
13 Piaget, J. (1953-4). Les relations entre l'intelligence et l'affectivité dans le développement de l'enfant. *Bull. de Psychol.*, 7, passim.
14 Piaget, J. (1954-5). Le développement de la perception de l'enfant à l'adulte. *Bull. de Psychol.*, 8, *passim.*
15 Piaget, J. (1954). La période des opérations formelles et le passage de la logique de l'enfant a celle de l'adolescent. *Bull. de Psychol.*, 7, 247-53.
16 Piaget, J. (1949). Le probléme neurologique de l'intériorisation des actions en opérations réversiblés. *Arch. de Psychol.*, 32, 241-58.
17 Piaget, J. (1953). Structures opérationelles et cybernétique. *Année Psychol.*, 53, 379-88.
18 Piaget, J. (1954). Les lignes générales de l'épistémologie génétique. *Proc. II. Int. Cong. Phil. Sci.*, 1, 26-45.


* Hull, C. L. : *A Behavior System.* (New Haven : Yale Univ. Press, 1952, pp. 347-50.)

† Bibliography, item 17.

# THE GENETIC APPROACH TO THE PSYCHOLOGY OF THOUGHT[1]

JEAN PIAGET
*University of Geneva, Switzerland*

From a developmental point of view, the essential in the act of thinking is not contemplation—that is to say, that which the Greeks called "theorema"—but the action of the dynamics.

Taking into consideration all that is known, one can distinguish two principal aspects:

1. The formal viewpoint which deals with the configuration of the state of things to know—for instance, most perceptions, mental images, imageries.

2. The *dynamic* aspect, which deals with transformations—for instance, to disconnect a motor in order to understand its functioning, to disassociate and vary the components of a physical phenomenon, to understand its causalities, to isolate the elements of a geometrical figure in order to investigate its properties, etc.

The study of the development of thought shows that the dynamic aspect is at the same time more difficult to attain and more important, because only transformations make us understand the state of things. For instance: when a child of 4 to 6 years transfers a liquid from a large and low glass into a narrow and higher glass, he believes in general that the quantity of the liquid has increased, because he is limited to comparing the initial state (low level) to the final state (high level) without concerning himself with the transformation. Toward 7 or 8 years of age, on the other hand, a child discovers the preservation of the liquid, because he will think in terms of transformation. He will say that nothing has been taken away and nothing added, and, if the level of the liquid rises, this is due to a loss of width, etc.

The formal aspect of thought makes way, therefore, more and more in the course of the development to its dynamic aspect, until such time when only transformation gives an understanding of things. To think means, above all, to understand; and to understand means to arrive at the transformations, which furnish the reason for the state of things. All development of thought is resumed in the following manner: a construction of operations which stem from actions and a gradual subordination of formal aspects into dynamic aspects.

The operation, properly speaking, which constitutes the terminal point of this evolution is, therefore, to be

[1] This paper, transmitted by Ernest Harms, is the text of an address made by Jean Piaget, from notes, at the New York Academy of Sciences' Conference on the Psychology of Thinking on April 28–29, 1960. The translation was made by Ruth Golbin, who has skillfully succeeded in retaining Piaget's individualistic style of expression.

JOURNAL OF EDUCATIONAL PSYCHOLOGY, 1961, Vol. 52, No. 6, pp. 275-281.

conceived as an internalized action reversible (example: addition and subtraction, etc.) bound to other operations, which form with it a structured whole and which is characterized by well defined laws of totality (example: the groups, the lattice, etc.). Dynamic totalities are clearly different from the "gestalt" because those are characterized by their non-additive composition, consequently irreversible.

So defined, the dynamics intervene in the construction of all thought processes; in the structure of forms and classifications, of relations and serialization of correspondences, of numbers, of space and time, of the causality, etc. One could think at first glance that space and geometry add to the formal aspect of thought. In this way one conceived of the geometric science in the past, considering it impure mathematics, but applicable to perception and intuition. Modern geometry, since *Le Programme d'Erlangen* by F. Klein, has tended, like all other precise disciplines, to subordinate the formal to the dynamic. The geometries are, indeed, understood today as relying all on groups of transformation, so that one can go from one to the other by characterizing one less general "subgroup" as part of a more inclusive group. Thus geometry too rests on a system of dynamics.

Any action of thought consists of combining thought operations and integrating the objects to be understood into systems of dynamic transformation. The psychological criteria of this is the appearance of the notion of conservation or "invariants of groups." Before speech, at the purely sensory-motor stage of a child from 0 to 18 months, it is possible to observe actions which show evidence of such tendencies. For instance: From 4–5 to 18 months, the baby constructs his first invariant, which is the schema of the permanent object (to recover an object which escaped from the field of perception). He succeeds in this by coordinating the positions and the displacements according to a structure, which can be compared to what the geometricians call "group displacements."

When, with the beginning of the symbolic function (language, symbolic play, imagerie, etc.), the representation through thought becomes possible, it is at first a question of reconstructing in thought what the action is already able to realize. The actions actually do not become transformed immediately into operations, and one has to wait until about 7 to 8 years for the child to reach a functioning level. During this preoperative period the child, therefore, only arrives at incomplete structures characterized by a lack in the notion of combinations and, consequently, by a lack of logic (in transitivity, etc.).

In the realm of causality one can especially observe these diverse forms of precausality, which we have previously described in detail. It is true that a certain number of authors—Anglo-Saxon above all—have severely criticized these conclusions, while others have recognized the same facts as we have (animism, etc.). Yet, in an important recent book (which will appear soon) two Canadian authors, M. Laurendeau and A. Pinard, have taken the whole problem up once again by means of thorough statistics. In the main points they have come to a remarkable verification of our views, explaining, moreover, the methodological reasons for the divergencies among the preceding authors.

At about 7 to 8 years the child arrives at his first complete dynamic structures (classes, relations, and numbers), which, however, still remain concrete—in other words, only at the time of a handling of objects (material manipulation or, when possible, directly imagined). It is not before the age of 11 to 12 years or more that operations can be applied to pure hypotheses. At this latter level, a logic of propositions helps complete the concrete structures. This enlarges the structures considerably until their disposition.

The fundamental genetic problem of the psychology of thought is hence to explain the formation of these dynamic structures.

Practically, one would have to rely on three principal factors in order to explain the facts of development: maturation, physical experience, and social interaction. But in this particular case none of these three suffice to furnish us with the desired explanations—not even the three together.

*Maturation.* First of all, none of these dynamic structures are innate, but they form very gradually. (For example: The transitivity of equalities is acquired at approximately 6½ to 7 years, and the ability of linear measure comes about only at 9 years, as does the full understanding of weights, etc.) But progressive construction does not seem to depend on maturation, because the achievements hardly correspond to a particular age. Only the order of succession is constant. However, one witnesses innumerable accelerations or retardations for reasons of education (cultural) or acquired experience. Certainly one cannot deny the inevitable role which maturation plays, but it is determined above all by existing possibility (or limitation). They still remain to be actualized, which brings about other factors. In addition, in the domain of thought, the factors of innateness seem above all limitative. We do not have, for example, an intuition of space in the fourth dimension; nevertheless we can deduce it.

*Physical Experience.* Experiencing of objects plays, naturally, a very important role in the establishment of dynamic structures, because the operations originate from actions and the actions bear upon the object. This role manifests itself right from the beginning of sensory-motor explorations, preceding language, and it affirms itself continually in the course of manipulations and activities which are appropriate to the antecedent stages. Necessary as the role of experience may be, it does not sufficiently describe the construction of the dynamic structures—and this for the following three reasons.

First, there exist ideas which cannot possibly be derived from the child's experience—for instance, when one changes the shape of a small ball of clay. The child will declare, at 7 to 8 years, that the quantity of the matter is conserved. It does so before discovering the conservation of weight (9 to 10 years) and that of volume (10 to 11 years). What is the quantity of a matter independently of its weight and its volume? This is an abstract notion corresponding to the "substance" of the pre-Socratic physicists. This notion is neither possible to be perceived nor measurable. It is, therefore, the product of a dynamic deduction and not part of an experience. (The problem would not be solved either by presenting the quantity in the form of a bar of chocolate to be eaten.)

Secondly, the various investigations into the learning of logical structure, which we were able to make at our International Center of Genetic Epistemology, lead to a very unanimous result:[2] one does not "learn" a logical structure as one learns to discover any physical law. For instance, it is easy to bring about the learning of the conservation of weight because of its physical character, but it is difficult to obtain the one of the transitivity of the relationship of the weight:

$$A = C \text{ if } A = B \text{ and } B = C$$

or the one of the relationship of inclusion, etc. The reason for this is that in order to arrive at the learning of a logical structure, one has to build on another more elementary logical (or prelogical) structure. And such structures consequently never stem from experience alone, but suppose always a coordinating activity of the subject.

Thirdly, there exist two types of experiences:

1. The physical experiences show the objects as they are, and the knowledge of them leads to the abstraction directly from the object (example: to discover that a more voluminous matter is more or less heavy than a less voluminous matter).

2. The logicomathematical experience supposes to interrelate by action individual facts into the world of objects, but this refers to the result of these actions rather than to the objects themselves. These interrelations are arrived at by process of abstractions from the actions and their coordinates. For instance, to discover that 10 stones in a line always add up to 10, whether they are counted from left to right or from right to left. Because then the order and the total sum have been presented. The new knowledge consists simply in the discovery that the action of adding a sum is independent of the action of putting them in order. Thus the logicomathematical experience does not stem from the same type of learning as that of the physical experience, but rather from an equilibration of the scheme of actions, as we will see.

[2] See *Etudes d'Epistomologie Genetique*, Vol. 7 and 10.

*Social Interaction.* The educative and social transmission (linguistic, etc.) plays, naturally, an evident role in the formation of dynamic structures, but this factor does not suffice either to entirely explain its development, and this for two reasons:

First, a certain number of structures do not lend themselves to teaching and are prior to all teaching. One can cite, as an example, most concepts of conservation, of which, in general, the pedagogs agree that they are not problematic to the child.

The second, more fundamental, reason is that in order to understand the adult and his language, the child needs means of assimilation which are formed through structures preliminary to the social transmission itself —for instance, an ancient experience has shown us that French-speaking children understand very early the expression "*quelques unes de mes fleurs*" [some of my flowers] in contrast to "*toutes mes fleurs*" [all my flowers], and this occurs when they have not yet constructed the relation of inclusion:

Some A are part of all B; therefore

$$A < B$$

In conclusion, it is not exaggerated to maintain that the basic factors invoked before in order to explain mental development do not suffice to explain the formation of the dynamic structures. Though all three of them certainly play a necessary role, they do not constitute in themselves sufficient reason and one has to add to them a fourth factor, which we shall try to describe now.

This fourth factor seems to us to consist of a general progression of equilibration. This factor intervenes, as is to be expected, in the interaction of the preceding factors. Indeed, if the development depends, on one hand, on internal factors (maturation), and on the other hand on external factors (physical or social), it is self-evident that these internal and external factors equilibrate each other. The question is then to know if we are dealing here only with momentary compromises (unstable equilibrium) or if, on the contrary, this equilibrium becomes more and more stable. This shows that all exchange (mental as well as biological) between the organisms and the milieu (physical and social) as composed of two poles: (*a*) of the *assimilation* of the given external to the previous internal structures, and (*b*) of the *accommodation* of these structures to the given ones. The equilibrium between the assimilation and the accommodation is proportionately more stable than the assimilative structures which are better differentiated and coordinated.

It is this equilibrium between the assimilation and accommodation that seems to explain to us the functioning of the reversible operations. This occurs, for instance, in the realm of notions of conservation where the invariants of groups do not account for the maturation and the physical experience, nor for the sociolingual transmission. In fact, dynamic reversibility is a compensatory system of which the idea of conservation constitutes precisely the result. The equilibrium (between the assimilation and the accommodation) is to be defined as a compensation of exterior disturbances through activities of the subject orientated in the contrary direction of these disturbances. This leads us directly to the reversibility.

Notice that we do not conceive of the idea of equilibrium in the same manner as the "gestalt theory" does, which makes great use of this idea too, but in the sense of an automatical physical equilibrium. We believe, on the contrary, that the mental equilibrium and even the biological one presumes an activity of the subject, or of the organism. It consists in a sort of matching, orientated towards compensation—with even some overcompensation—resulting from strategies of precaution. One knows, for instance, that the homeostasis does not always lead to an exact balance. But it often leads to overcompensation, in response to exterior disturbances. Such is the case in nearly all occurrences except precisely in the case of occurrences of a superior order, which are the operations of reversible intelligence, the reversible logic of which is characterized by a complete and exact compensation (inverted operation).

The idea of equilibrium is so close to the one of reversibility that G. Brunner, in a friendly criticism of one of our latest books appearing in the *British Journal of Psychology*, proposes to renounce the idea of equilibrium because the notion of the reversibility seems sufficient to him. We hesitate to accept this suggestion for the following three reasons:

First, reversibility is a logical idea, while the equilibrium is a causal idea which permits the explanation of reforms by means of a probabilistic schema. For instance, in order to explain the formation of the idea of conservation, one can distinguish a certain number of successive stages, of which each is characterized by the "strategy" of a progress of compensation. Now it is possible to show[3] that the first of these strategies (only bearing upon one dimension, to the neglect of others) is the most probable at the point of departure, and further, that the second of these strategies (with the emphasis on a second dimension) *becomes* the most likely—as a function of the result of the first. And, finally, that the third of these strategies (oscillation between the observed modifications upon the different dimensions and the discovery of their solidarity) *becomes* the most likely in the functioning of the results of the preceding, etc. From such a point of view the process of equilibration is, therefore, characterized by a sequential control with increasing probabilities. It furnishes a beginning for causal explanations of the reversibility and does not duplicate the former idea.

Secondly, the tendency of equilibrium is much broader for the operation than the reversibility as such, which leads us to explain the reversibility through the equilibrium and not the reverse. In effect, it is at this level of the obvious regulations and sensory-motor feedbacks that the process of equilibration starts. This in its higher form becomes intelligence. Logical reversibility is therefore conceivable as an end result and not as a beginning and the entire reversibility follows the laws of a semireversibility of various levels.

Thirdly, the tendency to equilibrate does not only explain this final reversibility, but also certain new synthesis between originally distinct operations. One can cite in this regard an example of great importance: the serial of whole numbers. Russell and Whitehead have tried to explain the basic set of numbers through the idea of equivalent classes, without recourse to the serial order. This means that two classes are believed to be equivalent, if one can put their respective elements into a reciprocal arrangement. Only when this relationship relies on the quality of the objects (an A put into relation with an A, a B with a B, etc.) one does not get the quantity. If this relationship is made exclusive of the qualities (an Individual A or B put into relationship with an Individual B or A) then there exists only one way to distinguish the elements from each other. In order not to forget one, or not to count the same twice, one must deal with them in succession and introduce the serial factor as well as the structure of classes. We may then say, psychologically speaking, that the sequence of whole numbers is synthesis between two groupings qualitatively distinct, the fitting of the classes and serialization, and that this synthesis takes place as soon as one excludes the qualities of the elements in question. But how does this synthesis occur? Precisely by a gradual process of equilibration.

On the one hand the child who develops his ideas from numbers is in possession of structures enabling him to fit them into classes (classifications). But if he wants to be exclusive of qualities in order to answer to the question "how many," he becomes unable to distinguish the elements. The disequilibrium which appears, therefore, obliges the child to resort to the idea of order and take recourse to arranging these elements into a lineal row. On the other hand, if the child arranges the elements as 1, 1, 1, etc., how would he know, for instance, how to distinguish the second from the third? This new disequilibrium brings him back to the idea of classification: The "second" is the element which

[3] *Logique et Equilibre*, Vol. 2 of *Etudes d'Epistemologie Genetique.*

has but one predecessor, and the "third" is one that has two of them. In short, every new problem provokes a disequilibrium (recognizable through types of dominant errors) the solution of which consists in a re-equilibration, which brings about a new original synthesis of two systems, up to the point of independence.

During the discussion of my theories, Brunner has said that I have called disequilibrium what others describe as motivation. This is perfectly true, but the advantage of this language is to clarify that a cognitive or dynamic structure is never independent of motivational factors. The motivation in return is always solidary to structural (therefore cognitive) determined level. The language of the equilibrium presents that activity, that permits us to reunite into one and the same totality those two aspects of behavior which always have a functional solidarity because there exists no structure (cognition) without an energizer (motivation) and vice versa.

# Development and Learning

JEAN PIAGET

*Center for Genetic Epistemology, Geneva, Switzerland*

My dear colleagues, I am very concerned about what to say to you, because I do not know if I shall accomplish the end that has been assigned to me. But I have been told that the important thing is not what you say, but the discussion which follows and the answers to questions you are asked. So this morning I shall simply give a general introduction of a few ideas which seem to me to be important for the subject of this conference.

First I would like to make clear the difference between two problems: the problem of *development* in general and the problem of *learning*. I think these problems are very different, although some people do not make this distinction.

The development of knowledge is a spontaneous process, tied to the whole process of embryogenesis. Embryogenesis concerns the development of the body, but it concerns as well the development of the nervous system and the development of mental functions. In the case of the development of knowledge in children, embryogenesis ends only in adulthood. It is a total developmental process which we must re-situate in its general biological and psychological context. In other words, development is a process which concerns the totality of the structures of knowledge.

Learning presents the opposite case. In general, learning is provoked by situations—provoked by a psychological experimenter; or by a teacher, with respect to some didactic point; or by an external situation. It is provoked, in general, as opposed to spontaneous. In addition, it is a limited process—limited to a single problem, or to a single structure.

So I think that development explains learning, and this opinion is contrary to the widely held opinion that development is a sum of discrete learning experiences. For some psychologists development is reduced to a series of specific learned items, and development is thus the sum, the cumulation of this series of specific items. I think this is an atomistic view which deforms the real state of things. In reality, development is the essential process and each element of learning occurs as a function of total development, rather than being an element which explains development. I shall begin, then, with a first part dealing with development, and I shall talk about learning in the second part.

To understand the development of knowledge, we must start with an idea which seems central to me—the idea of an *operation*. Knowledge is not a copy of reality. To know an object, to know an event, is not simply to look at it and make a mental copy or image of it. To know an object is to act on it. To know is to modify, to transform the object, and to understand the process of this transformation, and as a consequence to understand the way the object is constructed. An operation is thus the essence of knowledge; it is an interiorized action which modifies the object of knowledge. For instance an operation would consist of joining objects in a class to construct a

JOURNAL OF RESEARCH IN SCIENCE TEACHING, 1964, Vol. 2, pp. 176-186.

classification. Or an operation would consist of ordering, or putting things in a series. Or an operation would consist of counting, or of measuring. In other words, it is a set of actions modifying the object, and enabling the knower to get at the structures of the transformation.

An operation is an interiorized action. But, in addition, it is a reversible action; that is, it can take place in both directions, for instance, adding or subtracting, joining or separating. So it is a particular type of action which makes up logical structures.

Above all, an operation is never isolated. It is always linked to other operations, and as a result it is always a part of a total structure. For instance, a logical class does not exist in isolation; what exists is the total structure of classification. An asymmetrical relation does not exist in isolation. Seriation is the natural, basic operational structure. A number does not exist in isolation. What exists is the series of numbers which constitute a structure, an exceedingly rich structure whose various properties have been revealed by mathematicians.

These operational structures are what seem to me to constitute the basis of knowledge, the natural psychological reality, in terms of which we must understand the development of knowledge. And the central problem of development is to understand the formation, elaboration, organization, and functioning of these structures.

I should like to review the stages of development of these structures, not in any detail, but simply as a reminder. I shall distinguish four main stages. The first is a sensory-motor, pre-verbal stage, lasting approximately the first 18 months of life. During this stage is developed the practical knowledge which constitutes the substructure of later representational knowledge. An example is the construction of the schema of the permanent object. For an infant, during the first months, an object has no permanence. When it disappears from the perceptual field it no longer exists. No attempt is made to find it again. Later, the infant will try to find it, and he will find it by localizing it spatially. Consequently, along with the construction of the permanent object there comes the construction of practical or sensory-motor space. There is similarly the construction of temporal succession, and of elementary sensory-motor causality. In other words, there is a series of structures which are indispensable for the structures of later representational thought.

In a second stage, we have pre-operational representation—the beginnings of language, of the symbolic function, and therefore of thought, or representation. But at the level of representational thought, there must now be a reconstruction of all that was developed on the sensory-motor level. That is, the sensory-motor actions are not immediately translated into operations. In fact, during all this second period of pre-operational representations, there are as yet no operations as I defined this term a moment ago. Specifically, there is as yet no conservation which is the psychological criterion of the presence of reversible operations. For example, if we pour liquid from one glass to another of a different shape, the pre-operational child will think there is more in one than in the other. In the absence of operational reversibility, there is no conservation of quantity.

In a third stage the first operations appear, but I call these concrete operations because they operate on objects, and not yet on verbally expressed hypotheses. For example, there are the operations of classification, ordering, the construction of the idea of number, spatial and temporal operations, and all the fundamental operations of elementary logic of classes and relations, of elementary mathematics, of elementary geometry, and even of elementary physics.

Finally, in the fourth stage, these operations are surpassed as the child reaches the level of what I call formal or hypothetic-deductive operations; that is, he can now reason on hypotheses, and not only on objects. He constructs new operations, operations of propositional logic, and not simply the operations of classes, relations, and numbers. He attains new structures which are on the one hand combinatorial, corresponding to what mathematicians call lattices; on the other hand, more complicated group structures. At the level of concrete operations, the operations apply within an immediate neighborhood: for instance, classification by successive inclusions. At the level of the combinatorial, however, the groups are much more mobile.

These, then, are the four stages which we identify, whose formation we shall now attempt to explain.

What factors can be called upon to explain the development from one set of structures to another? It seems to me that there are four main factors: first of all, *maturation*, in the sense of Gesell, since this development is a continuation of the embryogenesis; second, the role of *experience* of the effects of the physical environment on the structures of intelligence; third, *social transmission* in the broad sense (linguistic transmission, education, etc.); and fourth, a factor which is too often neglected but one which seems to me fundamental and even the principal factor. I shall call this the factor of *equilibration* or if you prefer it, of self-regulation.

Let us start with the first factor, maturation. One might think that these stages are simply a reflection of an interior maturation of the nervous system, following the hypotheses of Gesell, for example. Well, maturation certainly does play an indispensable role and must not be ignored. It certainly takes part in every transformation that takes place during a child's development. However, this first factor is insufficient in itself. First of all, we know practically nothing about the maturation of the nervous system beyond the first months of the child's existence. We know a little bit about it during the first two years but we know very little following this time. But above all, maturation doesn't explain everything, because the average ages at which these stages appear (the average chronological ages) vary a great deal from one society to another. The ordering of these stages is constant and has been found in all the societies studied. It has been found in various countries where psychologists in universities have redone the experiments but it has also been found in African peoples for example, in the children of the Bushmen, and in Iran, both in the villages and in the cities. However, although the order of succession is constant, the chronological ages of these stages varies a great deal. For instance, the ages which we have found in Geneva are not necessarily the ages which you would find in the United States. In Iran, furthermore, in the city of Teheran, they found approximately the same ages as we found in Geneva, but there is a systematic delay of two years in the children in the country. Canadian psychologists who redid our experiments, Monique Laurendeau and Father Adrien Pinard, found once again about the same ages in Montreal. But when they redid the experiments in Martinique, they found a delay of four years in all the experiments and this in spite of the fact that the children in Martinique go to a school set up according to the French system and the French curriculum and attain at the end of this elementary school a certificate of higher primary education. There is then a delay of four years, that is, there are the same stages, but systematically delayed. So you see that these age variations show that maturation does not explain everything.

I shall go on now to the role played by experience. Experience of objects, of physical reality, is obviously a basic factor in the development of cognitive structures. But once again this factor does not explain everything. I can give two reasons for this. The first reason is that some of the concepts which appear at the beginning of the stage of concrete operations are such that I cannot see how they could be drawn from experience. As an example, let us take the conservation of the substance in the case of changing the shape of a ball of plasticene. We give this ball of plasticene to a child who changes its shape into a sausage form and we ask him if there is the same amount of matter, that is, the same amount of substance as there was before. We also ask him if it now has the same weight and thirdly if it now has the same volume. The volume is measured by the displacement of water when we put the ball or the sausage into a glass of water. The findings, which have been the same every time this experiment has been done, show us that first of all there is conservation of the amount of substance. At about eight years old a child will say, "There is the same amount of plasticene." Only later does the child assert that the weight is conserved and still later that the volume is conserved. So I would ask you where the idea of the conservation of substance can come from. What is a constant and invariant substance when it doesn't yet have a constant weight or a constant volume? Through perception you can get at the weight of the ball or the volume of the ball but perception cannot give you an idea of the amount of substance. No experiment, no experience can show the child that there is the same amount of substance. He can weigh the ball and that would lead to the conservation of weight. He can immerse it in water and that would lead to the conservation of volume. But the notion of substance is attained before either weight or volume. This conservation of substance is simply a logical necessity. The child now understands that when there is a transformation something must be conserved because by reversing the transformation you can come back to the point of departure and once again have the ball. He knows that something is conserved but he doesn't know what. It is not yet the weight, it is not yet the volume; it is simply a logical form—a logical necessity. There, it seems to me, is an example of a progress in knowledge, a logical necessity for something to be conserved even though no experience can have lead to this notion.

My second objection to the sufficiency of experience as an explanatory factor is that this notion of experience is a very equivocal one. There are, in fact, two kinds of experience which are psychologically very different and this difference is very important from the pedagogical point of view. It is because of the pedagogical importance that I emphasize this distinction. First of all, there is what I shall call physical experience, and, secondly, what I shall call logical-mathematical experience.

Physical experience consists of acting upon objects and drawing some knowledge about the objects by abstraction from the objects. For example, to discover that this pipe is heavier than this watch, the child will weigh them both and find the difference in the objects themselves. This is experience in the usual sense of the term—in the sense used by empiricists. But there is a second type of experience, which I shall call logical mathematical experience where the knowledge is not drawn from the objects, but it is drawn by the actions effected upon the objects. This is not the same thing. When one acts upon objects, the objects are indeed there, but there is also the set of actions which modify the objects.

I shall give you an example of this type of experience. It is a nice example because we have verified it many times in small children under seven years of age, but it is also an example which one of my mathematician friends has related to me about his own childhood, and he dates his mathematical career from this experience. When he was four or five years old—I don't know exactly how old, but a small child—he was seated on the ground in his garden and he was counting pebbles. Now to count these pebbles he put them in a row and he counted them one, two, three, up to ten. Then he finished counting them and started to count them in the other direction. He began by the end and once again he found ten. He found this marvelous that there were ten in one direction and ten in the other direction. So he put them in a circle and counted them that way and found ten once again. Then he counted them in the other direction and found ten once more. So he put them in some other arrangement and kept counting them and kept finding ten. There was the discovery that he made.

Now what indeed did he discover? He did not discover a property of pebbles; he discovered a property of the action of ordering. The pebbles had no order. It was his action which introduced a linear order or a cyclical order, or any kind of an order. He discovered that the sum was independent of the order. The order was the action which he introduced among the pebbles. For the sum the same principle applied. The pebbles had no sum; they were simply in a pile. To make a sum, action was necessary—the operation of putting together and counting. He found that the sum was independent of the order, in other words, that the action of putting together is independent of the action of ordering. He discovered a property of actions and not a property of pebbles. You may say that it is in the nature of pebbles to let this be done to them and this is true. But it could have been drops of water, and drops of water would not have let this be done to them because two drops of water and two drops of water do not make four drops of water as you know very well. Drops of water then would not let this be done to them, we agree to that.

So it is not the physical property of pebbles which the experience uncovered. It is the properties of the actions carried out on the pebbles, and this is quite another form of experience. It is the point of departure of mathematical deduction. The subsequent deduction will consist of interiorizing these actions and then of combining them without needing any pebbles. The mathematician no longer needs his pebbles. He can combine his operations simply with symbols, and the point of departure of this mathematical deduction is logical–mathematical experience, and this is not at all experience in the sense of the empiricists. It is the beginning of the coordination of actions, but this coordination of actions before the stage of operations needs to be supported by concrete material. Later, this coordination of actions leads to the logical–mathematical structures. I believe that logic is not a derivative of language. The source of logic is much more profound. It is the total coordination of actions, actions of joining things together, or ordering things, etc. This is what logical–mathematical experience is. It is an experience of the actions of the subject, and not an experience of objects themselves. It is an experience which is necessary before there can be operations. Once the operations have been attained this experience is no longer needed and the coordinations of actions can take place by themselves in the form of deduction and construction for abstract structures.

The third factor is social transmission–linguistic transmission or educational transmission. This factor, once again, is fundamental. I do not deny the role of any one of these factors; they all play a part. But this factor is insufficient because the child can receive valuable information via language or via education directed by an adult only if he is in a state where he can understand this information. That is, to receive the information he must have a structure which enables him to assimilate this information. This is why you cannot teach higher mathematics to a five-year-old. He does not yet have structures which enable him to understand.

I shall take a much simpler example, an example of linguistic transmission. As my very first work in the realm of child psychology, I spent a long time studying the relation between a part and a whole in concrete experience and in language. For example, I used Burt's test employing the sentence, "Some of my flowers are buttercups." The child knows that all buttercups are yellow, so there are three possible conclusions: the whole bouquet is yellow, or part of the bouquet is yellow, or none of the flowers in the bouquet are yellow. I found that up until nine years of age (and this was in Paris, so the children certainly did understand the French language) they replied, "The whole bouquet is yellow or some of my flowers are yellow." Both of those mean the same thing. They did not understand the expression, "some *of* my flowers." They did not understand this *of* as a partitive genitive, as the inclusion of some flowers in my flowers. They understood some of my flowers to be my several flowers as if the several flowers and the flowers were confused as one and the same class. So there you have children who until nine years of age heard every day a linguistic structure which implied the inclusion of a subclass in a class and yet did not understand this structure. It is only when they themselves are in firm possession of this logical structure, when they have constructed it for themselves according to the developmental laws which we shall discuss, that they succeed in understanding correctly the linguistic expression.

I come now to the fourth factor which is added to the three preceding ones but which seems to me to be the fundamental one. This is what I call the factor of equilibration. Since there are already three factors, they must somehow be equilibrated among themselves. That is one reason for bringing in the factor of equilibration. There is a second reason, however, which seems to me to be fundamental. It is that in the act of knowing, the subject is active, and consequently, faced with an external disturbance, he will react in order to compensate and consequently he will tend towards equilibrium. Equilibrium, defined by active compensation, leads to reversibility. Operational reversibility is a model of an equilibrated system where a transformation in one direction is compensated by a transformation in the other direction. Equilibration, as I understand it, is thus an active process. It is a process of self-regulation. I think that this self-regulation is a fundamental factor in development. I use this term in the sense in which it is used in cybernetics, that is, in the sense of processes with feedback and with feedforward, of processes which regulate themselves by a progressive compensation of systems. This process of equilibration takes the form of a succession of levels of equilibrium, of levels which have a certain probability which I shall call a sequential probability, that is, the probabilities are not established *a priori*. There is a sequence of levels. It is not possible to reach the second level unless equilibrium has been reached at the first level, and the equilibrium of the third level only becomes possible when the equilibrium of the second level has been reached, and so forth. That is, each level is determined as the most probable given that the preceding level has been reached. It is not the most probable at the beginning, but it is the most probable once the preceding level has been reached.

As an example, let us take the development of the idea of conservation in the transformation of the ball of plasticene into the sausage shape. Here you can discern four levels. The most probable at the beginning is for the child to think of only one dimension. Suppose that there is a probability of 0.8, for instance, that the child will focus on the length, and that the width has a probability of 0.2. This would mean that of ten children, eight will focus on the length alone without paying any attention to the width, and two will focus on the width without paying any attention to the length. They will focus only on one dimension or the other. Since the two dimensions are independent at this stage, focusing on both at once would have a probability of only 0.16. That is less than either one of the two. In other words, the most probable in the beginning is to focus only on one dimension and in fact the child will say, "It's longer, so there's more in the sausage." Once he has reached this first level, if you continue to elongate the sausage, there comes a moment when he will say, "No, now it's too thin, so there's less." Now he is thinking about the width, but he forgets the length, so you have come to a second level which becomes the most probable after the first level, but which is not the most probable at the point of departure. Once he has focused on the width, he will come back sooner or later to focus on the length. Here you will have a third level where he will oscillate between width and length and where he will discover that the two are related. When you elongate you make it thinner, and when you make it shorter, you make it thicker. He discovers that the two are solidly related and in discovering this relationship, he will start to think in terms of transformation and not only in terms of the final configuration. Now he will say that when it gets longer it gets thinner, so it's the same thing. There is more of it in length but less of it in width. When you make it shorter it gets thicker; there's less in length and more in width, so there is compensation—compensation which defines equilibrium in the sense in which I defined it a moment ago. Consequently, you have operations and conservation. In other words, in the course of these developments you will always find a process of self-regulation which I call equilibration and which seems to me the fundamental factor in the acquisition of logical–mathematical knowledge.

I shall go on now to the second part of my lecture, that is, to deal with the topic of learning. Classically, learning is based on the stimulus–response schema. I think the stimulus–response schema, while I won't say it is false, is in any case entirely incapable of explaining cognitive learning. Why? Because when you think of a stimulus–response schema, you think usually that first of all there is a stimulus and then a response is set off by this stimulus. For my part, I am convinced that the response was there first, if I can express myself in this way. A stimulus is a stimulus only to the extent that it is significant, and it becomes significant only to the extent that there is a structure which permits its assimilation, a structure which can integrate this stimulus but which at the same time sets off the response. In other words, I would propose that the stimulus–response schema be written in the circular form—in the form of a schema or of a structure which is not simply one way. I would propose that above all, between the stimulus and the response, there is the organism, the organism and its structures. The stimulus is really a stimulus only when it is assimilated into a structure and it is this structure which sets off the response. Consequently, it is not an exaggeration to say that the response is there first, or if you wish at the beginning there is the structure. Of course we would want to understand how this structure comes to be. I tried to do this earlier by presenting a model of equilibration or self-regulation. Once there is a structure, the stimulus will set off a response, but only by the intermediary of this structure.

I should like to present some facts. We have facts in great number. I shall choose only one or two and I shall choose some facts which our colleague, Smedslund, has gathered. (Smedslund is currently at the Harvard Center for Cognitive Studies.) Smedslund arrived in Geneva a few years ago convinced (he had published this in one of his papers) that the development of the ideas of conservation could be indefinitely accelerated through learning of a stimulus–response type. I invited Smedslund to come to spend a year in Geneva to show us this, to show us that he could accelerate the development of operational conservation. I shall relate only one of his experiments.

During the year that he spent in Geneva he chose to work on the conservation of weight. The conservation of weight is, in fact, easy to study since there is a possible external reinforcement, that is, simply weighing the ball and the sausage on a balance. Then you can study the child's reactions to these external results. Smedslund studied the conservation of weight on the one hand, and on the other hand he studied the transitivity of weights, that is, the transitivity of equalities if A = B and B = C, then A = C, or the transitivity of the inequalities if A is less than B, and B is less than C, then A is less than C.

As far as conservation is concerned,

Smedslund succeeded very easily with five- and six-year-old children in getting them to generalize that weight is conserved when the ball is transformed into a different shape. The child sees the ball transformed into a sausage or into little pieces or into a pancake or into any other form, he weighs it, and he sees that it is always the same thing. He will affirm it will be the same thing, no matter what you do to it; it will come out to be the same weight. Thus Smedslund very easily achieved the conservation of weight by this sort of external reinforcement.

In contrast to this, however, the same method did not succeed in teaching transitivity. The children resisted the notion of transitivity. A child would predict correctly in certain cases but he would make his prediction as a possibility or a probability and not as a certainty. There was never this generalized certainty in the case of transitivity.

So there is the first example, which seems to me very instructive, because in this problem in the conservation of weight there are two aspects. There is the physical aspect and there is the logical–mathematical aspect. Note that Smedslund started his study by establishing that there was a correlation between conservation and transitivity. He began by making a statistical study on the relationships between the spontaneous responses to the questions about conservation and the spontaneous responses to the questions about transitivity, and he found a very significant correlation. But in the learning experiment, he obtained a learning of conservation and not of transitivity. Consequently, he successfully obtained a learning of what I called earlier physical experience (which is not surprising since it is simply a question of noting facts about objects), but he did not successfully obtain a learning in the construction of the logical structure. This doesn't surprise me either, since the logical structure is not the result of physical experience. It cannot be obtained by external reinforcement. The logical structure is reached only through internal equilibration, by self-regulation, and the external reinforcement of seeing that the balance did not suffice to establish this logical structure of transitivity.

I could give many other comparable examples, but it seems useless to me to insist upon these negative examples. Now I should like to show that learning is possible in the case of these logical–mathematical structures, but on one condition—that is, that the structure which you want to teach to the subjects can be supported by simpler, more elementary, logical–mathematical structures. I shall give you an example. It is the example of the conservation of number in the case of one-to-one correspondence. If you give a child seven blue tokens and ask him to put down as many red tokens, there is a preoperational stage where he will put one red one opposite each blue one. But when you spread out the red ones, making them into a longer row, he will say to you, "Now, there are more red ones than there are blue ones."

Now how can we accelerate, if you want to accelerate, the acquisition of this conservation of number? Well, you can imagine an analogous structure but in a simpler, more elementary situation. For example, with Mlle. Inhelder, we have been studying recently the notion of one-to-one correspondence by giving the child two glasses of the same shape and a big pile of beads. The child puts a bead into one glass with one hand and at the same time a bead into the other glass with the other hand. Time after time he repeats this action, a bead into one glass with one hand and at the same time a bead into the other glass with the other hand and he sees that there is always the same amount on each side. Then you hide one of the glasses. You cover it up. He no longer sees this glass but he continues to put one bead into it while at the same time putting one bead into the other glass which he can see. Then you ask him whether the equality has been conserved, whether there is still the same amount in one glass as in the other. Now you will find that very small children, about four years old, don't want to make a prediction. They will say, "So far, it has been the same amount, but now I don't know. I can't see any more, so I don't know." They do not want to generalize. But the generalization is made from the age of about five and one-half years.

This is in contrast to the case of the red and blue tokens with one row spread out, where it isn't until seven or eight years of age that children will say there are the same number in the two rows. As one example of this generalization, I recall a little boy of five years and nine months who had been adding the beads to the glasses for a little while. Then we asked him whether, if he continued to do this all day and all night and all the next day, there would always be the same amount in the two glasses. The little boy gave this admirable reply. "Once you know, you know for always." In other words, this was recursive reasoning. So here the child does acquire the structure in this specific case. The number is a synthesis of class inclusion and ordering. This synthesis is being favored by the child's own actions. You have set up a situation where there is an iteration of one same action which continues and which is therefore ordered while at the same time being inclusive. You have, so to speak, a localized synthesis of inclusion and ordering which facilitates the construction of the idea of number in this specific case, and there you can find, in effect, an influence of this experience on the other experience. However, this influence is not immediate. We study the generalization from this recursive situation to the other situation where the tokens are laid on the table in rows, and it is not an immediate generalization but it is made possible through intermediaries. In other words, you can find some learning of this structure if you base the learning on simpler structures.

In this same area of the development of numerical structures, the psychologist Joachim Wohlwill, who spent a year at our Institute at Geneva, has also shown that this acquisition can be accelerated through introducing additive operations, which is what we introduced also in the experiment which I just described. Wohlwill introduced them in a different way but he too was able to obtain a certain learning effect. In other words, learning is possible if you base the more complex structure on simpler structures, that is, when there is a natural relationship and development of structures and not simply an external reinforcement.

Now I would like to take a few minutes to conclude what I was saying. My first conclusion is that learning of structures seems to obey the same laws as the natural development of these structures. In other words, learning is subordinated to development and not vice-versa as I said in the introduction. No doubt you will object that some investigators have succeeded in teaching operational structures. But, when I am faced with these facts, I always have three questions which I want to have answered before I am convinced.

The first question is: "Is this learning lasting? What remains two weeks or a month later?" If a structure develops spontaneously, once it has reached a state of equilibrium, it is lasting, it will continue throughout the child's entire life. When you achieve the learning by external reinforcement, is the result lasting or not and what are the conditions necessary for it to be lasting?

The second question is: "How much generalization is possible?" What makes learning interesting is the possibility of transfer of a generalization. When you have brought about some learning, you can always ask whether this is an isolated piece in the midst of the child's mental life, or if it is really a dynamic structure which can lead to generalizations.

Then there is the third question: "In the case of each learning experience what was the operational level of the subject before the experience and what more complex structures has this learning succeeded in achieving?" In other words, we must look at each specific learning experience from the point of view of the spontaneous operations which were present at the outset and the operational level which has been achieved after the learning experience.

My second conclusion is that the fundamental relation involved in all development and all learning is not the relation of association. In the stimulus–response schema, the relation between the response and the stimulus is understood to be one of association. In contrast to this, I think that the fundamental relation is one of assimilation. Assimilation is not the same as association. I shall define assimilation as the integration of any sort of reality into a structure, and it is this assimilation which seems to me to be fundamental in learning, and which seems to me to be the fundamental relation from the point of view of pedagogical or didactic applications. All of my remarks today represent the child and the learning subject as active. An operation is an activity. Learning is possible only when there is active assimilation. It is this activity on the part of the subject which seems to me to be underplayed in the stimulus–response schema. The presentation which I propose puts the emphasis on the idea of self-regulation, on assimilation. All the emphasis is placed on the activity of the subject himself, and I think that without this activity there is no possible didactic or pedagogy which significantly transforms the subject.

Finally, and this will be my last concluding remark, I would like to comment on an excellent publication by the psychologist Berlyne. Berlyne spent a year with us in Geneva during which he intended to translate our results on the development of operations into stimulus–response language, specifically into Hull's learning theory. Berlyne published in our series of studies of genetic epistomology a very good article on this comparison between the results obtained in Geneva and Hull's theory. In the same volume, I published a commentary on Berlyne's results. The essence of Berlyne's results is this: Our findings can very well be translated into Hullian language, but only on condition that two modifications are introduced. Berlyne himself found these modifications quite considerable, but they seemed to him to concern more the conceptualization than the Hullian theory itself. I am not so sure about that. The two modifications are these. First of all, Berlyne wants to distinguish two sorts of response in the S-R schema: (*a*) responses in the ordinary, classical sense, which I shall call "copy responses;" (*b*) responses which Berlyne calls "transformation responses." Transformation responses consist of transforming one response of the first type into another response of the first type. These transformation responses are what I call operations, and you can see right away that this is a rather serious modification of Hull's conceptualization because here you are introducing an element of transformation and thus of assimilation and no longer the simple association of stimulus–response theory.

The second modification which Berlyne introduces into the stimulus–response language is the introduction of what he calls internal reinforcements. What are these internal reinforcements? They are what I call equilibration or self-regulation. The internal reinforcements are what enable the subject to eliminate contradictions, incompatibilities, and conflicts. All development is composed of momentary conflicts and incompatibilities which must be overcome to reach a higher level of equilibrium. Berlyne calls this elimination of incompatibilities internal reinforcements.

So you see that it is indeed a stimulus–response theory, if you will, but first you add operations and then you add equilibration. That's all we want!

***Editor's note:** A brief question and answer period followed Professor Piaget's presentation. The first question related to the fact that the eight-year-old child acquires conservation of weight and volume. The question asked if this didn't contradict the order of emergence of the pre-operational and operational stages. Piaget's response follows:*

The conservation of weight and the conservation of volume are not due only to experience. There is also involved a logical framework which is characterized by reversibility and the system of compensations. I am only saying that in the case of weight and volume, weight corresponds to a perception. There is an empirical contact. The same is true of volume. But in the case of substance, I don't see how there can be any perception of substance independent of weight or volume. The strange thing is that this notion of substance comes before the two other notions. Note that in the history of thought we have the same thing. The first Greek physicists, the pre-socratic philosophers, discovered conservation of substance independently of any experience. I do not believe this is contradictory to the theory of operations. This conservation of substance is simply the affirmation that something must be conserved. The children do not know specifically what is conserved. They know that since the sausage can become a ball again there must be something which is conserved, and saying "substance" is simply a way of translating this logical necessity for conservation. But this logical necessity results directly from the discovery of operations. I do not think that this is contradictory with the theory of development.

*Editor's note: The second question was whether or not the development of stages in children's thinking could be accelerated by practice, training, and exercise in perception and memory. Piaget's response follows:*

I am not very sure that exercise of perception and memory would be sufficient. I think that we must distinguish within the cognitive function two very different aspects which I shall call the figurative aspect and the operative aspect. The figurative aspect deals with static configurations. In physical reality there are states, and in addition to these there are transformations which lead from one state to another. In cognitive functioning one has the figurative aspects—for example, perception, imitation, mental imagery, etc.

The operative aspect includes operations and the actions which lead from one state to another. In children of the higher stages and in adults, the figurative aspects are subordinated to the operative aspects. Any given state is understood to be the result of some transformation and the point of departure for another transformation. But the pre-operational child does not understand transformations. He does not have the operations necessary to understand them so he puts all the emphasis on the static quality of the states. It is because of this, for example, that in the conservation experiments he simply compares the initial state and the final state without being concerned with the transformation.

In exercising perception and memory, I feel that you will reinforce the figurative aspect without touching the operative aspect. Consequently, I'm not sure that this will accelerate the development of cognitive structures. What needs to be reinforced is the operative aspect—not the analysis of states, but the understanding of transformations.

HERMINE SINCLAIR

# Piaget's Theory of Development: The Main Stages

At first sight it would seem that a psychological theory that is regarded by its author as a "by-product" of his epistemological research and is therefore principally directed toward the investigation of knowledge and its changes in the history of mankind, as well as in the growing child, is ideally suited to educational applications. One of the aims of education is the fostering of knowledge, the endeavour to transmit to the next generation the experience of its forebears in the hope that the sum total of knowledge will be expanded. At the same time, for many different reasons, there is a general feeling that education is not good enough, that something should be changed, that not enough profit is derived from what is becoming a considerable number of years spent at school. It is thus not surprising that a number of educators have turned to Piaget's theory to seek help for new pedagogical approaches. Unfortunately, many of them have been disappointed; Piaget's theoretical approach has seemed too far removed from classroom reality. Recently, others have become very enthusiastic, seduced by the experimental situations Piaget has imagined, and there seems to be a regrettable tendency to take Piaget's problem situations and convert them directly into teaching situations.

Why I think this is regrettable is probably best explained by a metaphor: Piaget's tasks are like the core samples a geologist takes from a fertile area and from which he can infer the general structure of a fertile soil; but it is absurd to hope that transplanting these samples to a field of nonfertile soil will make the whole area fertile. A child's reactions to a few Piagetian tasks will enable a well-trained psychologist to give a fair description of that child's intellectual level; but teaching the solutions of these same Piagetian tasks to a group of children does not mean that

PIAGETIAN COGNITIVE-DEVELOPMENT RESEARCH AND MATHEMATICAL EDUCATION, National Council of Teachers of Mathematics, Washington, D.C., pp. 1-11.

the children will thereby attain the general intellectual level of the child who can solve the tasks independently.

Many modern school programs emphasize doing and point out that seeing and hearing are not enough; such programs are sometimes called Piagetian, and, indeed, one of Piaget's basic principles is the primacy of action. However, this does not mean that children should spend all their early school years digging in sandpits and making mud pies, progressing to constructing buildings out of bricks and then to making systems of pulleys and levers.

Educational applications of Piaget's experimental procedures and theoretical principles will have to be very indirect—and he himself has given hardly any indication of how one could go about it. His experiments cannot be modified into specific teaching methods for specific problems, and his principles should not be used simply to set the general tone of an instructional program.

It would thus seem necessary to study Piaget's theory as a whole before deciding which parts of it, if any, could be applied in the classroom. The theory is explicitly developmental and maintains that the explanation of the nature of adult knowledge is found by studying the way this knowledge has been built up; in other words, the adolescent explains the man, the child explains the adolescent, the toddler explains the child, and the infant explains the toddler. Even though all of you are familiar with parts of Piaget's work, a brief description of the psychological characteristics of cognitive development may be helpful. This will perhaps involve a certain amount of tedious repetition of facts known to all of you. My apologies!

According to Piaget, action, rather than perception, is the primary source of knowledge. To know objects, one has to modify them in some way—for instance, simply change their position. The main division into developmental stages is therefore based on the character of the actions that link the subject to the surrounding world.

## From Sensorimotor Intelligence to Concrete Operations

A first period is called the sensorimotor stage. It is a preverbal period, or, speaking more generally, a period of direct action without representation. During this stage (lasting until about the middle of the second year) the world around the subject becomes more and more stable and organized. While at first the newborn baby seems to have no awareness of himself as distinct from the objects around him, by the end of this period he can perform the actions that assure the direct dependencies between subject and objects. He has now acquired object permanency, a first cognitive invariant, as well as a first grouplike structure—the group of displacements, as Piaget has called it. In view of the paramount importance Piaget accords to actions that modify reality, it is no accident that his formalizations of the underlying cognitive structures are all in terms of groups of transformations—even at the level of sensorimotor intelligence. Constants, on the one hand, and action or operation structure, on the other, cannot be dissociated psychologically: at all stages of development they are no more than two sides of the same coin. However, it seems advisable to separate the invariants from their grouplike structures for the purposes of this brief sketch of the course of cognitive development toward the formal operations, which are the only ones that can be formally expressed in terms of group structures in the mathematical sense of the word *group*.

*Constants*

Let me start with the cognitive constants. Object permanency, achieved by the middle of the second year, means above all that the objects have now become "retrievable" or "retraceable"—the child no longer acts as if they disappear completely once they go out of his perceptive field; moreover, if they are hidden under several screens, he can recompose their successive displacements and find them again. Permanent objects are objects one can start "knowing"—they are no longer only objects to which one can react. A little later, objects acquire an identity that is no longer simply a function of the act of searching for them but that arises from the child's realization that several actions can be performed on the same object without its basic identity's being changed. For instance, a piece of wire can be twisted into the shape of a pair of glasses or scissors, but these different shapes do not alter the "sameness" of the piece of wire that was used to produce them. Although the child may put the glasses on his nose and pretend to look through them, he knows, and will say so if asked, that it is the same piece of wire that was used earlier for something else. The next step toward the establishment of quantitative constants is taken when the child begins to make a distinction between permanent and impermanent qualities of objects. The colour, suppleness, and material of the wire are permanent, but its shape is not. For children below the age of, say, seven, certain changes of shape imply a change in length. Nevertheless, the identity of objects has become more objective in the sense that it is now based on the objects' qualities rather than on the actions the subject performs on them.

The great novelty of the concrete-operational period is the change from qualitative identities toward quantitative constants. The first of these quantitative constants is numerical conservation, which manifests itself in correct answers to the well-known questions about the numerical equivalence of two collections of objects. For an example, consider the experiment in which red and blue counters are used. Starting from two rows, one red and one blue, arranged in a visual one-to-one correspondence, the experimenter spreads out the blue counters so that they go beyond the limits of the red row. The child is then asked whether there are still just enough red counters to cover the blue ones, or whether there will be some blue counters left over, or whether there will not be enough, and so on. Before the age of five or six, the child will say that there are not enough red counters to cover the blue, that some blue ones will be left over, that there are more blue ones than red ones, and so on. But from five or six onward, the child affirms that the number has not changed and he can give arguments to explain his judgment: "You didn't add any"; "You can put them back like they were"; "They're just spread farther apart"; and so on.

*Structures*

We now come to the second aspect, that of the structure of actions: the action group of displacements, which is completely bound up with object permanency, slowly becomes elaborated during the sensorimotor period from very elementary, often hereditary action patterns. These action patterns (sucking, looking, grasping) at first form isolated entities, but soon they assimilate other objects (sucking thumbs, toys, etc.) and become coordinated (grasping *and* looking, etc.). Gradually, instead of several little isolated actions, there are more and finer coordinations, which culminate in an intended connection between a definite goal and the action sequence necessary for reaching that goal. During the first period of postsensorimotor but preoperational intelligence, the child starts to build up what Piaget calls a *semilogic,* that is to say, a logic of one-way mappings. In psychological terms, this means that the child understands that when one pulls the cord of a curtain, the curtain opens; the farther one pulls, the farther the curtain opens. These functional dependencies imply a real, physical link between cause and effect just as much as a conceptual dependency. Pulling ($y$) makes the curtain move ($x$), where $x = f(y)$; but you also have to know how far to pull to make the curtain go all the way back—knowledge of $x$ depends on knowledge of $y$. These dependencies constitute a kind of semilogic, and their one-way character has been demonstrated in several studies.

In the following experiment, devised by N. van den Bogearts in 1968, the child is shown a toy truck which picks up counters in front of five different dolls. Each counter is put inside the truck in a line so that the arrangement of counters mirrors the itinerary. The colours of the counters correspond to those of the dolls' dresses. The dolls are arranged on the table in a fixed pattern, but neither in a straight line nor in a circle. The first questions concern the arrangement of the counters inside the truck: "Which will be first?" "Which will be last?" "Why is the red one next to the yellow one?" The four-year-old child understands and explains that the order of the counters in the truck is dependent on the itinerary of the truck: if it goes to the blue doll first, the blue counter is first; if it goes to the yellow doll next, the yellow counter will be next to the blue counter; and so on. But, surprisingly, if the child is asked to reconstruct the truck's itinerary, he is incapable of doing so: the mapping is only one way, and he does not understand that the order of the counters in the truck determines the itinerary just as the itinerary determines the order of the counters.

Incomplete though it may be, this semilogic is an important development and a necessary stage which the child has to pass through before he can acquire reversibility. The well-known experiment with the balls of clay can be reformulated in terms of functional dependencies. At first, a dependency is established between actions and their effects. If one rolls the clay $(x)$, it becomes longer $(y_1)$:

$$y_1 = f_1(x).$$

But if one rolls the clay $(x)$, it also becomes thinner $(y_2)$:

$$y_2 = f_2(x).$$

Both dependencies may be thought to covary; that is, if one rolls the clay, it gets longer and thinner. Finally, the child is able to express this covariation between $y_1$ and $y_2$ directly, without the necessity of linking it to the action of rolling, itself. A function $(f)$ that is reversible $(f^{-1})$ is seen to exist between $y_1$ and $y_2$, whereby getting longer is exactly compensated for by getting thinner, and vice versa:

$$y_1 = f(y_2) \quad \text{and} \quad y_2 = f^{-1}(y_1).$$

### From Concrete Operations to Formal Operations

Around the age of six or seven the semilogic of the preoperational period starts to turn into logic. At first this remains a limited logic—hence the term *concrete* operations—in contrast with the "full" logic of formal operations. However, this term does not mean that the child can think logically only if he can at the same time manipulate objects. Even less does it coincide with the (rather difficult to define) distinction between abstract and concrete. *Concrete,* in the Piagetian sense, means that the child can think in a logically coherent manner about objects that do exist and have real properties and about actions that are possible; he can perform the mental operations involved both when asked purely verbal questions and when manipulating objects. The latter situation is far preferable to the former, mainly for reasons of clarity, but the actual presence of objects is no intrinsic condition. Nor is the reverse—that is to say, the absence of objects—a condition for formal operations; these may indeed involve the solving of problems dealing only with propositions, but they may, and usually do, apply to quite concrete situations.

Among the many problems that come within the reach of adolescents at the level of formal operations, there is one (designed by B. Inhelder) that, I think, makes this aspect of the distinction quite clear. The experimenter shows the child a collection of metal bars (some made of brass, others of aluminum; some cylindrical, others with a square cross section; all of various lengths) which can be fixed above a board and then weighted at the end so that they will bend. The problem the child has to solve (which is unsolvable until about the age of twelve, i.e., the formal-operational period) is, Which bar bends most? The various questions are posed: "A long, brass, cylindrical one? A short, brass, cylindrical one? A long, aluminum, cylindrical one? A long, alumnium, square one? . . .?" To work out this problem, all the properties except one must be kept constant during the comparisons: for example, the child might compare two brass rods of the same length to see if the round (cylindrical) one bends more than the square one. The problem cannot be solved in any direct way. A direct, concrete solution would necessitate the existence of rods that are not made of anything at all, have no cross section and no length. Such rods do not exist—in fact, cannot exist—and one cannot even have a mental image of them. But by comparing two rods made of the same metal, with the same cross section and of different lengths, one *creates* impossible rods—in this case, rods that have only length. The concrete-operational child can do no such thing; he can manipulate and think about real objects, but he cannot work with hypothetical entities. He will not be able to solve the problem until about the age of twelve, when he attains the formal-operational period.

The stage of concrete operations results in an important change in children's manner of thought. They now possess what Piaget has called the structure of *groupement* (an incomplete but grouplike structure of transformations comprising invariants).

The term *structures* has given rise to many controversies. Questions such as the following are frequently asked in connection with Piaget's structural approach to intelligence: Have the structures any psychological reality? Or are they no more than a psychological artifice? What is the use, if any, of the search for such structures?

Many disciplines reach a point in history where their subject matter becomes so varied and the types of problems dealt with so large in number that the need is felt for some kind of unification. In mathematics, for instance, the foundations for organizational principles were laid in the beginning of the twentieth century and led to the mathematical theory of sets and mathematical logic. In psychological development, a similar need is at the basis of Piaget's search for structures.

At a certain stage the child becomes capable of dealing with a great variety of problems. Obviously, he is not aware that he is reasoning according to certain well-defined principles, much less that he is using structures. But the way in which he reasons clearly indicates that there is some kind of organisation. What type of organisation and what sort of general mental operations can account for the way a child at a particular stage solves certain problems and yet fails to solve others? It is easy to observe whether a child gives the right answer to a certain problem; it is much more difficult to observe how he goes about solving it. To account for the method of solving (or of failing to solve) a variety of problems, one has to go beyond observation and suppose the existence of an underlying system of operations (a structure).

*Concrete operations*

The operations that form the concrete "grouping" are of the most general kind (putting objects together into a class, separating a collection into subclasses, ordering elements, ordering events in time, etc.). These operations are transformations that are reversible, either through annulment (as in the case of adding, annulled by subtracting) or through reciprocity (as in the case of relationships: *A* is the son of *B*, *B* is the father of *A*).

The importance of the concept of group structures goes beyond the realm of mathematics. In the natural sciences one can, in certain cases, postulate the existence of a grouplike structure. When one then considers the effect of certain transformations on a set of object states (elements), it becomes possible to hypothesize the existence and even the nature of some previously unobserved object states.

Groups of transformations possess an identity operation. Similarly, when one deals with actual problem situations where objects are displaced or changed in form, certain modifications have no effect on certain quantitative properties. For example: pouring a liquid into a different glass has no effect on its volume; kneading a substance has no effect on its mass; spreading out counters does not change their total number.

In Piaget's approach, one learns about the structures of thought by studying, for instance, at what age and in what manner children conceptualize the invariance of quantitative properties such as weight and volume. These are, of course, the famous "conservation experiments." Because of the fact that invariants are always invariants of a system of operations, the acquisition of the conservation concepts is an excellent indicator of the level of intellectual development.

For the concrete-operational period, Piaget distinguishes the basic transformational structures of classes on the one hand and those of relations on the other. *Classification* implies the grouping of objects according to their similarities; *seriation* implies the ordering of objects according to their differences.

The system of operations that accounts for the problems in classification that eight- or nine-year-olds can deal with can be formalized as follows:

If $A, B, C$, and so on, are classes that are included one in the other and $A', B', C'$, and so on, their complementary classes, the following operations pertain.[1]

1. $A + A' = B; B + B' = C;$ and so on.
2. $B - A' = A; C - B' = B;$ and so on.
3. $A + 0 = A.$
4. $A + A = A; B + B = B;$ and so on.
5. $(A + A') + B = A + (A' + B')$, but $(A + A) - A \neq A + (A - A)$.

In this system of operations, reversibility is annulment: adding $A'$ to $A$ gives $B$; subtracting $A'$ from $B$ gives $A$.

This structure accounts for the success achieved by children at this

---

1. EDITOR'S FOOTNOTE. It is instructive to translate Piaget's language and symbolism into current mathematical language and symbolism. Readers with a mathematics background will be more familiar with the latter. There are certain correspondences between symbols and words which should first be made clear: class $\longleftrightarrow$ set; $+ \longleftrightarrow$ $\cup$; "′" corresponds to set difference—that is, $A'$ is not the complement of $A$ but is the set difference relative to a set $B$; and $A' = B - A$, where "$B - A$" denotes a set consisting of those elements of $B$ that are not elements of $A$.

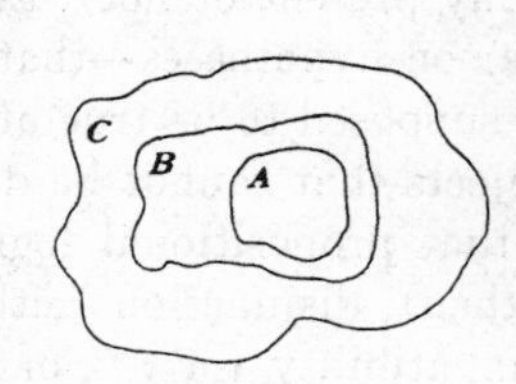


| *Piaget's language* | *Mathematical language* |
|---|---|
| 1. $A + A' = B$ | 1. $A \cup (B - A) = B$ |
| $B + B' = C$ | $B \cup (C - B) = C$ |
| 2. $B - A' = A$ | 2. $B - (B - A) = A$ |
| $C - B' = B$ | $C - (C - B) = B$ |
| 3. $A + 0 = A$ | 3. $A \cup \emptyset = A$ |
| 4. $A + A = A$ | 4. $A \cup A = A$ |
| $B + B = B$ | $B \cup B = B$ |
| 5. $(A + A') + B' = A + (A' + B')$ | 5. $(A \cup (B - A)) \cup (C - B) = A \cup ((B - A) \cup (C - B))$ |
| but $(A + A) - A \neq A + (A - A)$ | but $(A \cup A) - A \neq A \cup (A - A)$ |

level when dealing with several problems in classification: (1) the quantification of class inclusion—they can answer questions on the relative numerical extension of a general class $B$ compared with a subclass $A$; (2) multiplication of classes—they can find missing elements in double-entry tables; and (3) intersection problems—given, for instance, a collection of pictures of green objects and a collection of pictures of leaves, they can find the green leaves which form the intersection.

Seriation implies reversibility by reciprocity and not by annulment. For instance, in seriating lengths, one has to understand that element $E$ is simultaneously bigger than all the preceding ones and smaller than the succeeding ($E > D$, and, the reciprocal relationship, $D < E$). Moreover, once this problem is clearly understood, a new deductive way of composition becomes possible through the application of a transitivity argument: if $A(\mathrm{R})B$ and $B(\mathrm{R})C$, then $A(\mathrm{R})C$.

The existence of this structure, very similar to that of classification, accounts for the success achieved from seven years onward in problems such as: (1) ordering sticks in an operational manner—that is, first taking the smallest (or biggest) of all, then the smallest (or biggest) of those left, and so on; (2) ordering dolls, walking sticks, and rucksacks of different sizes so that one obtains corresponding seriations; and (3) ordering according to two different properties—for instance, counters of various shades of blue and various sizes to be arranged in a double-entry matrix (e.g., keeping size constant horizontally, colour ordered from pale to dark, and keeping colour constant vertically, size ordered from small to big).

This concrete-operational period stretches from age seven to age twelve and at the same time constitutes a complete elaboration of the types of reasoning made possible by these operations, an application of their power to more and more difficult contents, and a preparation for the much more powerful formal operations.

*Formal operations*

Since the concrete operations, as I have just said, bear only on reality in the sense that they are applicable to true and observable situations (whether the situation is actually present or not), the novelty of formal operations is that they can bear on hypotheses—that is to say, on statements that are not known, nor supposed to be true at the outset—and on behaviour and properties of objects that cannot be directly observed. In formalized terms, this means that propositional logic becomes possible, admitting implication (if . . . then), disjunction (either or both . . . or), exclusion (either . . . or), incompatibility (or . . . or . . . or neither nor), and so on, between propositions. In terms of groups of transformations, this implies that annulment by inversion and reciprocity become combined and that therefore every transformation is now at the same time the inverse of another and the reciprocal of a third.

Let me give just one example of the possibilities that are now opened up as far as the reasoning of children at this level is concerned. In a situation where an object is shown to move and to stop while a light comes on or goes out, a child of this age is capable of the following reasoning—which can be observed through the experiments he does, since he can manipulate the object. The first hypothesis might be that the light is the cause of the stops ($l \Rightarrow s$). This would mean that $l \,.\, \bar{s} = 0$. But there could still be stops without light ($\bar{l} \,.\, s$ need not be 0).[2] If, on the other hand, the stop causes the light, then there could not be a stop without light ($\bar{l} \,.\, s = 0$), but there could be light without stop ($l \,.\, \bar{s}$ need not be 0). Therefore: (1) if $l \Rightarrow s$, then $l \,.\, \bar{s} = 0$; and (2) if $s \Rightarrow l$, then $\bar{l} \,.\, s = 0$. If, on the one hand, the light occasionally comes on without the object's stopping, then hypothesis (1) is invalidated; if, on the other hand, the object stops occasionally without a light, then hypothesis (2) is invalidated. In Piaget's formalization, these operations constitute a group of four transformations such that N = RC, R = NC, C = NR, and I = NRC. Here I represents the *identity* transformation; N represents the *negation* transformation; R represents the *reciprocity* transformation; and C represents the *correlativity* transformation. The group table is shown in figure 1. From the table one sees, for example, that RC = N (from the R-row and C-column intersection), NC = R, and (NR)C = I. This system unites both inversions and reciprocities, which remained separate in the incomplete grouplike structure of the concrete operations.

| | I | N | R | C |
|---|---|---|---|---|
| I | I | N | R | C |
| N | N | I | C | R |
| R | R | C | I | N |
| C | C | R | N | I |

Fig. 1

This very brief sketch of the main stages of cognitive development leaves many aspects untouched. In particular, nothing has been said about what is called the *semiotic function,* the peculiarly human capacity to represent objects and events by something else. This "something else" is not necessarily language, although language is certainly the most important part of the semiotic function; mental images, gestures, symbolic play, and, even before any of these behaviours can be observed or inferred,

2. EDITOR'S NOTE. Here "." means *and* and "0" means *false*.

imitation in the absence of the model, are all part of this capacity to represent reality (in the largest sense of the word). Evidently, this capacity of re-presenting reality—that is to say, of rendering it present—extends the field of mental action enormously. It liberates the child from the limiting constraints of the here and now: it enables him to recapitulate past events and to anticipate future events. In short, from an organism that reacts and acts in the face of present circumstances (according to the actual situation), the infant becomes an individual who can begin to "know" and to plan.

I have been asked to devote one period to the Genevan language experiments, and a longer discussion on the semiotic function is needed as an introduction to that paper. However, the representation of reality will also be discussed (in the case of mental images and their observable expression, drawings) when I talk about the different types of knowledge. In fact, if this first sketch has given the impression that cognitive development is primarily or even uniquely a development of logic, I hasten to emphasize that this is not the case. There are many different types of operational structurations, and certain types are theoretically distinguished one from the other.

HERMINE SINCLAIR

# Different Types of Operatory Structures

Having given a brief sketch of what Piaget considers the characteristics of the main stages in intellectual development, I shall now deal with some of the problems that arise from this theory. Granted that children are, of course, totally unaware of these structures and that the operations only formalize what children can do and how they go about doing certain tasks, it still looks as if these operations are mainly logico-algebraic in character. Are they applied in other fields of activity also? Or, to narrow the question, are they applied in such subjects as physics, chemistry, geometry? If so, how?

It seems useful to introduce a distinction on which Piaget has often insisted, that of the two poles of knowledge. The two types of knowledge that exemplify these two poles are called *logical knowledge* and *physical knowledge*. In the case of logic, our knowledge stems mainly from our own actions or operations and their coordination. To take Piaget's example: a child is playing with a number of pebbles; he arranges them first in small groups, say 2, 4, 6; and then rearranges them so that there are 5, 3, 4; from this he discovers that the total number of pebbles does not change. But the properties of the pebbles have little or nothing to do with this knowledge. The same actions could have been performed upon, and the same conclusion drawn from, a collection of sweets, dolls, and so forth. Only one condition pertains to the objects themselves: they should be clearly separate and should stay where one puts them. Water or milk would not be much good!

By contrast, when a child wants to find out something about floating, it is imperative that the properties of the objects used in the experiment be taken into account. In fact, it is the properties that become the main

PIAGETIAN COGNITIVE-DEVELOPMENT RESEARCH AND MATHEMATICAL EDUCATION, National Council of Teachers of Mathematics, Washington, D.C., pp. 53-65.

source of knowledge. Nothing can be found out about floating without observing how solid and liquid interact. This physical type of knowledge is much less "pure" than the former; in fact, observations by themselves lead only to fragmentary, ad hoc knowledge. To be able to induce laws and regularities and to imagine experiments, a logical framework is necessary. As far as actual situations are concerned, either in real life or in the tasks psychologists propose to children, the two aspects are usually both present but in different ratios. Furthermore, one and the same situation can frequently be used to explore knowledge of different kinds. For instance, the well-known concept of conservation of weight is at first only a conservation of an invariant property of objects; logical operations of addition and composition are sufficient to maintain that weight does not change with a change in shape. But the conservation of weight is all the same more difficult than that of simple substance, a global quantitative concept; and with their growing knowledge of the physical world, children begin to see difficulties they had not considered in the conservation-of-weight problem. Apparent regressions may occur, as in the case of children who begin to wonder whether the ball of clay divided into little bits does not weigh less than the whole ball, since the little bits "press" on more of the surface of the scale, as if an intensive property like pressure were equivalent to an extensive property such as weight. They also often think that the weight of an object diminishes when its movement increases. When one asks the same questions for conservation of weight—(1) after putting the two quantities of plasticine on a double scale; (2) after hanging them underneath the scales; and (3) after hanging two balls at the same height on one side and two balls, one underneath the other, on the other—the children's answers will be quite different at certain stages and there may be apparent regressions. The distinction of the two opposite poles of knowledge is therefore to be seen as theoretical and heuristic; in real situations the type of reasoning applied is somewhere in between the two extremes.

Another question comes to mind concerning this distinction. Given the fact that, starting in the sensorimotor period, all knowledge proceeds from action and that all action implies the transposing or transforming of objects (including the subject's own displacements in space), is the distinction valid at all levels, right from the start of the development of intelligence?

According to Piaget, even at the very early stage of sensorimotor intelligence, that is to say around six months of age, it is possible to distinguish the roots of the two types of knowledge. In one, which will later develop into logical operations, it is mainly the action patterns themselves that become coordinated and integrated. This occurs whenever the baby has a specific goal and combines two movements to reach it. In the other, coordination also occurs, but the new knowledge comes mainly from the objects themselves, as in the case of the baby who discovers that if a certain object is pushed and starts swinging, it not only moves (he follows the movement with his eyes) but also makes a sound (he listens to the sound). In a research project on symbolic behavior, carried out in collaboration with Irene Lezine and Myra Stambak, we have examples of children from the age of thirteen or fourteen months onward performing actions that can be classified according to the two types: sometimes they push one object with another; they shake the objects; they tap the floor with them; they explore them carefully with their forefinger. In other instances they spend quite some time (that is, a minute or so) aligning the objects, putting one on top of another, and so on. In the one case, they are learning about the properties of the objects themselves—soft, supple, prickly, and so on—or about the effect of one object on another—one can push the spoon right inside the bristles of a brush but not inside a mirror. In the other case, they seem to be introducing some organization into the objects around them—they put a spoon next to a toy broom and a feather duster—and contemplate the patterns that result from their own organizing action. But most of the time the two types of activity seem at that age to be inextricably interwoven. It is only with continuing development that the activities leading to the two types of knowledge can be more easily distinguished.

There is, apart from the theoretical reasons, an educational use to be made of the distinction. In the case of knowledge of the physical type, reality flatly contradicts an incorrect idea; it is possible to show the child that he is wrong. If a six-year-old thinks that a small piece of iron will float "because it's so light," one has only to perform the experiment for him to see that his prediction is not correct. This does not, of course, mean that he will give up his idea; at first the child is incapable of forming a different hypothesis and will regard counterexamples as "funny" cases. But such a demonstration is totally impossible in the case of a logical problem. For example, if a child affirms that there are more apples than *fruit* (items of fruit) in the bowl, making him count first the fruit and then the apples is not going to have any influence at all. If he can already count and finds that there are six items and four apples, that does not prove to him that there is more fruit than apples. Counting, in this case, can be compared to naming; the fact that the last person named is called Peter does not tell anyone anything about the number of people in the room.

However, there seems to be a bit of a paradox here, which I cannot resolve. Since "wrong" ideas in physics seem to be easily demonstrable and "wrong" ideas in logic very difficult, why do educational curricula always introduce physics so much later than arithmetic? Is it because every day we make use of technological marvels that only a few of us really understand, whereas our daily contact with mathematics is limited to fairly simple problems such as adding and subtracting money or working out how many rolls of wallpaper are necessary to cover a certain surface? Or is it precisely because wrong ideas in physics are so obviously wrong that it seems hopeless to start teaching physics early? When one constructs the syllogism "Johnny has two eyes; Johnny is a boy; therefore all boys have two eyes," one has all one's facts right, but the logic is way off. On the other hand, when one says, "All boys have two noses; Johnny is a boy; therefore Johnny has two noses," the logic is impeccable, but one of the premises is false. The first type of reasoning, wrong as it is, seems somehow less false than the second!

In his epistemological work Piaget seems to indicate a more profound reason. In many cases, it is only after many aspects of a branch of science have been elaborated that science discovers (or at least explicitly formulates) basic concepts that are acquired early in cognitive development. Such is the case with topological structures. Topology became a branch of mathematics well after Euclidian geometry, but we find that the child can handle relationships of closure as opposed to openness of figures, of being adjacent as opposed to nonadjacent, of overlapping, and so on, well before he can deal with the relations between parallel as opposed to intersecting, curves as opposed to straight lines, and so on. Similarly, one-to-one correspondence, which is at the base of set theory (another recently formulated theory), is one of the earliest established concepts in the child. Possibly awareness and explicit formulation of deeply ingrained, basic concepts comes later than that of more complex achievements. However that may be, a similar phenomenon exists as regards physics, where certain of the most difficult notions of modern physics seem to exist in a primitive, intuitive form in children—but then they look completely "wrong." The concept of time seems to provide an example of this. Very young children have an intuition of speed; this is based purely on the eventual "overtakings" or "catchings up." Time, however—that is to say, duration—remains linked to distance covered or to the amount of work done. Until nine years of age there is confusion when comparing two moving objects or persons as regards the time taken and the distance covered; going further usually implies having taken more time. It is very difficult for children of this age to admit that time is something that can be measured independently of what has been accomplished during the time. In fact, they think that a watch does not work in the same way when it is worn by someone who is running as when it is on the wrist of someone who is walking slowly. For them, there is no common, homogeneous time. The insufficiency of this postulate in physics became clear only when Einstein used the constancy of the velocity of light, as demonstrated in the Michelson-Morley experiment, to derive his principle of relativity. It seems that, once again, children's intuition has something in common with late developments in science.

The findings of developmental psychology indicate a very clear parallel between the child's reasoning in logico-mathematical problems and his way of attacking problems in physics (generally, to start with, in simple mechanics). For instance, even in the preoperational period, when his logic is still a semilogic of one-way mappings, when a child is asked about the respective lengths of a piece of string in the situation pictured in figure 1, he knows very well that if one pulls on the extremity of $A$ (for instance, by hanging a weight on it), $A$ will get longer and $B$ will get shorter; but since he is as yet incapable of quantification, he will not suppose that $\Delta A = \Delta B$. In general, the child thinks that the gain in the length of $A$ is more than the loss in the length of $B$; after all, $A$ is "where the pull is" (Piaget et al. 1968). To take another example, where the

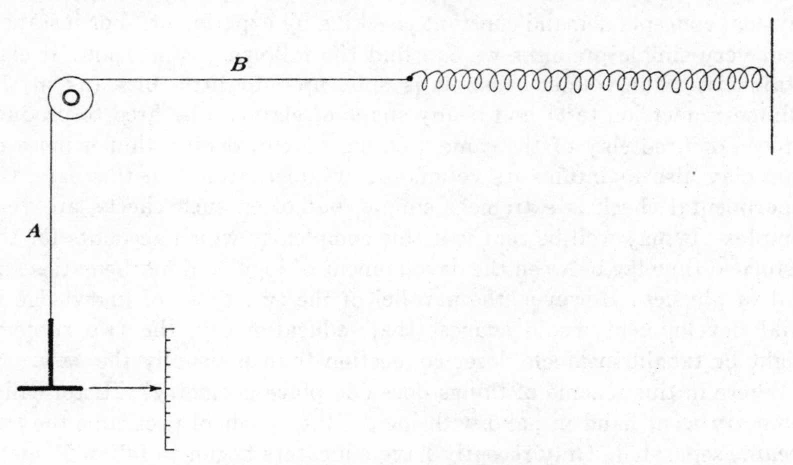

Fig. 1. Spring, string, and pulley task operations

apparent discrepancy between knowledge of physical phenomena and logico-mathematical reasoning is more striking, at the stage of concrete operations, in the following situation (Piaget 1970) a rubber band is marked with a clip at one third of its length and then is stretched out. Children initially think that the stretching occurs only at the ends and then, shortly afterward, at the end of each segment. However, applying the additive compositions of which they are capable at this stage, they think that the change in length is the same for both parts, despite their initial inequality. They can then observe that their predictions were wrong; but since at this stage they are still incapable of understanding proportion, they will content themselves with the following explanation: "The long bit gets more added to it, the small bit less." The logic of this reasoning is perfectly comprehensible, but it is combined with the idea, as regards the physics of the phenomenon, that the "pull" is not distributed over the whole rubber band but seems to result in "bits" added at the ends. Somehow or other, this idea seems to many people more "wrong" than the corresponding logical concepts, which do not yet enable children to deal with proportionality. Interestingly, as soon as children understand proportionality, they correctly predict the length in this problem and then (as regards the physical aspect) immediately maintain that the "pull" goes through the whole rubber band and that therefore the force is evenly distributed over the whole length.

However, despite this close parallel, a certain time lag in the construction of physics concepts is comprehensible. The logical operations open the way to deduction and do not need any checking with reality, but the physical concepts demand constant checking by experiment. For instance, from very simple premises we can find the following conclusion: if clay retains its total volume when it is split up into little bits (as in the volume-immersion test) and if any shape of clay can be fired to produce a piece of fired clay of the same volume, we can deduce that a piece of fired clay also maintains its volume on fragmentation. In this case, the experimental check is extremely simple, but often such checks are very complex. It may well be that it is this complexity which accounts for the historical time lag between the development of logic and mathematics and that of physics. However, the parallel of the two types of knowledge in child development would suggest that, educationally, the two subjects might be taught in much closer connection than is usually the case.

Where in this scheme of things does one place geometry? Historically, geometry went hand in hand with logic. But in school programs the two became separated. Only recently have educators begun to follow Piaget's practice of amalgamating logic and mathematics (and therefore geometry) in one whole: logico-mathematical knowledge. Once again, experimental psychological findings reveal a remarkable parallel; cognitive development is an indivisible entity, and its laws and the progression of its structures may have different manifestations in different types of problems but nevertheless remain basically the same. In fact, in many experiments a child's physical explanations and logical and geometrical solutions are inextricably linked (as was the case in the experiment on the pulling of the rubber band).

To take an example that has clearer geometrical implications, consider the following experiment (Piaget and Inhelder [a] 1947). The child is shown a squat, angular bottle of ink (see fig. 2*a*). This bottle is put into a cover so that the level of ink is invisible. The child is then asked to draw, in a prepared frame that shows the bottle and the table (see fig. 2*b*), the ink level (i.e., indicate where it is), then to draw its level if the bottle is tilted, put on its side, or turned upside down (all the positions are shown, but with the cover). The first drawings (in the preoperational

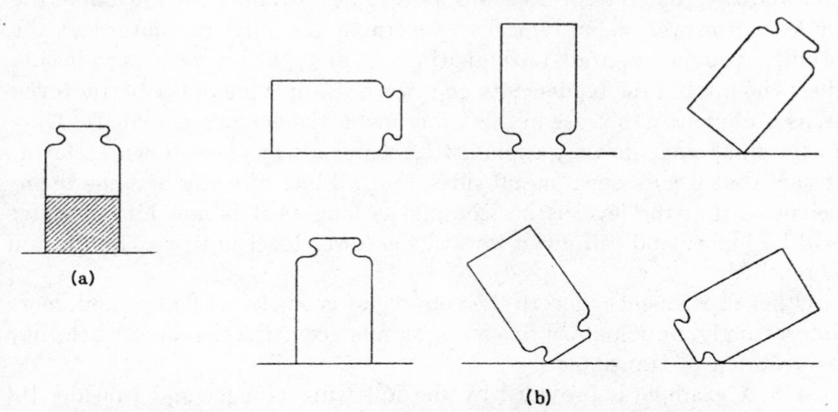


Fig. 2. (*a*) Bottle with ink. (*b*) Frame positions showing line of the table.

stage) show scribbles that fill the whole bottle (and go beyond as well!). At a second stage, the level of the ink is drawn in all situations as parallel to the bottom of the bottle, and in the upside-down position the ink may be hanging from the top (see fig. 3). In the next stage, certain modifications are introduced, mainly by having the ink go toward the opening and drawing oblique lines that connect the corners (see fig. 4). Finally, of

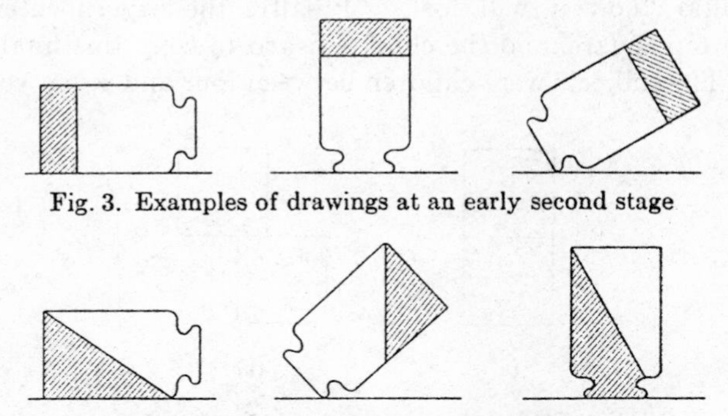

Fig. 3. Examples of drawings at an early second stage

Fig. 4. Examples of drawings at late second stage

course, at about the age of nine or ten, all the drawings are correct. Now these different drawings can be interpreted in a quasi-geometrical way: at first, the only relationship that counts is that the ink be inside (or mainly inside) the bottle. Secondly, the child keeps the intrafigural relationships constant: the level always keeps its relation to the shape of the bottle. It is only at the third stage that extrafigural indications are taken into account and the drawing of the table in the model sketch begins to attract their attention. Finally, a system of coordinates is established, and the children say that the level should always be "straight" or "just like the table." However, their remarks concerning the physical nature of the problem provide a parallel explanation: at first, the ink just stays inside; then, the ink has the tendency to go toward the opening of the bottle (even if, as is obviously the case in this experiment, the opening is sealed). Only in the final stage do they explain that water always goes down as far as it can, that it goes down on all sides, that all bits of water arrange themselves so that the level is horizontal—as long as it is not, bits of water will be higher and roll down toward the lower level until an equilibrium is reached.

Other experiments concern the copying of geometrical figures and, more interestingly, anticipatory images of simple geometrical shapes when they are rotated or translated.

A first example is provided by the following (Piaget and Inhelder [b] 1966). The child is shown two cardboard squares (5 cm by 5 cm), one placed above the other, touching along one side (see fig. 5*a*). He is then asked to copy this situation, and only if he can make a more or less correct copy is he retained for the rest of the experiment. Now the child is asked to imagine something: "How would it look if I pushed the top square a little bit to the right?" (the gesture is sketched but the square is not moved). Once the child has understood this instruction, he is asked to draw (and sometimes to indicate by gestures, but we shall not go into those results) "how it will look." Finally, the experimenter actually pushes the top square, and the child is asked to copy this final situation, figure 5*b*. The subjects were children between four and seven years of age.

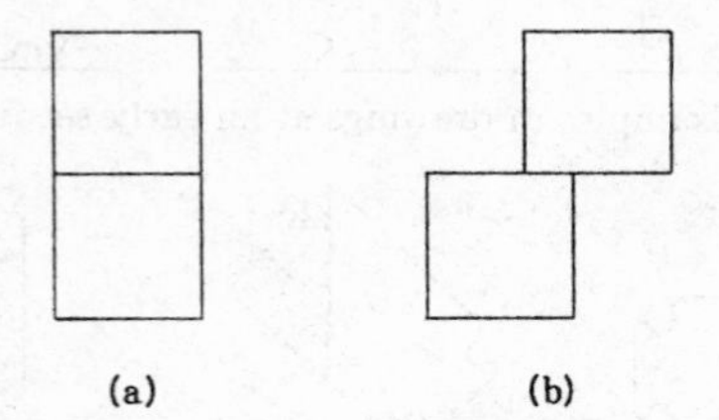


Fig. 5. Task with two squares, 5 cm by 5 cm

Surprisingly, the drawing by anticipation is correct (77 percent success rate) only at the age of seven. Interestingly, even the simple copy of the final state is correct (76 percent) only at five-and-a-half years. Even more interestingly, the deformations introduced in the copy are of exactly the same type as those in the anticipatory drawing, but they appear two years earlier. This fact alone is full of interest and proves once again that it is not sufficient to have the model in front of one's eyes to be able to reproduce its structure. The following types of drawings were observed (here reproduced schematically):

1. The very simplest solution consists in a simple copy of the initial situation, or in a horizontal recombination (see fig. 6).

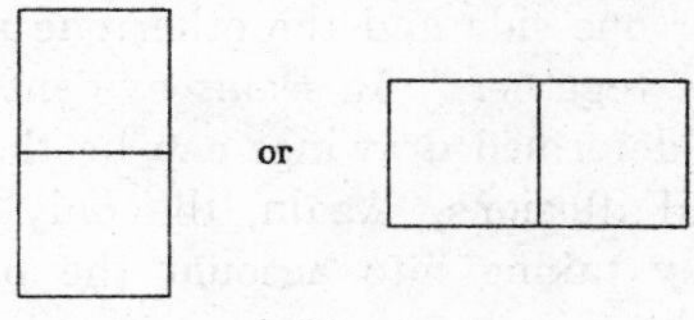


Fig. 6

2. Next (at about the same ages) the two squares are drawn one apart from the other and the top square is moved up instead of sideways (see fig. 7). Fifty-five percent of the drawings of the five-year-olds are of this type.

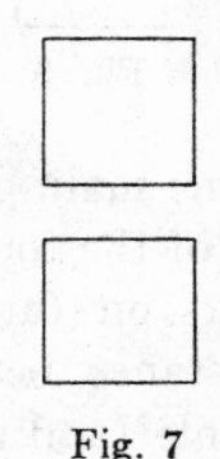

Fig. 7

3. A very interesting series of drawings is found at the next level (see fig. 8). They seem to indicate that the main difficulty resides in the prob-

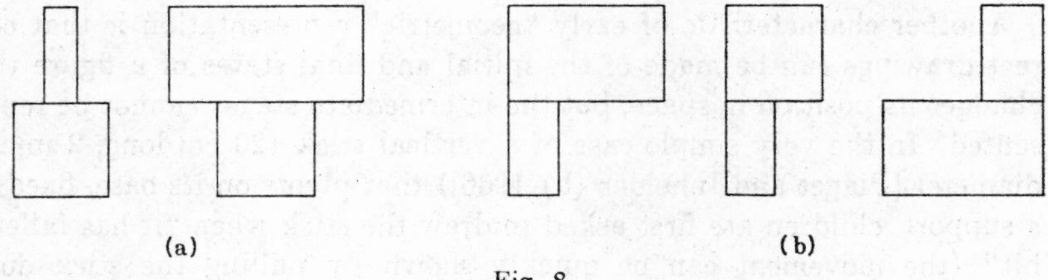


Fig. 8

lem of what happens to the right vertical side of the top square when its left vertical side is displaced away from the corresponding left side of the bottom square. The displacement of the right side is represented either as symmetrical to that of the left or vice versa (drawing *8a*). In other cases, one of the top square's sides is correctly placed relative to the corresponding side of the bottom square, but the top square's other side is drawn in vertical extension of the corresponding bottom square's side (original position), as in drawing *8b*.

4. Finally, of course, the problem is solved. However, when little vertical strokes are drawn on the squares, on the bottom one to the right of the top side and on the top square to the left of the bottom side, the problem becomes more difficult (see fig. 9). As one of the subjects said: "One of the strokes is near one side and the other one near the other side, so they can never come together." It seems evident that neither remarks such as this nor the deformed drawings can be the result of faulty perception, or of optical illusions. Again, the only way to explain them would seem to be by taking into account the particular character of preoperational thought.

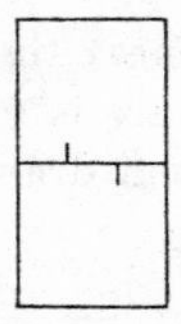

Fig. 9

The solutions indicate that the main problem is ordinal. The relationship between the vertical sides of the top square and those of the bottom square is what the child works on (and fails to solve before the age of seven). The horizontal distance between the two vertical sides is neglected; the shape of the whole (and all children of this age recognize a square when they see one!) is sacrificed. Either the intrafigural relationships are conserved, as in the first stages, or an attempt is made to represent the interfigural relationships, but the two cannot yet be coordinated.

Another characteristic of early "geometric" representation is that correct drawings can be made of the initial and final states of a figure that changes its position in space, but the intermediate stages cannot be represented. In the very simple case of a vertical stick (20 cm long, 2 mm in diameter [Piaget and Inhelder (b) 1966]) that pivots on its base, fixed by a support, children are first asked to draw the stick when "it has fallen a bit" (the movement can be quickly shown by pulling the stick down through an angle of 20° and 30°). After this drawing, the child is asked to draw the stick in several positions: first when it is upright, then at several points "on the way down," and finally when it "has fallen right down, flat on the wooden support." The experimenter directs the child's attention to the pivot and makes it clear that the stick cannot move away from that point. There is little difficulty, even at the age of four-to-five years, in drawing the two extreme positions. The interesting errors concern the intermediary positions. Figure 10 shows schematized representations of typical errors in indicating the intermediary positions of the stick; the dotted lines represent the (correct) initial and final positions. Solution 3 is particularly popular at four and five years of age. Solutions 4 to 8 are more or less contemporaneous (at five-to-six years of age), and they all show the difficulty of coordinating the movement of the top extremity of the stick (which describes a quarter of a circle) and the successive positions of the whole stick. The curves in solutions 6 and 7 are particularly interesting and represent an incapacity to conciliate the (curved) trajectory of the extremity and the fact that the stick itself does not change its shape.

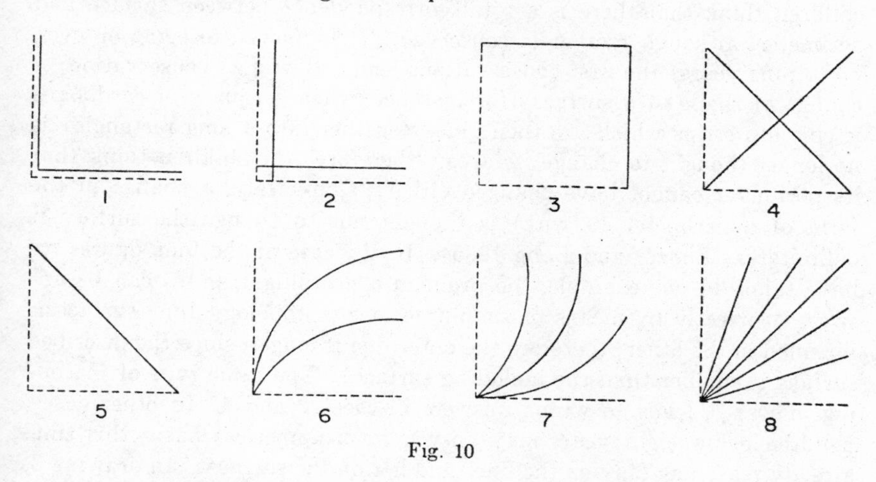

Fig. 10

Should we conclude that geometry follows exactly the same developmental line as that of logical and arithmetical operations? What about the famous mathematical intuition and its supposed reliance on mental images? According to Piaget, this is partly true—especially for the early period—until the first grouplike structure of transformations is firmly established. However, geometry remains a case apart because of the very close correspondence between its operations and their spatial representations (drawing, models). Other experiments have shown how, once the attachment to the initial and final states is overcome, children around seven or eight years can solve problems with complete and elegant reasoning, whereas young children, though often able to answer correctly, either cannot justify their answers or else cite the wrong reasons. In one experiment the children were presented with a number of drawings (Piaget and Inhelder [b] 1966) such as those in figure 11. They were

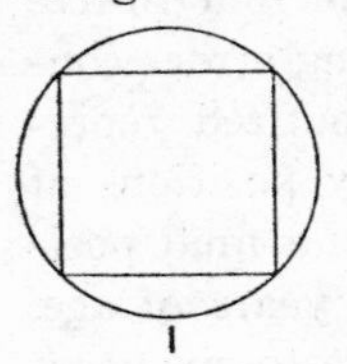

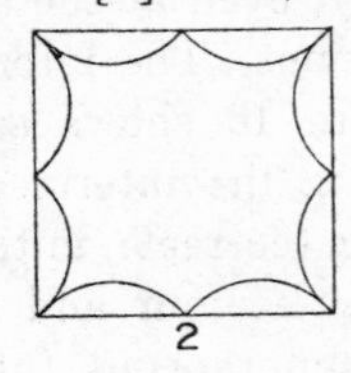

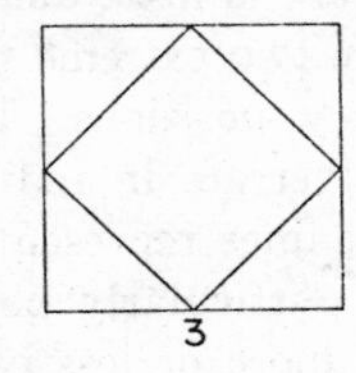

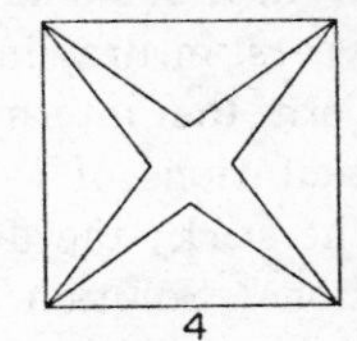


Fig. 11

asked which one of the two lines (two roads, two bits of string) in each drawing was longer, or were they the same? Without giving a detailed analysis of the various stages that characterize children's responses, the following are the main points. At first, from the age of four-to-six years, children think that there is a total correspondence between surface and perimeter, although neither is conserved. Then (seven-to-eight or even up to nine years) the first conservations lead to "wrong" conservation: a change of shape of a surface (for instance, when a square of cardboard is cut into strips which are then glued together into a long rectangle) is no longer thought to change its area, "therefore" the children think that its perimeter cannot have changed either! Conversely, a change in the form of a perimeter (a wire) is thought not to change the surface it delimitates (Lunzer and Bang 1965). In the case of the four figures we have taken in our example, the problem concerning 1 and 3 can be answered correctly by means of simple notions of topology (one surface is included in the other; therefore the outer line is longer, since the inscribed surface is smaller than the including surface). The same type of reasoning, however, leads to wrong answers in cases 2 and 4. In other cases, children below eight years may answer on a numerical basis, this time already reasoning only on the lines and not on the surfaces. In drawing 3, for instance, this may lead to the answer that both lines are the same length: "They each have four bits."

From seven years onward, correct answers are given to situations 2 and 4, and the arguments become based on the possible transformations that would permit a direct comparison: "If you put one of the lines in straight bits like the other, you know it's longer."

It seems clear that in a certain sense geometry constitutes a special case, where representation and mental images are much more adequate than in problems involving classifications or number. Geometrical operations bear on the description of figures in space and their transformations, and in this special case there is a very close resemblance between operations and their actual representations. Geometrical intuition, according to Piaget, has a privileged position, since its two aspects—one operational, the other representational and imagined—give rise to a much closer synthesis than in any other domain.

## REFERENCES


Lunzer, E., and V. Bang. *Conservations spatiales.* Paris: Presses Universitaires de France, 1965.

Piaget, J. *L'épistémologie génétique.* Paris: Presses Universitaires de France, 1970.

Piaget, J., J.-B. Grize, A. Szeminska, and V. Bang. *Épistémologie et psychologie de la fonction.* Paris: Presses Universitaires de France, 1968.

Piaget, J., and B. Inhelder (a). *La représentation de l'espace chez l'enfant.* Paris: Presses Universitaires de France, 1947.

——— (b). *L'image mentale chez l'enfant.* Paris: Presses Universitaires de France, 1966.

HERMINE SINCLAIR

# Representation and Memory

In the short sketch of the main stages of cognitive development, I mentioned only briefly an important complex of behaviors that all belong to what is called the semiotic, or symbolic, function. At the end of the sensorimotor period we observe the emergence of symbolic play, language, and, in general, activities that could not take place without some kind of representation of absent objects or events that are not taking place at the precise moment. One of Piaget's well-known examples concerns Jacqueline (Piaget 1935), who, at the age of twenty months, comes into a room with a bunch of grass in each hand; to open the door (which opens inward), she puts down the grass, turns the handle, pushes, picks up the grass again, and enters. A little later she wants to go outside; she puts the grass down again in the same way as she had when she entered the room, that is to say, at the threshold. However, she changes her mind, picks it up, and moves it farther back into the room so that it is not hit by the door when it opens. Such behavior, of which many examples have been observed, does not occur before the beginning of the second year and cannot be interpreted without supposing that some kind of representation (e.g., of the door's movement in the above example) has taken place.

Post-sensorimotor intelligence acquires a new dimension, which frees the action from the strict *hic et nunc* and—importantly, in view of what is one of the main characteristics of formal operations (the insertion of the actual into the full range of the possible)—it now becomes possible to perform one action while envisaging the performance of others. Representation enlarges the field of action immensely, both in space and in time; actual actions can be accompanied by representations which almost simultaneously encompass actions and events in the past or the present, in the immediate vicinity or a long way away.

PIAGETIAN COGNITIVE-DEVELOPMENT RESEARCH AND MATHEMATICAL EDUCATION, National Council of Teachers of Mathematics, Washington, D.C., pp. 125-135.

These new representational capacities of the child in his second year are expressed in many different types of behavior. On the one hand, there is imitative behavior, not (as during the sensorimotor period) in the presence of the model, but in its absence. In fact, this imitative behavior seems to be a common aspect of all representations: in symbolic play (where the child can use objects to stand for other objects), in intelligent acting (such as Jacqueline's pushing the grass out of the way of the door's trajectory) which necessitates some kind of mental image, and in the beginnings of language. If we say that imitation is the common factor, this does not mean that representational behavior is a simple copying of reality. On the contrary—and far more than is usually supposed—the subject constructs his own representations according to his particular needs and capacities. Since the means of knowing is essentially through actions performed on reality, representation far more often reflects the way a person deals with a problem in action than a simple copy-image of the situation involved.

In his well-known studies on children's drawings, Luquet (1927) showed the existence of a period of what he called "intellectual realism," when the six- or seven-year-old draws what he knows rather than what he sees. In this period we observe drawings of faces seen in profile but with two eyes, of a field with flowers and with potatoes visible in the soil, or of trucks with four complete wheels as if they were transparent. In the same way, whatever the children cannot yet apprehend cognitively is deformed; for example, there is no coordination of different points of view, and in one drawing one can observe a table top as seen from above, with a toy car on top of it as seen from the side, and so on. Moreover, it is not only the drawings that are made spontaneously without a model that exhibit these characteristics but also those of figures that are in front of the child as he draws. Before the age of four, all closed figures (squares, rectangles, ellipses, circles, etc.) are copied as a curved, closed line, while crosses, *l*'s, curved lines, and so forth, are copied as "open" figures. But with children as young as three years of age, one can observe copies of drawings that essentially represent topological relationships (such as inside, next to, on the boundary of) which correctly represent these relations (see fig. 1).

In all education we rely heavily on representation. Actual demonstration with pupils manipulating is rather restricted in scope; and, even when applicable, its pertinent aspects are underlined verbally or through algebraic, geometric, or other notation. If the child himself represents reality in a distorted way, how does he apprehend information which the adult presents to him in a representational manner? An extensive series of experiments on memory images (observed either through drawings,

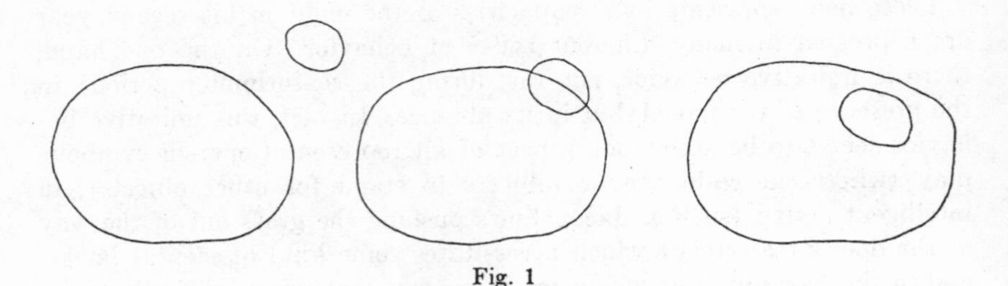

Fig. 1

gestures, or verbal explanation) has revealed many distortions—in fact, there often was as much distortion when the memory was tested immediately after presentation as there was one hour later, one week later, and even several months later (Piaget and Inhelder 1968). In every case, the deformations were due to a different way of interpreting the situation and not to simple memory factors; it is always possible to check for this eventuality by presenting similar situations that are cognitively "easier" but perceptually equivalent. For instance, in verbal memory "The table is laid by Mary and Peter" gives occasion for deformations, whereas "Peter lays the table, and Mary makes the salad" does not. Similarly, to draw a little circle on the perimeter of a bigger one does not seem to be "easier" than to draw a rectangle, however clumsily; in fact, to me the reverse would seem to be true.

Before giving a few examples of how children distort situations that they have been asked to memorize, it seems worthwhile to say a few words on the general subject of memory, another crucial factor in education.

There exist two types of memory. The first one is recognition; that is to say, of an object or situation already encountered. Recognition memory is very primitive: it exists even in nonvertebrates and, of course, in babies during the sensorimotor period. The second type of memory belongs to a higher level of development and does not seem to exist before the beginnings of representation; in fact, it is a kind of representation and consists in the evocation of situations already encountered but absent at the moment of recall. When we claim to have an excellent memory of faces but a bad memory for names, we are really saying that on seeing somebody, recognition memory works well (we recognize the face) but we cannot evoke the name; in fact, as soon as we are told the name, we recognize it just as well.

Piaget and Inhelder's book (1968) on memory concerns evocation memory and deals with a special aspect of it; that is, its relationship to different levels of cognitive development. Mental images are symbols of reality and can be used either intellectually (to solve a problem), for play and fantasy, or for art. Mental images also serve memory for the reconstitution of past events. In this sense, memory is a type of knowledge, not attached to the present (as is perception) and not bearing directly on the solving of new problems (as is intelligence), but on the past. Developmentally, it has often been thought that fundamentally memory mechanisms are the same in the adult as in the child. There are obvious differences, because the child is not interested in certain problems and he does not understand certain situations; therefore he does not store them. However, if he does understand them, the mechanisms of retention are supposed to be the same as those of the adult, the only differences being quantitative, pertaining to span, extinction curves, and so on.

Piaget, on the other hand, maintains that there is a qualitative difference according to developmental levels; encoding and decoding processes depend on the code used by the subject, and it is precisely this code that changes with cognitive development. In fact, the amount of information transmitted by a certain number of signals depends on the number of elements and the rules of the code. To give a very simple example: if I am shown a bottle held obliquely with wine running out of it, I do not have to "remember" that the bottle was not corked and sealed. Knowing what happens to open bottles when one turns them upside down makes the information of the absence of the cork redundant. If it is true that intelligence changes the code according to which memory encodes and decodes, the same situation presented to children at different levels will carry a different information load and will be encoded in a different way.

In many experiments on memory, striking examples were found in the schematization of the situations presented. One example concerned number. The child was shown the arrangement of counters of figure 2. A collection of differently colored counters was used to demonstrate (after having asked the child to anticipate the result) that the same six counters can exactly cover all three lines in the arrangement to be memorized. Finally, the subject's cognitive level was determined by the numerical conservation test. A few minutes after presentation and once again a

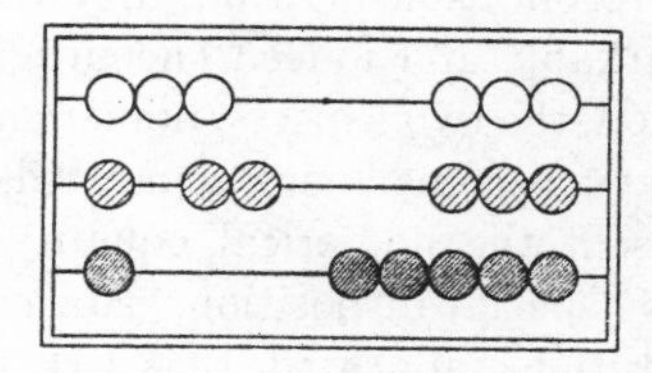

Fig. 2

week later, the child was asked to reproduce the situation by a drawing, by gestures, and by reconstituting what he had seen with a collection of counters.

Types of memory productions were closely linked to operational levels.

A first type, observed with the youngest children (four-year-olds), was the following: no numerical equivalence between the three lines and no attempt to make the lines more or less the same length. Both in the drawings and reconstitutions, the number of counters in the three lines was very different: 12, 8, and 9, or even 4, 13, and 15, and so on. But there was usually (at least in two lines) a division into groups.

A second type was more involved (four years six months to five years): three lines with more or less the same number of counters and coincidence of their extremities (15, 13, and 13 or 7, 6, and 6, etc.). In a way, these reproductions are figuratively less "true" to the model, since in this type there is absolutely no indication of the subgroups. However, there is progress in that there is an indication of numerical equality.

A third type reveals further progress. Once again the lines have coinciding extremities, and the numerical equality is more marked: at least two of the lines have the same number. Moreover, this time the subgroups are marked, although in a peculiar way: in the lines with exact numerical equality, the subgroups are also equal, for example, twice 1 and 4 or twice 1 and 3. The synthesis between the spatial disposition in subgroups (present in an isolated manner in type 1) and numerical equality (indicated in type 2) is not yet possible.

Finally, at five to six years, numerical equality is correct; all three lines have the same number of counters. But only one child (out of eight) reproduced 6 counters per line and exactly the arrangement of the original. The other seven associated the numbers in their own personal way ($3 + 3$, $2 + 4$, and $1 + 5$; or $3 + 3$, $1 + 4 + 1$, and $1 + 5$; etc.).

All children who produced type 4 drawings or reconstitutions succeeded in the numerical conservation task (also one child of only four years and nine months).

It is interesting to see what happens to this memory some six to ten months later. Without any new presentation of the situation, almost all the children had some recollection of what they had been shown. This, in itself, is rather remarkable and indeed encouraging for educators. At the end of this long period, the two aspects, numerical equality and spatial disposition, seem to have become more separated. Again, most of the children tried to represent the numerical equality but seemed to have completely forgotten the spatial disposition. However, two new types of drawings and reconstitutions appeared that are of particular interest (see fig. 3). The first type is a *seriation:* we find lines of 6, 5, 4, 3, 2, and 1

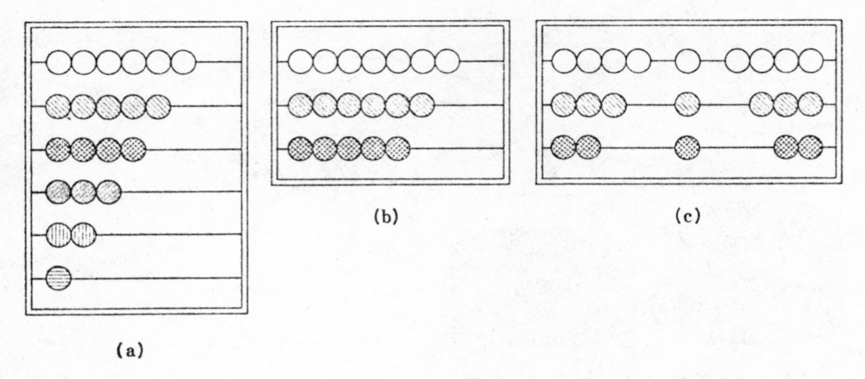


Fig. 3

counters, placed one above the other as in figure 3*a*. More often, there are only three lines as in the model, but again seriation; for instance, in figure 3*b* the top line has 7 counters, the next 6, and the last 5. The second type (fig. 3*c*) is a symmetrical arrangement: 4, 1, 4; 3, 1, 3; 2, 1, 2.

As might be expected, memory of the situation becomes increasingly schematized as time goes by. However, the remarkable appearance of seriations and symmetries (which are a type of figurative classification) is more interesting than a schematization. According to Piaget's analysis of the concept of number, this concept is attained by a synthesis of the two types of grouplike structures, that of seriation and that of classification.

In another experiment, a problem of transitivity was involved. If there is more liquid in glass *B* than in glass *A* and more liquid in *C* than in *B*, is there more liquid in *C* than in *A?* However, it is not the logical problem (which is difficult to solve and to remember even after the age of seven) that I want to present here, but a curious phenomenon that reveals how even a simple action such as the pouring of liquid from one glass to another can be deformed in memory. The experiment involved four glasses—one with red liquid, one with yellow, and two empty. The experimenter pours the yellow liquid into an empty glass and the red liquid into another empty glass. Then the yellow liquid is poured into the glass that originally contained the red and vice versa, so that at the end, the contents of two differently shaped glasses are interchanged. (See fig. 4.)

When the children were asked to tell us what they had seen, the four- and five-year-olds maintained that we had poured the yellow liquid into the glass with the red liquid and vice versa. We wondered whether this was a kind of abbreviated description of what had really happened, and we showed them the four glasses with the liquids in their original positions. To our surprise, the children actually took up the two glasses that

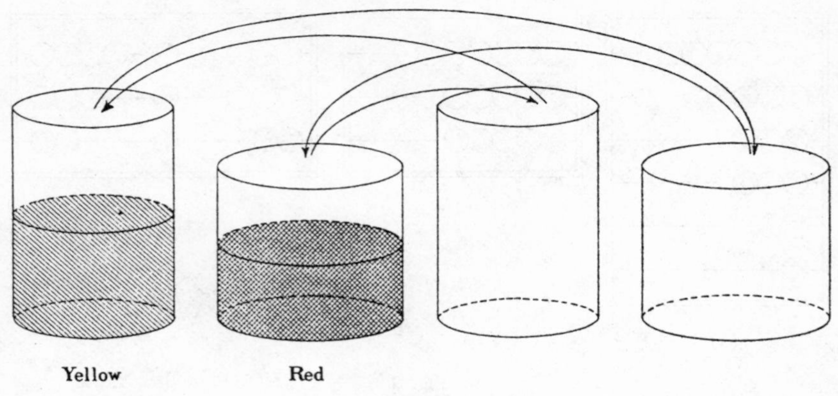


Fig. 4

were filled with liquid and tried to pour, simultaneously, the yellow liquid into the glass with the red liquid and the red into the glass with the yellow. Questioned as to whether they really thought that this could be done, they maintained their answer: "Yes, if you're clever enough." "Won't the yellow and red get all mixed up?" was our next question. Many hesitated or simply said "no." One child said, "Yes, maybe, but it will unmix itself in the end."

Another memory study concerned a double-entry table and involved wooden buttons (round and square, blue and red) glued onto a piece of heavy paper as shown in figure 5. (The experiment was designed by J. Bliss.)

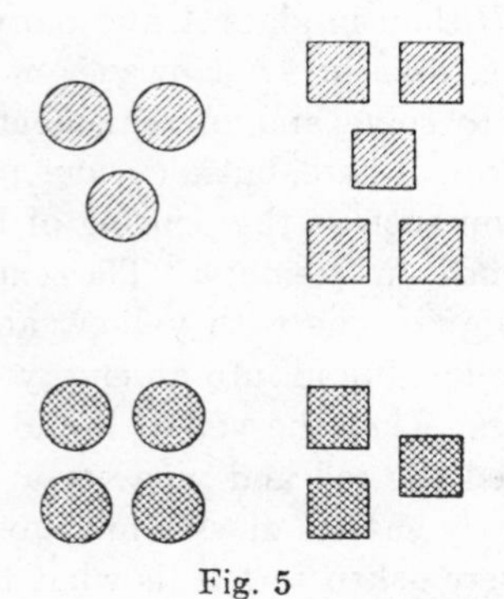

Fig. 5

The children's recollections were of the following types. A first type, found only at four to five years, was a simple agglomeration of buttons, sometimes only red (or only blue) ones. Neither the figurative disposition nor the classificatory principle was represented (see fig. 6).

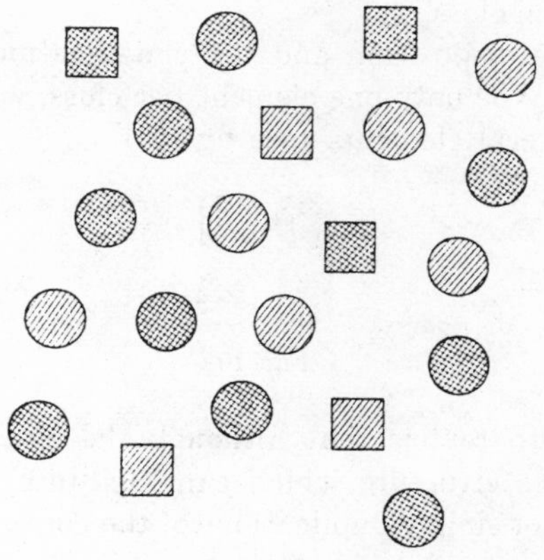

Fig. 6

A second type, more involved, showed the beginnings of a classificatory principle in the sense that two classes were present (red and blue squares for instance), but instead of an arrangement into four groups, there was a line (a circle or haphazard arrangement) made up of either just two buttons (a red square and a blue square or a red round and a blue round) or a great number of such couples (see fig. 7).

Fig. 7

A third type had the correct spatial arrangement in four groups, but again only two classes were represented (very exceptionally three) as in figure 8. Sometimes there were groups of buttons and sometimes only one.

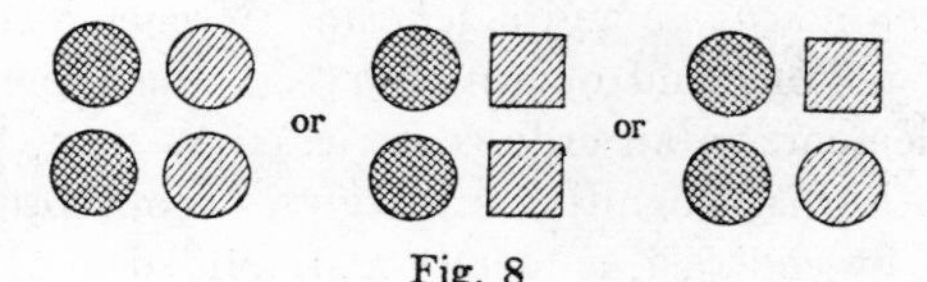


Fig. 8

A fourth type revealed considerable progress, since the multiplicative structure was present: all four classes were represented (fig. 9). How-

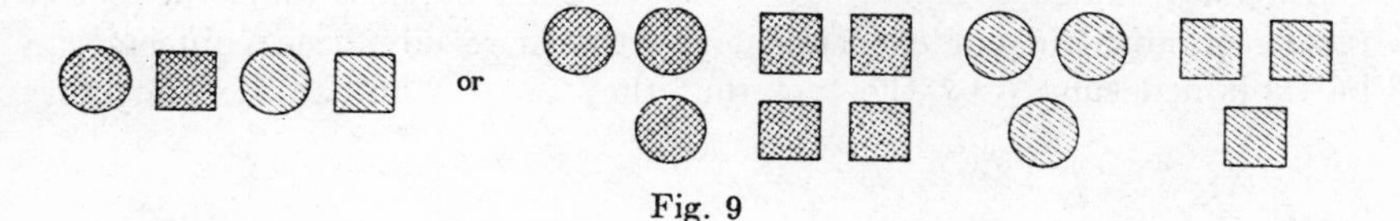


Fig. 9

ever, the double-entry-table arrangement was absent; there was an alignment either of one element of each class or of small groups of three or four elements of each class.

Finally, both the disposition and the classification were remembered, but again there may be only one element per class, which seems to represent a group of several elements (see fig. 10).

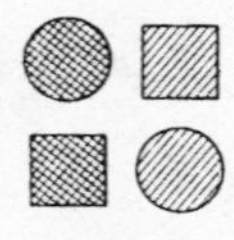

Fig. 10

It is important to realize that although the situations we presented all have a cognitive structure which can facilitate memorization, these experiments were not simple duplications of the corresponding tasks where the child himself has to classify elements, seriate sticks, and so on. In a very broad sense, *memory* also includes the cognitive structures that permit the solving of new problems. But *memory* in a more limited sense concerns only recognition, reconstitution, or, especially, evocation of events located in the past by the subject himself. In a sense, in these memory experiments the relationship between memory in the broad and strict senses was studied. In all cases, the results indicate that it is the level of cognitive development, that is to say, the particular cognitive structure of a certain stage or substage, that determines not so much the amount as the organization of the information remembered. Usually, our younger subjects do not remember "less" than the older ones; in certain cases they seem to remember more. But they remember differently. Remembering differently in this case does not mean that the younger children picked on certain details and the older children on others; it means that the total situation was differently organized according to developmental level. In this connection, it is useful to mention Piaget's distinction between a *scheme* and a *schema*. A scheme concerns the general structure of actions and operations (e.g., the scheme that permits one to arrange elements in an ordered series). As such, Piaget's schemes include such entities as "cognitive strategies," "conceptual frames," and so on. A schema, by contrast, is merely a simplified imagined representation of the result of some organizatory activity. A model unites the two: it is a schema insofar as it is a simplified representation of a particular situation, but it is a scheme insofar as it is a means of generalization.

All our findings suggest that we should not suppose that the better results obtained in our experiments by the more advanced subjects can be explained simply by the fact that they possess both more and more accurate schemata of representation. Of course, they have encountered more situations and accumulated more of these schemata, but more importantly, they approach the situation with different schemes, that is to say, with a different cognitive organizatory capacity. The active functioning of this organizatory ability makes mnemonic encoding and decoding possible and determines its form. In this sense, the mnemonic code itself is structured and restructured along with general cognitive development.

In general, our results strengthen the educational tendency away from rote learning. It could well be that with excessive emphasis placed on rote learning, pupils would cease to use their organizatory capacity (which alone permits economical encoding and decoding) and come to rely only on a figurative, copy type of memory, which does not attain the efficiency of cognitively organized remembering. On the other hand, we do not want to equate all memory with our particular situations, which appeal specifically to this organizing mnemonic capacity. In many subjects taught in school, a certain amount of rote learning is, in the present system, inevitable. But as regards mathematics and allied disciplines, it appears that it is the concept formation itself that should be fostered by all possible means and that all representation is liable to be deformed by those pupils who are as yet incapable of a cognitive grasp of the problem involved. On the other hand, the deformations they introduce in what seemed to be a perfectly clear model can be precious indicators of their cognitive level.

Some deformations found in verbal memory are similar, although they are often less clearly linked to cognitive level. One of the difficulties in the presentation of verbal material is that a certain construction can be perfectly well understood in some instances and not at all in others. What Slobin has called *reversible* sentences are a good example of this. "John kicks Jack" is reversible in the sense that "Jack kicks John" is also a semantically possible expression; on the other hand, the permutation of subject and object in "John kicks the table" results in the impossible (or at least very improbable) expression "The table kicks John." This distinction explains many phenomena in children's comprehension of sentences such as "This is the house that Jack built" and the noncomprehension of sentences such as "This is the boy that Jack kicked." In an experiment on passive sentences, this difference was also found between sentences such as "The car is washed by the man" and "The car is followed by a truck." In an immediate-memory experiment, we found that half of the four-year-olds quite correctly repeated sentences of the second type, but without being capable of understanding the relationship between "actor" and "acted-upon." At five, these correct repetitions without understanding began to disappear and in their place we noted different expressions that correctly indicated the relationship but did not reproduce the passive construction. Many children simply turned the passive into the corresponding active but were convinced that that was what the experimenter had said (Sinclair and Ferreiro, forthcoming).

In general, it seems that representational ability is closely linked to cognitive level, but with important differences as regards the information represented. Probably because in mathematics representation is so close to operations, in that discipline the influence is the clearest. Moreover, although as yet not much is known about the development of the different aspects of the symbolic function, it seems that this development varies more from one individual to another than does that of cognitive structures. There are important individual differences in the use of language—and the same can be said about painting, music, and acting. In contrast with mathematical notational systems, these symbolic representations can, up to a point, be dissociated from what they express. The language of poets is not more beautiful than that of other people because they have better concepts to express. Inversely, poor language and clumsy drawings do not necessarily indicate low conceptual levels.

## REFERENCES


Luquet, A. *Le dessin enfantin.* Paris: Alcan, 1927.

Piaget, J. *La naissance de l'intelligence.* Paris and Neuchâtel: Delachaux & Niestlé, 1935.

Piaget, J., and B. Inhelder. *Mémoire et intelligence.* Paris: Presses Universitaires de France, 1968.

Sinclair, H., and E. Ferreiro. *Étude génétique de la compréhension. production, et répétition des phrases au mode passif.* forthcoming. Archives de psychologie.

HERMINE SINCLAIR

# Piaget's Theory and Language Acquisition

It may seem rather contradictory that Genevan psychologists should be interested in the acquisition of language. Piaget himself has always stressed the fact that language is *structured* by thought rather than being its source, and since it is in the development of thought that he is interested, he has paid very little attention to language. Even if one of his first publications *The Language and Thought of the Child* (Piaget [a] 1923) had the word *language* in the title, this does not mean that at that time he accorded a more important status to language. He was then studying thought through the verbal interchange that takes place among children and between the child and an adult. In his later work, he found methods better suited to his purpose, although dialogue between child and experimenter always plays a part.

It was Piaget who dethroned language from the central position it had occupied in the minds of those who wanted to study thought, and it was Piaget who put language in its place by showing that it is part of a much more general capacity—that of representation or the symbolic functions, which appear in the middle of the second year in a number of different behaviors (symbolic play, delayed imitation in the absence of the model, mental images, etc.). However, he did not suppose that language acquisition would therefore follow the same line of development as the other manifestations of the symbolic function. He pointed out that language dealt with *signs,* that is to say, symbols that have no resemblance to, or other links with, the objects and events they symbolize.

On the other hand, because of the spectacular achievements of a linguist, Chomsky, language is now being reinstated as the key to the understanding of human thought. Furthermore, since it was shown conclusively that

PIAGETIAN COGNITIVE-DEVELOPMENT RESEARCH AND MATHEMATICAL EDUCATION, National Council of Teachers of Mathematics, Washington, D.C., pp. 203-214.

language could not possibly be acquired in an associationist manner, it was concluded that the fundamental linguistic structures must therefore be innate. It may seem paradoxical in the light of these theoretical differences to say that it is Chomsky's work that is making possible the study of language acquisition within a Piagetian framework.

However, despite the important differences, Chomsky's and Piaget's theories have several points in common. Both men are nonempiricists, both are interested in underlying structures that can be formalized, both are dealing with competence rather than with performance. Also, it is through Chomsky's studies that the difference between language and the other manifestations of the symbolic function has become much clearer. In symbolic play and images, symbols may be linked in a common framework, but they do not form a system. Language, by contrast, is structured into a system, and although it is, on the one hand, a way of representing what is known, it is, on the other hand, itself an object to be known. The child has to infer regularities and rules and arrive at an *interiorized* grammar that will enable him to construct and understand an unlimited number of sentences in his mother tongue. It is in this sense that the study of language acquisition cannot be undertaken in the same manner as that of other modes of representation; but it is also in this sense that language is an object of knowledge and that its acquisition can be studied in the constructivist manner in which Piaget studies the development of other types of knowledge.

## Theoretical Framework and Experimental Methods

Genevan research in language is based (as is most research) on certain theoretical principles. The basic ones are the following:

1. It is not language that explains human thought, but rather cognitive patterns and operations that will eventually provide the basis for explaining language.
2. It is not an explicit description of language as a fully acquired system that will throw light on acquisition mechanisms and provide a model for comprehension and production mechanisms, but rather a better knowledge of the long process of acquisition that will elucidate the functioning of the fully acquired system. This functioning of the system is not to be equated with a search for the psychological factors that distort "performance"; it concerns the mechanism through which *ideal* performance under optimal conditions is attained (in comprehension as well as in production), leaving aside the flaws caused by deficits in perception, memory, attention, and so on.

The above principles stem directly from Piaget's epistemological approach, of which the following are two of the aspects:

1. The development of thought is an autonomous process, but that of the symbolizing and representative functions is not.
2. The structure of adult thought can be understood only through the study of its formation, that is, the study of cognitive development in the child.

However, our guiding principles do not imply that we have a reductionist attitude toward language. We certainly do not think that language acquisition can be explained by the laws of cognitive development alone; the structure of language itself is a necessary part of an acquisition model.

This catalogue of basic convictions is no more than an explanation of our experimental methods. We are very far from having any coherent theories on acquisition, and our experimental studies are only just beginning. The most complete study to come out of the Geneva school is a doctoral thesis by Emilia Ferreiro (forthcoming) on the temporal relationships in children's language. Several projects are still being carried out, and it is not possible to give more than an indication of the implications we see in our results. However, before giving some examples, something more has to be said about our methods.

We try to investigate comprehension as well as production. We study comprehension in the following way: the experimenter pronounces a verbal pattern (such as "The boy is pushed by the girl"), and the child is asked to act it out using a number of toys. In many ways, this technique is superior to the one in which the subject is asked to choose among pictures. In several of our experiments the children understood the utterance in an unforseen way that we could not have represented pictorially. Some examples are given below.

In the production tasks we try to elicit a certain verbal pattern by asking the child to describe an event the experimenter has acted out with toys. Production is obviously very much more difficult to study than comprehension. In fact, since there are almost always several ways of describing an event, it is difficult to devise a situation that imposes a particular structuration. For example, how does one go about obtaining relative clauses from a child? In the case of adult subjects, one simply explains and asks for a particular pattern. But such methods are not possible below the age of eight or nine, before certain grammatical terms have been learned in school. We cannot, in general, decide from its nonappearance at certain ages that the children are incapable of producing the pattern in question. We are, however, less interested in success and failure than in types of errors and patterns. Evidently, we are not interested in errors that are due to such superficial factors as lack of attention or of memory. We try to exclude them by keeping the child interested, by rephrasing the instructions, and, in the case of comprehension tasks, by repeating the utterance in question as often as seems necessary. Moreover, the appearance of a certain type of error or pattern at one point of development and not another, or that of a new type of error that seems to derive from the preceding one, cannot be explained by memory or attention factors. Such findings directly touch on the problem of determining the rules children's productions follow at different moments in development and how later rules are derived from earlier ones. In fact, when we speak of errors, this is not the right description for many of the verbal patterns we find. Often, the children's descriptions are quite adequate in themselves but different from adult expressions, and if grammatical errors are present, we can regard them as expressions of the type of child grammar our subjects work with, in which case they become precious indications of rule-bound behavior that simply follows different rules. The term *error* is applicable only when in the comprehension tasks children give a wrong interpretation of an unambiguous sentence.

In both comprehension and production tasks, we try to apply the Piagetian exploratory method; although we make sure that all the children are asked certain questions, we adapt the interview to each child's individual level. This exploratory method is much more difficult in language experiments than in others, one reason being that what Bärbel Inhelder calls *verification sur le vif* is often impossible. This *verification sur le vif* occurs when, on the basis of his knowledge of cognitive development, the experimenter makes a hypothesis on the thought pattern (scheme) that may underlie the child's answer. From there, the experimenter makes up a new question, a new situation, or a problem which will enable him to test his hypothesis. In other words, as soon as a subject reacts in an unforeseen way, the experimenter tries to find out what is behind the answer. Since we still know very little about an eventual sequence in the acquisition of particular patterns, it is difficult to invent new situations; since we cannot ask questions without using a certain verbal pattern, we may unwittingly influence the child's answer; and, finally, at the age at which we are working, children are incapable of understanding questions about language itself. In our language experiments we usually introduce an exploratory period at the end of the procedure; but we may also take advantage of children's spontaneous remarks such as "I think I got it upside down" and questions such as "Should I take the boy first?" With children who spontaneously start playing with our toys, we may change the order of our items to suit the framework of their play activity.

It is obvious that this kind of procedure leads to a certain loss in quantitative information. However, in our view this loss is more than compensated for by a corresponding gain in qualitative information.

In certain cases, the children are also asked to repeat something the experimenter has said, in a context where they have to make an effort to understand the utterance. For instance, from time to time during a comprehension task, we ask the child to repeat what we have said before he acts it out with the toys. Interestingly, as can be seen in the examples below, these repetitions often resemble the answers we obtain in production tasks. They also may throw light on the peculiar reactions that occur during the comprehension task. A comparison of reactions to all three tasks is therefore often fruitful. Incidentally, the repetition task provides a kind of check on memory factors.

Before giving some examples of Genevan research in language, I should like to bring up a question that is often asked: How is it possible to hope to find a parallel between the mechanisms of cognitive development (as they have been interpreted by Piaget) and those of language acquisition if the latter seem to take place in a continuous, direct manner without any discernible stages and, especially, if the main linguistic structures are all present at about the age of five, as is often maintained?

There is no language in the proper sense before the culmination of the sensorimotor period. Communication, however, starts right from birth (cries of distress and simple signalling by the baby of its presence in a certain place). Communication soon becomes bipolar: distress is signalled by generally high, nasalized sounds, produced with tense muscles; contentment is signalled by low, nonnasal sounds, produced with a relaxed musculature.

Little by little, vocalisations take on some of the phonetical and prosodical characteristics of the mother tongue, under the influence of many different factors (such as the development of recognition-memory, adoption of a sitting position which allows the child to look directly at another person's face, the beginnings of imitation in the presence of a model, sensorimotor coordinations between sight and hearing, development of the muscular tonus in the lips, etc.).

With the acquisition of object permanency and the first grouplike structure, the infant becomes able, in our view, to start communicating with language. In fact, object permanence means that objects are now becoming things to be known and not only things to be reacted to. This development at the same time *necessitates* some kind of representation and *makes it possible.* Language is, among other things, a capacity to substitute a signifier for real events and objects. It is therefore comprehensible that these realities have first to be established as having an existence divorced from the subject's actions before they can be represented by a signifier. At this point, Piaget's stages and periods of language acquisition converge. As I have said, language proper starts at the end of the sensorimotor period and coincides with the advent of other representational behavior.

One characteristic that distinguishes the first verbal period from what went before is that instead of a direct communication between interlocutors (which continues to exist, of course, even between adults—e.g., expressions such as *ssht* or *brrr*), communication now includes a reference to some event or object signified in an as yet very global but already conventional manner, in sounds that the adult recognizes as a word (or a combination of several words) from his language.

Evidently, the very first manifestations of language, the famous first words, are difficult to place exactly. As with all imitative behaviors, they have to be recognized as such by the observer. For example, if I had not seen a seventeen-month-old girl look intently at a butterfly beating its wings against a window, I would not have interpreted her behavior, on a visit a week later, when she went straight to that window and flapped her arms, as a delayed imitation of a past event. Also, there is a great danger of interpreting the first words in an adultomorphic way (e.g., interpreting them as nouns, or verbs) and parochial manner (e.g., fitting them forcibly into the word classes of a certain language). Without going into the controversy of the precise nature of this holophrastic speech, I should like to allude to Piaget (1959) who considers holophrases to be *l'enounce d'une action possible* ("expressing a possible action") and *jugement d'action* ("action judgment"). In other words, he emphasizes their predicative function; that is, they say something *about* something.

A second characteristic of the first verbal productions is the discovery of the principle of syntactic combination. First, sometimes in the form of a simple juxtaposition of two separate elements, then in the expression of genuine relations ("daddy car"), syntax begins to develop. The two- or three-word phrases—such as "read book", "that cat fish", "no come eat", "Johnny truck"—announce grammatical relations such as attribution, possession, localisation, and so on. The first vocalisations seem to be phonetically universal (all babies produce the same sounds, whatever the language spoken in their environment); the first holophrastic or two-word utterances seem to be structurally universal. But very soon, with the introduction of the first grammatical markers, the particular system of the mother tongue appears.

It has been amply demonstrated that although imitation obviously plays a role, these first productions are not shortened and clumsy copies of adult sentences but are active creations on the part of the child. An older child's saying "I'll smile up my painting" (putting a smiling mouth in the face of the sun) is a quasi-poetical extension of a semantic field.

By the age of five, it seems that the child has acquired most of the adult's syntactic structurations. If this were true, all language acquisition would take place during Piaget's preoperational period. The precocity of this achievement is often taken as an argument for the innateness of linguistic structures. However, in the first place, as Hans Furth (1969) has said, "There is no reason to believe that other knowing and symbolic behavior that the child acquires as early as language does not require equally complex activities on the part of the child". Indeed, the recent work of Piaget et al. (1968) on the preoperational period with its semi-logic of unidirectional dependencies has made the achievements of this stage much clearer. Moreover, many of the typical conquests of the concrete-operational period are already present, in isolated thought patterns, much earlier. The four-year-old *knows,* and will say so if asked, that in the liquid-pouring experiment nothing has been added or taken away; he perceives that the glasses have different dimensions; he knows by that age that if you pour the liquid back into the original glass, it will attain the original level (*renversabilite*). But what he cannot do is to derive from all this that the quantity of the liquid must therefore be the same. This conclusion will become logically necessary only with the establishment of the operational structure. In the second place, many linguistic structurations are not understood until the age of nine or ten; the acquisition period of a number of fundamental and frequent patterns stretches well into the concrete-operational stage.

Our hypothesis is that the linguistic competence of children of four to five years of age has the same functional characteristics as their cognitive competence and that it does not necessitate the intervention of concrete operations. This hypothesis does not imply that the one-way mappings of this period *explain* the verbal acquisitions; in fact, one of the experiments, which I shall discuss later, shows clearly that many problems remain to be solved.

In what way, then, does the period of concrete operations elaborate language acquisition? It would seem that several new capacities start to lead to new verbal behavior at this level.

In the first place, a certain reflexion on language itself becomes possible, since sentences can now be dissociated from their content. When asked to make a sentence with the words "coffee" and "salt", a six-year-old will no longer say, "You can't, nobody puts salt in coffee!" He will be able to answer questions on sentences such as "How many words do I say when I say, 'Mary has seven dolls'?" The four-year-old will announce, "Seven words"; the six- to seven-year-old will count on his fingers and get the right answer (or the wrong answer, but it won't be seven).

In the second place, this detachment will make it possible for him to find different formulations describing the same event. It now becomes possible to *conserve* the semantic content of an utterance while changing its form. This may sound like a facile allusion to conservation concepts, but although I believe that it has a more profound significance, I cannot as yet explain it further. For instance, in our own experiment on the passive sentence (Sinclair and Ferreiro 1971), five-year-olds often behaved as follows: when the experimenter had shown them a truck pushing a car and asked them to describe this event by starting to speak about the car, they said, "No, I can't; otherwise it would be the wrong way round, the car pushing the truck". Similarly, in Ferreiro's experiment on temporal relationships, when five-year-olds were asked to describe two events acted out, such as a girl doll going up a staircase and then a boy doll entering a garage, they rigidly adhered to this temporal succession in their description. They either refused to start with "the boy" or if they tried to do so, they were incapable of introducing temporal indicators to reestablish the correct order. They finished by admitting that when one starts with the second event, "It's the wrong way round", or, straightforwardly, "It's wrong" and claiming that it could not be done. Younger children (four-year-olds) did not express these perplexities. They simply complied with our instructions and inversed agent and patient ("The car pushes the truck" instead of "The car is pushed by the truck") and also reversed the order of the two events without hesitation (maybe they expected reality to be adjusted to their description).

For the moment, we cannot yet go beyond a description of such new acquisitions that take place during the concrete-operational period. However, from our few experiments we are convinced that these acquisitions concern not only lexical but also syntactic acquisitions. We hypothesize that the new structure of thought makes these acquisitions possible and that it will be possible to show parallels. The operational period would in this view constitute a restructuration of the acquisitions in the preoperational period.

## Two Experiments

After this long introduction, I shall briefly indicate some of our findings from two experiments on passive sentences and on the ordering of three words that are not linked by a syntactic structure. The technique for the study of passive sentences has already been described: comprehension, through the acting out of passive sentences said by the experimenter; production, following the instruction to describe an event acted out by the experimenter by first naming the patient; and repetition of the sentence said by the experimenter before acting it out. In general—and we conducted the experiment with both French- and German-speaking children—our results are the same as those found by Harry Beilin (1969) with subjects of English mother tongue.

Our criterion for success in the comprehension task was the correct acting out of what Slobin calls *reversible sentences,* such as "The boy was washed by the girl", in contrast with such sentences as "The car was washed by the boy". In the first example, agent and patient can be interchanged without rendering the semantic content of the sentence impossible or improbable. Girls can wash boys and boys can wash girls. In the other example, only one version is possible, since cars don't wash boys!

Comprehension results indicated that by six years and six months to seven years, most of these sentences are understood. Before then, the main tendency is to take the first noun as the agent and the second as the patient. The five-year-olds hesitated a great deal, and there were some interesting compromise solutions. For instance, some of them introduced a kind of reciprocal action, and for the sentence "The boy is washed by the girl", they made the boy wash the girl *and* the girl wash the boy. Interestingly, apart from the difference between reversible and irreversible sentences, the particular action presented (or the verb chosen) influences both the average age at which success is achieved and the type of utterance produced. A durative verb such as *laver* ("to wash") is not treated in the same way as verbs such as *renverser* ("to knock down"). Passive sentences with the verb *suivre* ("to follow") are often not understood by children of eight and even beyond that age.

The repetition task showed that at four years of age children are perfectly capable of repeating passive sentences correctly, but their comprehension is incorrect. As mentioned above, they act as if the subject of the passive sentence was the agent. They also introduce certain modifications in the model that are difficult to interpret. These modifications, however, concern either the verb form (*a lavé,* "has washed", instead of *est lavé,* "is washed", for instance) or the preposition (*avec,* "with", instead of *par,* "by") or both, but never nouns.

At the age of five, comprehension gets better, but repetition seems to deteriorate. In fact, this apparent deterioration is an improvement; parrot-like correct repetitions disappear, and different modifications are introduced. The most interesting are those that transform the passive sentence into an active one, keeping the semantic content constant ("The boy is washed by the girl" repeated as "The girl washes the boy") or those that substitute another verb form for the passive ("The boy got washed by the girl"). Only from six years of age are literally correct repetitions always accompanied by correct actions.

The production task showed that our instruction (to start with the patient instead of the agent) is interpreted by the four-year-olds as a suggestion to "say something about" the patient, which in many cases leads to a truncated passive or an intransitive sentence that does not mention the agent; for example, "The boy gets clean", "The boy is washed", "The car moves", and so on. The five-year-olds are capable of centering their attention on both the patient and the agent, but they do this in two juxtaposed sentences, of which one describes the patient and the other the action; for example, "The boy is clean and the girl washed him". Around the age of six, the first passive constructions are regularly used, although (in French) our children prefer the formula *il s'est fair laver par la fille* (which can be translated roughly as "he got himself washed by the girl").

In this experiment, the results of the comprehension, production, and repetition tasks converge. They also reveal a phenomenon of decentration, which is one of the characteristics of the concrete-operational period.

The other experiment is much more difficult to interpret. Having observed that word order is an important semantic indicator for young children, we wondered how they would interpret a sequence of three lexical items not linked by a syntactic structure and, especially, whether the order in which the three items were presented would have some influence on their interpretations. We chose three combinations:

1. Two nouns and one transitive verb, such as boy-girl-wash or boy-box-open (reversible and nonreversible), presented in the six possible orders (boy-girl-wash; girl-boy-wash; girl-wash-boy; boy-wash-girl; wash-boy-girl; wash-girl-boy)
2. Two nouns and one intransitive verb, such as horse-pig-run
3. Two verbs and one noun, such as bear-jump-grunt

In this experiment, our youngest subjects were three years old. We warned the children that we were going to "talk rather funnily, not at all as the teacher would talk" and that they should try to "find out what we meant and show us what they thought". Almost all the subjects accepted this instruction and only a few three-year-olds did not seem to be able to do anything but choose the toys named in the combination, without making them act.

A first surprise was that there was a definite difference in the children's behavior according to whether a transitive or an intransitive verb was used. The latter did not give rise to any hesitations. The children made the horse and the pig jump, or the bear (provided with a grunting mechanism) jump and grunt, often in the order in which we had pronounced the items, but often not. On the other hand, the combinations with a transitive verb gave rise to hesitation and periods of reflexion. It seemed as if as early as the age of three, there is some awareness of the difference between transitive and intransitive verbs, and moreover, the children behaved as if in the case of a transitive verb, word order becomes important.

Since the experiment is not yet finished, I can do no more than give some indications of what happens with transitive verbs. A definite change does seem to take place between four and seven.

The nonreversible combinations (such as boy-wash-car) are at all ages preponderantly interpreted in the most probable way, in whichever order they were presented. However, a few five-year-olds, in the case of the order car-wash-boy, put our little sponge on top of the car and made the car wash the boy. This very strong conviction that "the first noun is the subject" is also attested to by the fact that in the reversible combinations (such as boy-wash-girl) all the children, of all ages, took the first word as the agent. However, the age differences appeared when the order was not noun-verb-noun but either noun-noun-verb or verb-noun-noun.

The youngest subjects showed a strong tendency in the case of verb-noun-noun to introduce an agent from outside: for instance, when we said "wash-boy-girl", they themselves took the sponge and washed both dolls or took a third doll and made her wash the others. Sometimes, in the case of noun-noun-verb they introduced a patient. This behavior again seems to indicate a very strong awareness of the subject-verb-object construction; if a possible subject in the form of a noun is not present as the first word pronounced, they introduce one.

The slightly older subjects (four and five) had different solutions to this problem. Sometimes, we again observed the reciprocal solutions, as in the passive sentences. For "boy-girl-wash", the children made the boy and girl wash each other. Two other solutions seem to become preponderant around the age of five. The first is to consider the noun immediately following the verb as its object. For example, "wash-boy-girl" is interpreted as "The girl washes the boy". The other solution is to regard the first of the two nouns as the subject and the other as the object. Thus, "wash-boy-girl" is understood as "The boy washes the girl". The last solution seems to be preferred at all later ages. In the first solution it is the verb that is picked out by the child and interpreted in terms of its position in relation to the nouns; in the other, it seems to be the order of the two nouns that is decisive for the subject-object relationship.

These first results seem to us rather more mysterious than those of the experiment on the passive sentences. In view of the predominance of ordinal relationships during the preoperational period, the early awareness of order for the interpretation of utterances may not be so surprising. However, the systematic nature of our young subjects' interpretations was astonishing. Moreover, the differentiation between transitive and intransitive verbs and the shift from a verb-centered to a noun-centered interpretation is difficult to understand. We conducted this experiment in a rigid way and have not yet introduced any supplementary questions or situations to explore the mechanism behind the behavior. As always, we hope that the children's own explanations will give us some more ideas.

In conclusion, it can only be said that the mystery of language acquisition is far from solved. Obviously, the small number of experiments performed in Geneva and elsewhere cannot possibly lead us immediately to a comprehensive theory of acquisition mechanisms, which could then be tested against new facts. However, it would seem that by taking into account the laws of cognitive development we shall be able to get some idea of the kind of inferences children at different stages of development are capable of making from the adult utterances they hear. No theory of acquisition can afford to ignore the important work done in linguistic theory; but neither can such theories ignore the stages in cognitive development, which, in our opinion, will give the clue to the nature and form of the linguistic structures children are able to produce and understand.

## REFERENCES


Beilin, H. "Active-Passive Confirmation and Operational Reversibility." Paper presented at a meeting of the Society for Child Development, 1969, at Santa Monica, Calif.

Ferreiro, E. *Les relations temporelles dans le language de l'enfant*. Geneva: Droz, forthcoming.

Furth, H. *Piaget and Knowledge*. Englewood Cliffs, N.J.: Prentice-Hall, 1969.

Piaget, J. (a). *Le language et la pensée chez l'enfant*. Neuchâtel and Paris: Delachaux & Niestlé, 1923.

——— (b). *Formation du symbole*. Neuchâtel and Paris: Delachaux & Niestlé, 1946.

Piaget, J., J.-B. Grize, A. Szeminska, and V. Bang. *Épistémologie et psychologie de la fonction*. Paris: Presses Universitaires de France, 1968.

Sinclair, H., and E. Ferreiro. "Temporal Relationships in Children's Language." *International Journal of Psychology* 6, no. 1 (1971).

# PART III: CRITICAL ISSUES IN THE THEORY

# The Theory of Stages in Cognitive Development

JEAN PIAGET
University of Geneva
*Translation by Sylvia Opper, Cornell University*

Ladies and Gentlemen:

I should first like to thank the organizers of this small conference on the role of ordinal scales in the problem of development for having invited both my collaborator and friend, Bärbel Inhelder, and me to participate in your meeting. To be quite honest, I am not an expert in ordinal scales. Since you do me the honor of inviting me to address you, however, I feel that the problem of stages is one that should serve as an introduction to the discussions to be held on ordinal scales.

There are two reasons for this. First, a theoretical one: If ordinal scales do indeed have some basis in reality, then a succession of stages must exist in some form or another. And second, as you all know full well, no general agreement has as yet been reached about the existence of these stages. Our own hypotheses about the existence and the necessary sequence of these stages are not accepted by everybody. Consequently, I feel that it might be useful for Bärbel Inhelder and me if I were to discuss the question of stages with you and thus come to know your criticisms, objections, and the problems involved. Generally speaking, however, I feel that it is this working group, whose objective is to study ordinal scales, that will eventually solve the problem of stages. Today, therefore, I shall merely outline the problem and make a few brief comments.

Each time that a specific problem is studied, as for instance that of causality which is currently receiving our attention, the analysis of the responses and reactions of children of different ages seems to point to the existence of relatively well-defined stages in this limited area. The important point, however, is to discover whether there are any general overall stages in development, and whether the different stages found in these more limited and specific areas

An address to the ETB McGraw-Hill invitational conference on ordinal scales of development, Monterey, California, February 9, 1969.

contain any elements in common. In other words, is it possible to detect broad periods in development with characteristics that can be applied in a general manner to all the events of these periods? This is the hypothesis that we are trying to investigate.

We postulate four major periods in development. First there is a sensorimotor period which occurs before the advent of language. This period is characterized by what we call "sensorimotor intelligence," which is a type of intelligence resulting in a certain number of performances, such as the organization of spatial relationships, the organization of objects and a notion of their permanence, the organization of causal relationships, etc. After the sensorimotor period, at around the age of 2 years, comes another period which starts with the symbolic or semiotic function. This is called the period of "preoperational thought" since the child is now capable of having representational thought by means of the symbolic function. At this stage, though, the child cannot perform operations in the way that I define this term. In my terminology "operations" are internalized actions which are reversible; that is, they can be performed in opposite directions. Finally, they are coordinated into overall structures, and these structures give rise to a feeling of intrinsic necessity.

The third major period starts at around the age of 7 or 8 years and is characterized by the inception of operations. Initially these operations are concrete; that is, they are used directly on objects in order to manipulate these objects. For instance, the child can classify concrete objects, or order them, or establish correspondences between them, or use numerical operations on them, or measure them from a spatial point of view. The operations remain concrete until the child is about 11 or 12 years of age. Then, at approximately this age, the fourth major period begins. This period can be characterized by formal or propositional operations. This means that the operations are no longer applied solely to the manipulation of concrete objects, but now cover hypotheses and propositions that the child can use as abstract hypotheses and from which he can reach deductions by formal or logical means.

If these four major periods do indeed exist, then we should be able to characterize them in a precise manner. What we have tried to do in the past, and what we are still trying to do, is to describe the characteristics of these stages in terms of general overall structures which become integrated. With development, the more elementary structures become incorporated into higher level structures, and these in turn are incorporated into structures of an even higher level.

Not everyone believes that it is necessary to characterize stages in terms of overall structures. For example, Freud's stages of emotional development are characterized by their dominant traits. There is the oral stage, or the anal stage, or the narcissistic or primary stage, and so forth. The different characteristics exist at all the stages, but at any particular moment one of the characteristics predominates. Freud's stages can therefore be described in terms of dominant characteristics.

Such a characterization is not, I believe, adequate for the cognitive functions. In this area we should attempt to go beyond this. If we were to remain satisfied with the notion of dominant characteristics for the cognitive functions, it would always be somewhat arbitrary as to what exactly is dominant and what is not. This is why we are trying to discover the overall structures in cognition rather than specify the dominant characteristics. This means that we are looking for total structures or systems with their own laws, systems which incorporate all their elements and whose laws cover the entire set of elements in the system. It would be these structures which become integrated with development. I shall stop here, but before ending I should like to repeat that this is an important problem, because there is no consensus as to the existence of such structures. I shall therefore try to support my views in the remainder of my address.

The existence of these overall structures raises a problem: do they in fact really exist in the mind of the subject being studied, or are they merely an invention of the psychologist who studies children or adults? The notion of overall structures presents two difficulties. First, the subject is not conscious of the existence of his cognitive structures. For example, he does not know what a seriation is, or a classification, or a relationship of correspondence. He himself has never given a thought to the nature of these overall structures. He acts, he operates, he behaves. And from this behavior we, the psychologists, detect the structures. But the structures are unconscious. They are expressed in regular forms of responses that we believe we are discovering in the subject's behavior. We also feel that if the underlying structures did not exist, we would not be able to explain such behavior. But the subject himself is not aware of these structures. He is neither a professor of psychology nor a professor of logic. He does not reflect upon the structures that he uses. He simply uses them. This, then, is the first difficulty: do the structures really exist in the subject's mind, or have we perhaps invented them?

The second difficulty is this: if we are to be convinced of the existence of these structures, we should be able to formalize them in logical terms. We then try to adapt this formalization to what we are able to observe in the child. But we can never be sure whether we have invented the formalization or whether it really is an expression of what is to be found in the mind of the child. So you see I am very much aware of the various problems involved in the notion of overall structures. Let me, however, deal with some of them by means of a simple example.

I refer here to the example of seriation. Seriation consists of the ordering of a series of sticks from the smallest one to the tallest. Bärbel Inhelder, Mimi Sinclair, and I have once again returned to this problem of seriation in our recent studies on memory, and our findings confirm the stages discovered in our earlier work. For instance, we found that during the initial stage, which we may call stage A, the youngest subjects maintain that all the sticks are of equal length. During the next stage (stage B), the subjects divide the sticks into two categories, large and small, with no ordering of the elements. At stage C, the children talk of the large ones, the middle-sized ones and the small ones. At stage D, the child constructs a series in an empirical fashion, by trial and error, but he is not able to produce immediately a faultless construction. And finally, at stage E, the child discovers a method: he chooses the largest of all the sticks and he sets this on the table, then he takes the largest of all the remaining sticks and places this beside the first stick, then the largest of the remaining ones, until he has placed all the sticks on the table. At this stage, he constructs a correct ordering without any hesitation, and this construction presupposes a reversible relation. That is to say, an element *a* is both smaller than the ones which have gone before it and larger than the ones to follow. This is a good example of what I mean by a structure.

But let us see what the logicians have to say about this problem. What is a seriation from the formal point of view? Can we discover any relationship between the logician's formalization of a seriation and the child's structure of the same notion? For the logician, a seriation is a chaining of asymmetrical, connex, and transitive relations. As far as asymmetry is concerned, this seems obvious in the present example. This means that one element is larger than another. As for connectivity, this means that all the elements are different and that there are no two alike. And lastly, there is the transitivity relationship. This means that if *A* is larger than *B* and *B* larger than *C*, then *A* is automatically larger than *C*. In the above-mentioned seriation problem, we did not see any evidence of transitivity. Is it part of the structure? Does it exist? Here we can do some separate experiments on the problem by taking three sticks of unequal length. We compare the first with the second, and then hide the first under the table. Then we compare the second with the third, and we say to the child, "You saw beforehand that the first was larger than the second, and now you can see that the second is larger than the third. What is the one under the table like compared to the third one? Is it larger, smaller, or just the same?" Experience has shown that very young children are not able to use the deductive method and are thus unable to solve the problem of transitivity. They reply, "I don't know. I haven't seem them next to each other. I need to see all three together at the same time before I can answer your question."

For the older children, however, who use the deductive method, transitivity is evident. Not only is it evident, but it also is necessary. And here we touch upon the real problem of overall structures: the problem of the appearance at a particular point in development of the feeling of necessity. Until this point, a certain occurrence was either absent or simply probable; now it becomes necessary. How can one explain the apparition of necessity from the psychological point of view? This, I feel, is the real problem of overall structures. How is it that a phenomenon which until then had been merely noted empirically, or else had been felt to be simply probable, now becomes logically necessary from the subject's point of view?

One first reply could be to say that it is an illusion. Hume, in his studies on the notion of causality, maintained that the necessary cause-effect relationship was in fact not necessary at all, but simply due to our associations of ideas or to our habits. So one could say that this feeling of necessity is simply a habit. However, the striking thing here is that the child reaches this feeling of necessity as soon as he has understood the phenomenon in question. One can sometimes witness the precise moment when he discovers this necessity. At the beginning of his reasoning, he is not at all sure of what he is stating. Then suddenly he says, "But it's obvious." In another experiment where Bärbel Inhelder was questioning a child on a problem which is not that of seriation but of recurrent reasoning, but which also involves the feeling of necessity, the child was at first very uncertain. Then suddenly he said, "Once one knows, one knows forever and ever." In other words, at one point the child automatically acquires this feeling of necessity. Where does this necessity come from?

My personal feeling is that there is only one acceptable psychological explanation: this feeling of necessity comes from the closure or completion of a structure. One could, of course, also maintain that necessity is simply an awareness of an idea which was predetermined in the mind, an innate or a priori idea. But this is not a true psychological solution, for it defies verification. Also, if this were indeed true, the feeling of necessity would appear much earlier than it actually does.

This is why I believe that the feeling of necessity is neither a subjective illusion nor an innate or a priori idea. It is an idea which is constructed at the same time as the overall structures. As soon as a structure is sufficiently complete for closure to occur or, in other words, once the internal compositions of the structure become interdependent and independent of external elements and are sufficiently numerous to allow for all types of arrangements, then the feeling of necessity manifests itself. I believe that it is this feeling of necessity which constitutes evidence of the existence of the overall structures which characterize our stages.

I do not want to describe here all the overall structures that can be found. They naturally vary according to the four major stages mentioned earlier. At the sensorimotor level we find composite actions which are performed in a step-by-step or contiguous manner, since the child is not capable of representation which would allow for more complex relationships. His compositions are simply actions which are chained to one another but which nevertheless still form some kind of structure. We find, for instance, in the organization of space, an organization of movements and of positions which mathematicians call the group of displacements. This is one example of a structure, with its characteristic of necessity. That is to say, it is possible to return to the point of departure, and this is a necessary return. Also it is possible to reach one point by a variety of different routes, and these are called detour behaviors. So already in these two types of behavior, return and detour, we see the characteristic of necessity and the existence of overall structures.

At the level of preoperational thought we find other overall structures. These are not yet operational structures in the sense that I described earlier; that is, they are not yet reversible, but they are nonetheless structures with their own laws. Take for example the notion of a function. As an example, we have a piece of string, B, which can be pulled over a spring. If you tie a weight to a segment called A, the segment A′ will become shorter. When A becomes shorter, A′ becomes longer; when A′ becomes shorter, A becomes longer. So the lengthening of A is a function of the shortening of A′. At this point of development the child has not yet acquired conservation. If we were to ask the child if the whole string (B) were equal to the sum of the two parts (A and A′), that is, $B = A + A'$, in both cases (when the string has been pulled down with the weight or not), the child would not give the correct answer because he cannot conserve. This is an example of a function but without reversibility.

In other experiments we also find functions, as for instance in the many-to-one relationship, but this is not accompanied by the reverse relationship of one-to-many. In the one-to-many relationship, or the many-to-one, the child reaches only a partial logic; he has not yet acquired the other half of logic which would be reversibility. Other examples of structures at this level are those of qualitative identity. For example, if one pours liquid from one glass to another as in the well-known experiments on conservation, the child at this stage does not accept the conservation of quantity, but he already admits to the qualitative identity. He will say that it is the same water in both cases, but not the same quantity. Qualitative identity is far easier to achieve. All the child needs to do is to isolate the qualities, whereas for conservation the child must construct the quantities, and this is another matter.

I do not need to remind you that at the level of the concrete operations we find a great many overall structures which are much richer than those of the preoperational level and which we have called groupings. Examples are the notion of seriation mentioned previously, classification, one-to-one correspondence, and many-to-one or one-to-many correspondences. At this level quantification becomes possible as a result of the overall structures, and consequently so, too, do the notions of conservation which were lacking at the preoperational level. Even identity changes and becomes operational and additive. For example, in the conservation problem, the child will say, "It's the same quantity, because you haven't added anything or taken anything away." Nothing has been added and nothing taken away; this is an additive identity and therefore a quantitative one, and no longer simply qualitative identity as when the child says, "It's the same water. It's the same color," etc.

There is no need for me to remind you that at the level of formal or propositional operations we also find even richer structures which are a synthesis of the previous ones. For instance, we have the group of four transformations which combines into a single system the structures of inversion ($A - A = 0$) and the structures of reciprocity ($A = B$ therefore $B = A$). These formal structures incorporate the preceding ones and constitute the termination of the construction of overall structures which has been going on throughout the entire period of childhood. The stages are therefore characterized by successive structures which do not replace each other, but which are integrated into one another. The simplest ones become incorporated into later, more complex ones. For example, the preoperational functions, or identities, are integrated into the concrete operations; then later, these concrete operational structures become incorporated into the formal operational structures.

At this point of our study I should like to note that these two notions of stages and overall structures, which I believe are necessarily closely bound together, have a meaning which is not only a logical and formal one. Despite their formalization, these structures have essentially a biological meaning, in the sense that the order of the stages is constant and sequential. Each stage is necessary for the following one. If this were not the case, one would be in no position to talk of stages. Naturally, the ages at which different children reach the stages may vary. In some social environments the stages are accelerated, whereas in others they are more or less systematically retarded. This differential development shows that stages are not purely a question of the maturation of the nervous system but are dependent upon interaction with the social environment and with experience in general. The order, however, remains constant.

Furthermore, the accelerations or retardations raise one problem which has not yet been studied sufficiently but which will have to be considered in the future. This is the problem of the optimal speed of development. What advantages are to be gained from speeding up the stages? I am often asked the following question in this country: "Can one accelerate the stages indefinitely?" My reply is to ask: "Is there any advantage to be derived from such acceleration?" Take experiments like those of Gruber where he finds that kittens acquire the requisite reactions towards the permanent object by the age of 4 months; that is, they search for objects hidden under a screen. It takes the human baby 9 months to reach this self-same point of development. One can consequently ask whether it would be advantageous for the human baby to reach this point at 4 instead of 9 months. I do not think so, because the kitten does not go very much further. Once it reaches a certain level, it scarcely progresses beyond this point. The human baby, on the other hand, develops more slowly, but in the long run he goes much further. One must remember that the higher the zoological species the longer is its period of infancy. There is a reason for this, and it may be that there is an optimal speed of development for each species. So we return to biology.

Our stages are very similar to those described by Waddington when he speaks of necessary courses which lead to a certain result. He calls these necessary courses or channels "creodes." He also describes certain forms of equilibrium which occur when there is a deviation from the creode due to unforeseen circumstances. In this case some force acts to bring the development back to its normal course. Waddington calls this "homeorhesis." It is a dynamic equilibrium, as opposed to homeostasis which is static. And finally, Waddington stresses what he calls the "time tally." This particular notion of a time tally raises the problem of the optimal speed of the stages of development. One last point is that the stages in embryology have a sequential ordering, with each stage being necessary for the following one. It is not possible to miss a stage in development.

If this were true of psychology, then there would be a relationship or a very close analogy with embryological development. I repeat that this does not mean that everything is genetically or internally determined within a hereditary program, since accelerations or retardations can occur in mental development which appear to be of an even greater magnitude than in embryology.

The present basic problem in the question of stages is that of the passage from one stage to the next. What mechanisms are responsible for this passage? Bärbel Inhelder and her collaborators have been dealing with this specific problem in their study of the possibility of certain forms of learning. These are not the types of learning that take place as a result of repetition or of the external reinforcements as in habit learning. Rather, she has been studying the type of learning which consists of isolating the factors which we believe are active in normal development in order to show how variations in these factors can produce accelerations in certain areas of development, and, more particularly, can result in certain correlations between the various learning experiences.

But I do not wish to discuss this problem here since it is currently in the process of investigation and the results will shortly be published in a book by Inhelder and her collaborators. What I would like to do is to raise the general problem of the passage from one stage to the next. I should like to approach this problem in the following manner. Three models can be used to describe this passage from one stage to the next. First, one could maintain that the successive acquisitions which characterize the stages mentioned earlier are acquisitions which are purely and simply due to environmental pressures, to experience, or to more or less random encounters with certain aspects of the daily social and physical environment. In this case, the succession of the stages would no longer be necessary. It might be a regular succession, with some regularities being more or less emphasized or attenuated depending upon the environment, but there would be no necessary succession.

The second possibility would be that the stages are internally determined; that is, they are predetermined. The succession of stages would be somehow preformed in the hereditary equipment of each individual. This approach is a return to the conception of innate ideas, and this notion, which was not very popular some years ago, has now become fashionable again. I refer in particular to the work being carried out in psycholinguistics by Chomsky, and to work done by certain psychologists who maintain that they are able to find notions of conservation very early in life, and that these notions then deteriorate—I am not quite sure how—only to reappear eventually at a later stage in development. I would classify this second solution as one of predetermination.

And then there is a third approach which is the one to which we subscribe. This solution is difficult to prove. It is even difficult to express or to explain. But once one has understood it, it seems that it is a compelling one, although it still remains to be proved. This third solution is that the stages result in a certain number of overall structures which become necessary with development, but are not so at the beginning of life. For example, the formal structures become necessary once the child possesses the concrete operations. As soon as he can perform the concrete operations, sooner or later he will begin to coordinate reversibility by inversion with reversibility by reciprocity and hence construct the group of four transformations. Similarly, once he is able to manipulate the classifications, sooner or later he will construct a classification of all the classifications, and thus he will end up by producing the combinatorial, which is a necessary form of formal thought.

Thus stages are characterized by overall structures which become necessary but which are not so initially. Formal structures become necessary when the concrete structures are complete; concrete structures become necessary when the structures of identity, of functions, etc., are complete; and these in turn become necessary when the sensorimotor functions are complete. But nothing is given in an a priori or innate fashion; nothing is preformed or predetermined in the activity of the baby. For instance, we could search far and wide in the behavior of the baby without finding even the rudiments of the group of four transformations, or of the combinatorial. These are all constructed and the construction—this I find to be the great mystery of the stages—becomes more and more necessary with time. The necessity is at the end of development, not at the point of departure. This, then, is the model upon which we are trying to base our work and our experiments.

There are still two more remarks that I should like to add before closing. First, that the stages which I have just discussed are those of intelligence, of the development of intelligence, and more particularly of the development of the logico-mathematical operations. They refer to those operations of which the subject is, in a way, the master or the director and which he can apply at will, in such a manner as he deems suitable, to a particular group of objects. When we study other cognitive functions, things naturally become more complex and the stages may be far less evident. In the field of perception, for example, we find hardly any stages as far as the primary or field effects are concerned. We do find some semistages in the perceptual activities, but these are not nearly as well defined as the stages of intelligence.

With mental imagery, we find essentially two periods. There is one preceding the concrete operations when mental images are mainly reproductory and static. During this period children have great difficulty in representing or imagining transformations or movements. The anticipatory images which are necessary for the representation of transformations only make their appearance at the level of the concrete operations. So here we find the beginnings of a stage, but again far less evident than in the field of intelligence.

In our recent research into memory, we find three distinctions. These are: recognitive memory, which is by far the earliest type of memory to appear and which is found right at the beginning of the sensorimotor level; evocative memory, which only appears with the semiotic function from the age of two or three years onwards; and then, between the two, there is a level of reconstructive memory which is still bound up with movement, with action, but which is more than simple recognition. These are very elementary distinctions which don't go very far in the differentiation of stages.

Even in the area of intelligence, as I mentioned before, the stages which I have just described are those of the logico-mathematical operations. Because here the subject does what he wants, in a manner of speaking. For the notion of causality, on the other hand, which we are studying at present, knowledge is physical and no longer logico-mathematical, and so the resistances of the object present all sorts of new problems. Consequently the stages are far less clear. At first, we had the impression that there were very few stages in the development of the notion of causality. Now we are slowly finding some. However, we are not yet at the point of being able to describe these stages in terms of the characteristics of overall structures such as described earlier. This is the first of my two concluding remarks.

Finally, a fairly important problem for the theory of stages is that of time lags. At certain ages the child is able to solve problems in quite specific areas. But if one changes to another material or to another situation, even with a problem which seems to be closely related, lags of several months are noted, and in some cases even of 1 or 2 years. Let us take one example, the problem of inclusion. The child is given a bunch of flowers, some of which are primroses, while others are tulips, daisies, or any other flowers. If you were to ask the child, "Are all the primroses flowers?" he will reply, "Of course." If you then ask, "Are there more flowers or more primroses in this bunch?" the child, instead of comparing the primroses with all the flowers, will compare them with all the flowers which are not primroses. And he will answer, "There are more," or "There are less," or "There are the same number," depending upon the result of this comparison, as if he were not able to include the part in the whole. This is the problem of class inclusion.

This problem is solved at approximately the age of 8 years for the flowers. But Bärbel Inhelder and I have noted that if one uses animals, for example, the problem becomes more complicated. If one asks the child, "Are all sea gulls birds?" he will reply, "Of course." If you ask, "Are all the birds sea gulls?" he will reply, "Of course not. There are also blackbirds, sparrows, etc." Then if you ask, "If you look out of the window, can you tell me whether there are more sea gulls or more birds in Geneva?" the child finds this more difficult to answer than for the flowers. Why is this? Is it because one cannot make a bunch with the sea gulls as with the flowers? I do not know. But this is one example of the problem. It is possibly a poorly chosen one, but there are any number of these problems of time lags between the solution of a problem with a certain material and the solution of the same problem with another material.

I have often been reproached for not having produced a sufficiently precise theory of these time lags in the same way as one can try to produce a theory of the overall structures or of the positive characteristics of stages. But time lags are a negative characteristic which form an obstacle to the construction of the overall structures. My reply to such a reproach is merely the following: time lags are always due to an interaction between the person's structures on the one hand, and the resistances of the object on the other. The object may be flowers, which offer little resistance; one places them on the table, and one makes a bunch of them. But there are other objects which offer more resistance, as for instance the birds. One cannot put them on the table. Some resistances of objects are unpredictable. When one encounters them, one can explain them, but always after the event. It is not possible to have a general theory of these resistances.

And so, in concluding, I should like to find some sort of an excuse for this failure by a comparison with physics. Physics is a much more advanced science than psychology, a more exact science which permits mathematical theories in almost all areas. But there is one area where physicists have not yet managed to produce a general theory. This is the problem of friction. Friction is the resistance of an object when you make it move along a surface. Physicists explain the role of friction in such and such a situation, but they have not yet come up with a general theory for this phenomenon. Time lags are somewhat analogous; they are comparable to all the concrete situations where friction is involved. Some areas are manipulated with ease; others offer all sorts of resistances. This problem still remains to be solved.

As you see, I have tried to be honest in my address by pointing out the various problems and difficulties which still remain. But I repeat, I am counting especially on the work that you are going to do here in your meeting on ordinal scales to shed some light on the difficult question of stages.

# Cognitions and Conservations: Two Views

**Jerome S. Bruner, Rose R. Olver, Patricia M. Greenfield, *et al.***

***Studies in Cognitive Growth.*** New York: Wiley, 1966. Pp. xvi + 343 $7.95.

*Reviewed by* JEAN PIAGET

JEROME BRUNER and his eleven collaborators have given me great pleasure in dedicating to me the fine book they have written on cognitive development and I thank them most heartily for it. I thus find it embarrassing to write a critical review of their work, but, as they say themselves, fundamental agreement on the important problems does not exclude disagreement on certain specific interpretations. Such points of disagreement are useful, for they are conducive to new experiments, and we still need a great number of new facts to confirm or invalidate our various hypotheses.

The two central problems which to my mind dominate all questions of cognitive development are (1) to determine whether knowledge consists only in copying or imitating reality, or whether to *understand* reality it is necessary to *invent* the structures which enable us to assimilate reality, and consequently (2) to determine whether the actions performed by the subject on reality consist simply in the construction of appropriate images and adequate language, or whether the subject's actions, and, later, his operations *transform* reality and modify objects. I cannot help being astounded that psychologists from large countries which, like the USA and the USSR, intend to transform our world, have no greater ambition than to describe the activity of the subject as the mere construction of adequate images and sufficient language; I find it hard to believe that we can build sputniks or plan trips to the moon with no more than good copies of observable or already observed data to guide us.

Bruner has no faith in logic (except in the concept of identity) and he has not understood the role of operational structures. No doubt he believes that this is the main difference between us.

CONTEMPORARY PSYCHOLOGY, 1967, Vol. 12, pp. 532-533.

But it goes deeper than that. It is a matter of indifference to me whether or not one uses the language of modern logic to describe the operations of subjects; but if one ignores these operations it seems to me that one can understand neither Euclid, nor Newton, nor Einstein, nor the child, because cognitive development is a continuous building of new *transformational structures* and not the making of cameras or talking machines.

Bruner does say that I "missed the heart of the conservation problem," a problem on which I have been working for the last 30 years. He is right, of course, but that does not mean that he himself has understood it in a much shorter time. We are beginning to discover that for a thorough understanding of the mechanism of operations we have to start with an analysis of functions (in the mathematical sense) and of identity itself at a pre-operatory level, and this study of identity, which we started two or three years ago, has already given some surprising results that lead to interpretations very different from Bruner's.

BEFORE considering Bruner's interpretations, however, it is necessary to point out three misconceptions which recur throughout the volume and distort the whole discussion. (1) In the screening experiments (and Bruner forgets that we published screening experiments in 1963) it is necessary to distinguish true conservation from pseudo-conservation. Pseudo-conservation is easy to spot by a simple check which Bruner has not applied: when a child says that there will be the same quantity to drink, one should ask him to pour the same amount of liquid into two different, empty glasses, one low and wide, and one tall and narrow; in case of pseudoconservation the child will pour liquid into both glasses up *to the same level,* without paying attention to the difference in width, which shows clearly that his (correct) answer was not based on conservation of quantity. Without this check many of Bruner's results cannot be used. (2) Bruner also confuses co-variance of dimensions with compensation; this leads him to maintain, wrongly, that compensation can be present without conservation. In fact, co-variance can be acquired by direct perceptive recording of real situations without comprehension, and here again Bruner omitted to apply checking experiments that would decide the matter. (3) He also continuously confuses "renversabilité," or empirical return, with reversibility. "Renversabilité" is a physical concept (e.g., when one notes that an elastic or a spring can become longer and then become shorter) whereas reversibility is a logico-spatial or operatory concept (movement from A to B is nullified by returning from B to A) and, here again, careful experimentation is necessary to distinguish the two concepts.

When Bruner claims that neither reversibility nor compensation are necessary for conservation, he is being equivocal in three ways: the three central notions in this discussion (conservation, compensation and reversibility) are poorly defined and poorly tested in a book that sets out to give an accurate theory of conservation, superior to our own. . . .

The main contention of the book is that conservation is due to learning which liberates the concept of identity from the conflicts induced by perceptual cues, and this learning is supposed to take place thanks to manipulation ("renversibilité") and, especially, to language.

As regards language, Bruner believes that learning consists in relating innate syntactic structures (syntactic maturity) to reality, but he does not give any experimental data on linguistic development itself, nor on its relationship with cognitive structure. H. Sinclair succeeded in showing experimentally that the child's language is actually transformed along with the construction of operational structures. Verbal training, however, results in progress in conservation with only 10% of subjects, though after such training 65% of subjects show a grasp of co-variance of dimensions (again, co-variance must not be confused with compensation). This goes to show that operations direct language acquisitions rather than vice versa.

As regards identity, what sets it apart from the concept of conservation is that identity is only qualitative, and can therefore be acquired by the dissociation of a perceptive quality from other perceptive qualities: e.g., with liquids if $a$ = color, $b$ = the quality of being a liquid and $c$ = shape, then $abc$ stays "the same water" for the subject because $a$ and $b$ have not changed and only $c$ is modified. Conservation, however, involves quantities that are not perceptive, but have to be constructed by compensation between different dimensions (co-variance is acquired much earlier in development, even in the shape of "function"). These quantities call for progression from ordinal scales to hyperordinal scales (Suppes), and to extensive or numerical scales. A detailed study of the different forms of identity shows that the problem is far more complex than Bruner supposes.

As regards Bruner's experimental approach, I am surprised by its recurring superficiality and the considerable lacunae due to the absence of checks. For instance, nowhere is there to be found a precise determination of the initial and final developmental levels in the pre-tests and post-tests, though different levels may be indicated by the child's arguments, by the possible links with other structures and by the durability of the acquired behavior. These lacunae are the more serious since the learning sessions were concerned with the exact same problems: for instance (p. 198) when the liquid is poured into a glass with a different diameter, 100% of the 7-year-olds are said to possess conservation but only 30% correctly predict the level of the liquid in the second glass: obviously they did not possess conservation at all.

On page 189 we are told that 36% of the children who showed conservation on the initial test think that the duck, when it goes to swim in a different pond, no longer has the same quantity of water: it is clear in this experience that for the child the quantity of liquid "to drink" is not the same as the quantity of liquid "to swim in" (depth of the water, etc.), a point that should have been analysed. Furthermore, in this otherwise attractive experiment, many other factors intervene that also are left unanalyzed. In particular, the direct and immediate pouring of a liquid from two identical glasses (one remaining untouched as a means of comparison) is not the same thing as pouring a liquid from a single receptacle into others while a continuity is being suggested by the accompanying story told to the child. It would have been necessary to study this factor, as is being done presently by Inhelder, Bovet and Sinclair. Bruner's experiments need to be repeated with greater care. Certain replications have already been undertaken by Mermelstein, Arc, Mills and Swartz, and give different results.

To sum up, neither Bruner's conceptualization, nor (unfortunately and principally) his experimental methods seem convincing to us. This is a pity indeed, for Bruner is exceptionally gifted for inventing new experiments and ingenious apparatus; but the analysis and the interpretation of his results are always too hurried. Remarks such as these are moreover instructive, and show that adults— even great psychologists—just like children, need time to reach the right ideas. This is the great mystery of development, which is irreducible to an accumulation of isolated learning acquisitions. Even psychology cannot be learned or constructed in a short time. . . .

# Reversibility in nonconservation of weight[1]

*FRANK B. MURRAY and PAUL E. JOHNSON*

*Contrary to Piaget's position (Piaget, 1960, 1967, 1968), we argue that reversibility is both logically and psychologically irrelevant to conservation, because logically, simply inverting the conservation transformation provides no information about the property being conserved, and psychologically, because nonconservers give evidence of reversibility. Specifically, the data indicate that nonconservers think that an increase in a clay ball's temperature reduces its weight, and a decrease in its temperature increases weight.*

The pivotal concept in Piaget's account of the intelligent behavior of young children is that of the "operation," which by his definition is a covert act that is reversible and part of a system of such acts (Piaget, 1960). "The criterion for the appearance of such operational systems is the construction of invariants or concepts of conservation" and conversely, "... when the most elementary forms of conservation are absent, it is a consequence of the absence of operational reversibility [pp. 8, 12]." This somewhat circular relationship of conservation and reversibility is the subject of this paper.

Other than conservation, the behavioral criteria for reversibility are difficult to specify. Piaget describes reversibility metaphorically as the child's mental capacity to undo, nullify, cancel, or invert a mental operation. When a child understands an operation, Piaget insists that "he also understands, by this very fact, the possibility of its inverse [Tanner & Inhelder, 1960, p. 80]." That is, if the S understands, or acts as if he understands, an operation leading from A to B, he understands the inverse operation B to A. If S possesses the additive operation he possesses as well the subtractive form of the same operation.

It is argued that in the conservation problem when a round clay ball is flattened into a pancake, the nonconserving child is mentally unable to undo the operation or transformation, and consequently he is unable, as well, to understand that the ball and the pancake have the same amount of clay, weigh the same, or take up the same amount of space. The conserving child, on the other hand, is able to undo the transformation mentally, and in fact he often supports his correct judgment with the explanation that the pancake could be rolled into the original ball, and because of that nothing has really changed.

The argument of this paper, in part, is that on purely logical grounds the reversibility of the transformation is irrelevant to the conservation judgment since it provides no evidence that the property of the object in question did not, in fact, change while it was in the transformed state. That an ice cube or a clay pancake can be returned to its original state as a quantity of water or as a clay ball is no guarantee at all that its volume, etc., as an ice cube or pancake was the same as its volume, etc., as a quantity of water or as a clay ball. Because a stretched rubber band can be returned to its original shorter length clearly does not mean that it was not longer when it was stretched. When the child offers a reversibility reason to justify a conservation response, his argument is irrelevant and, strictly speaking, incorrect.

In fact, knowing that a transformation can be empirically or even logically undone should be of no real help in the solution of the conservation problem, since that solution in some sense depends upon a consideration of the relevant and irrelevant transformations of the concept in question (Johnson & Murray[2]; Murray & Johnson, 1968). One might, in this regard, expect that the nonconserver, if his nonconservation has any validity at all, would show reversibility and consistency in his error. If the nonconserver really thinks that flattening a pancake decreases its weight, he might very well think that rolling back into a ball

PSYCHONOMIC SCIENCE, 1969, Vol. 16, pp. 285-287.

Table 1
Number of Ss in Each Group (1, 2, 3, 4) Responding Same, More, Less to Each Problem. (N = 120)

| Problem | Group 1 | | | Group 2 | | | Group 3 | | | Group 4 | | |
|---|---|---|---|---|---|---|---|---|---|---|---|---|
| Number | Same | More | Less | Same | More | Less | Same | More | Less | Same | More | Less |
| 1 | 0 | 29 | 1 | 4 | 0 | 26 | 1 | 29 | 0 | 1 | 0 | 29 |
| 2 | 1 | 29 | 0 | 1 | 0 | 29 | 2 | 28 | 0 | 1 | 0 | 29 |
| 3 | 10 | 18 | 2 | 17 | 3 | 10 | 9 | 20 | 1 | 7 | 4 | 19 |
| 4 | 9 | 19 | 2 | 15 | 4 | 11 | 11 | 17 | 2 | 7 | 3 | 20 |
| 5 | 9 | 3 | 18 | 18 | 8 | 4 | 12 | 1 | 17 | 11 | 18 | 1 |
| 6 | 11 | 3 | 16 | 17 | 10 | 3 | 14 | 1 | 15 | 9 | 14 | 7 |

increases its weight; that is, this particular shape transformation changes an object's weight for him just as an addition or substraction transformation changes an object's weight for most adults.

The particular transformation investigated in the data reported here to support the speculations above was an imagined temperature transformation and its effect on second graders' conservation of weight.

SUBJECTS

From four schools in Minneapolis and St. Paul that had been using the MINNEMAST curriculum unit on weight, 120 second-grade Ss were randomly selected. The mean age of the sample was 8:1.5 years, all Ss were white. The sample was randomly assigned to four groups with the restriction that there be 15 boys and 15 girls in each group.

MATERIALS

The materials for the conservation problems reported in this paper were: one blue clay ball (4.5 cm in diam), one green clay ball (7.5 cm in diam), and a beam balance.

PROCEDURE

All Ss were tested individually in a small office at each school, and each S was presented with 18 conservation-of-weight problems in a different random order. Only 6 of those problems will be discussed here since only these are relevant for the topic of this paper. Ss were randomly assigned to four groups which differed in these ways: Groups 1 and 3 received the problems in the forward form, i.e., the transformation of a clay ball from A to B; Groups 2 and 4 received the problems in reversed form, B to A; Groups 3 and 4 had a beam balance present to refer to, and Groups 1 and 2 had no beam balance.

Subjects in all groups were shown two wooden blocks, one larger than the other, and were told, "These are two building blocks; would you hold one in each hand. I'd like to know what you think about how much they weigh. Can you tell me, is this one heavier than this one, or is this one heavier than this one, or do they both weigh the same?" (E pointed to the block in question each time it was mentioned). All children in the sample correctly answered the question.

In addition, the balance groups (3 and 4) were asked, "How would you use this balance to find out which was heavier?" All children in these groups used the balance appropriately.

Before the conservation problems were presented, Ss were shown a ball of clay and asked, "Do you know what this is?" and were permitted to manipulate it before they were told, "Today we're going to play with this clay in different ways, and I'm going to ask you what you think about it." Ss in Group 1 were presented with the following six problems and asked the following questions:

(1) The child was told to watch as E added a piece of blue clay to the blue ball, and asked, "Do you think the clay ball weighs more now than it did before, or does it weigh less now than before, or does it weigh the same now as it did before?"

(2) Problem 1 was repeated with the green ball.

(3) Subjects were shown the blue ball, and were directed, "Imagine that we left this clay outside in the winter, and when we came back it was hard and cold. Do you think it would weigh more when it was hard and cold that it does now, or do you think it would weigh less, etc., or do you think it would weigh the same, etc.?"

(4) Problem 3 was repeated with the green clay ball.

(5) Subjects were shown the blue clay ball, and were directed, "Imagine that we left this clay outside in the summer and when we came back it was hot and very soft. Do you think it would weigh more when it was hot and soft than it does now, or do you think it would weigh less, etc., or do you think it would weigh the same, etc.?"

(6) Problem 5 was repeated with the green ball.

Essentially the same problems were

Table 2
Number of Nonconserving Ss (More, Less) in Each Group Who Shifted and Were Consistent Between Problems 3 and 5 and Problems 4 and 6

| | | Problem 3 | | | | | | | |
|---|---|---|---|---|---|---|---|---|---|
| | | Group 1 | | Group 2 | | Group 3 | | Group 4 | |
| | | More | Less[1] | More | Less[4] | More | Less[1] | More | Less[1] |
| Problem 5 | More | 1 | 1 | 0 | 5 | 0 | 1 | 2 | 15 |
| | Less | 16 | 1 | 1 | 2 | 14 | 0 | 1 | 0 |
| | | Problem 4 | | | | | | | |
| | | More | Less[1] | More | Less[4] | More | Less[2] | More | Less[3] |
| Problem 6 | More | 3 | 0 | 2 | 5 | 0 | 1 | 3 | 7 |
| | Less | 13 | 2 | 1 | 1 | 11 | 0 | 0 | 7 |

*Binomial test:* [1]$p = .001$, [2]$p = .003$, [3]$p = .008$, [4]$p = .109$

presented to the Ss in Group 2 (reversed form) except that in Problems 1 and 2 a piece of clay was removed from the ball; in Problems 3 and 4 Ss were told that a cold ball was brought inside where it was warm, and the question was, "Do you think it weighs more inside than it did outside, etc.," and in Problems 5 and 6 Ss were told that the ball that had been left out in the heat was brought inside where it was cooler, and were asked, "Do you think the ball weighs more inside than it did outside where it was hot, etc.?"

Group 3 was presented the forward and Group 4 the reversed problems with the addition that the expression, "would weigh more (less or same)," in each question was preceded by the expression, "if we weighed it on the balance would it . . . ."

## RESULTS

The number of Ss in each group who responded that the clay ball weighed more than, less than, or the same as, the same clay ball after each problem's transformation is presented in Table 1. Those Ss on Problems 3, 4, 5, and 6 who said that the ball weighed the same are conservers, by definition, and those who said the ball weighed more or less are nonconservers for the same reason. The data from Problems 1 and 2 indicate clearly that nearly all Ss, conservers and nonconservers, were aware that added clay increased weight, and that subtracted clay decreased the weight of the ball in question.

The differences in the proportions of *more* and *less* responses among the nonconserving Ss were found to be significant (chi square, $p < .001$) between the forward and reversed forms of the transformations of Problems 3, 4, 5, and 6 for the balance groups (3 and 4) and nonbalance groups (1 and 2; $p < .01$ for Problems 5 and 6). Nonconserving Ss thought that increasing a clay ball's temperature (moving it from cold to warm) reduced its weight, and consistently that decreasing its temperature (moving it from warm to cold) increased its weight.

Within each group, Problems 3 and 5 and Problems 4 and 6 required the same Ss to judge the effects of increasing and decreasing temperature on the same clay ball. In all but Group 2, where the data are clearly in the expected direction, significant numbers (binomial test, $p < .01$) of the same Ss who judged that decreasing temperature increased weight judged, on the other hand, that increasing temperature reduced weight (Table 2).

There was high reliability between the blue and green clay ball forms of each problem in that the following number of Ss out of 30 gave the same response between Problems 1 and 2, 3 and 4, and 5 and 6: Group 1, 28, 25, 25, respectively; Group 2, 27, 26, 25, respectively; Group 3, 29, 27, 28, respectively; and Group 4, 28, 24, 21, respectively.

## DISCUSSION

The nonconserving child is apparently quite "logical" and consistent in his error. In fact, the principle source of his error seems not to be an unawareness of the inverse of the transformation, but a misjudgment of the relevancy of the transformation he is asked to evaluate. In other words, it would seem that conservation is much more a subject matter variable than it is a logical or inferential variable.

Bruner and his colleagues (1966) have argued, for different reasons than those presented here, that reversibility is not at the heart of the conservation problem. Piaget (1967, 1968) has responded that Bruner has confused reversibility with "renversabilité," or empirical reversibility, which, he argues, is a physical concept, such as the awareness that a spring or elastic can return to its original state. In empirical reversibility, the return may be incomplete (i.e., the spring never returns exactly to its former state), or the transformation from A to B may be different sufficiently from the transformation from B to A (or A′ in the case of incomplete physical return) to be considered a separate operation. In the present study, we would argue that cooling and warming are as much the same operation as are addition and subtraction (the most often cited example of reversibility), and that the transformations examined in the present investigation were not empirical and physically performed, but were imagined and abstracted transformations that were uncontaminated by the physical constraints of the empirical situation. There is also little doubt that the nonconservers of this study possessed the addition-subtraction operation or schema. In any event, the burden is upon the Genevans to provide the behavioral criteria that distinguish reversibility from "renversibilité," and to specify more clearly the kind of "careful experimentation ... necessary to distinguish the two concepts [Piaget, 1967, p. 533]."

It may very well be that reversibility is a property solely of the logical model that Piaget has constructed to describe intellectual development, and, like the formal grammar of language, it need not have a reference in the behavior it best describes. In that event, it is not a category of behavior, and as such it requires no explanation in psychology.

REFERENCES

BRUNER, J. et al. *Studies in cognitive growth.* New York: Wiley, 1966.

MURRAY, F., & JOHNSON, P. A model for relevant and irrelevant transformations in children's concept of weight. In H. Hausdorf (Ed.), *A.E.R.A. Paper Abstracts, 1968 Annual Meeting.* P. 308.

PIAGET, J. *Logic and psychology.* New York: Basic Books, 1960.

PIAGET, J. Review of Bruner et al, *Studies in cognitive growth.* Contemporary Psychology, 1967, 12, 532-533.

PIAGET, J. *On the concept of memory and identity.* Barre, Mass.: Clark University Press, 1968.

TANNER, J., & INHELDER, B. (Eds.), *Discussions on child development.* Vol. 4. New York: International Universities Press, 1960.

NOTES

1. This work was supported in part by a grant to the MINNEMAST Center at the University of Minnesota from the National Science Foundation (GE-3), and in part by grants to the University of Minnesota Center for Research in Human Learning from the National Science Foundation (GS-1761), the National Institute of Child Health and Human Development (HD-01136-04), and from the Graduate School of the University of Minnesota.

2. Johnson, P., & Murray, F. A framework for the analysis of the child's concept of weight.

## Cognitive Capacity of Very Young Children

JACQUES MEHLER

THOMAS G. BEVER

J. Piaget has investigated the mistakes which children make in solving simple problems (*1*). In the most often quoted of Piaget's experiments, a child sees two identical arrays of material and is asked if he, in fact, thinks they are "the same." For example, a child of four characteristically replies that the two identical rows of four pellets in Fig. 1a are, in fact, "the same." The experimenter then adds or subtracts some material in one of the arrays and changes its shape at the same time. He again asks the child if both arrays have the same amount of material, or if one has "more." If the array is like the one in Fig. 1b, the same child reports incorrectly that there are now "more" in the upper row. However, a child of 5 correctly indicates that it is the array with the added material which has "more."

Various experimental techniques have been used to isolate the ages at which children develop the ability to ignore particular kinds of changes and to recognize when material is "conserved" (that is, not perceived as modified in quantity), in spite of those apparent changes. The development of the different kinds of quantity conservations is interpreted by Piaget as a behavioral reflection of the development of general cognitive capacities. For example, the 4-year-old's failure to conserve quantity in the above pellet experiment indicates that he does not have the cognitive capacity to "reverse" situations; hence, he cannot transform Fig. 1b back to Fig. 1a and then recall which particular row had the two pellets added to it. He instead responds to the momentary "appearance" of the two rows in Fig. 1b and incorrectly reports that the longer row has "more."

All of the well-known experiments on the conservation of quantity have ignored children below the age of 4. The exclusion of younger children has appeared rational because 4-year-old children do not have quantity conservation. If a 4-year-old does not have conservation, why should we expect an even younger child to exhibit it? Although this argument was reasonable, it was also misleading. The present study of over 200 children shows that under 3 years 2 months (3-2), children exhibit a form of quantity conservation; they lose it as they get older and do not exhibit it again until they are about 4 years 6 months (4-6).

Seven age groups of children from 2-4 to 4-7 were tested in individual sessions with two experiments involving quantity judgments. Each experiment used two pairs of rows like those shown in Fig. 1, a and b. One of the experimental sequences for each child had clay pellets while the other had M & M candies (candy-coated chocolate pellets). In each experimental sequence the child was first presented with adjacent rows of four, as in 1a, and he was asked if they were the "same." The experimenter then modified the arrays into a situation like 1b, in which a short row of six is adjacent to a longer row of four. In the experiment with clay pellets he was then asked which row had "more." In the experiment with M & M's the responses to situation 1b were nonverbal: instead of asking the child to state a quantity judgment, the experimenter asked him to "take the row you want to eat, and eat all the M & M's in that row." The order in which the M & M experiment and clay experiment were presented was balanced for each age group, as was the orientation of the arrays on the table in front of the child (*2*). Each session took about 10 minutes. The experimenter wrote down the response of the subject, and a tape recording was taken for subsequent analysis.

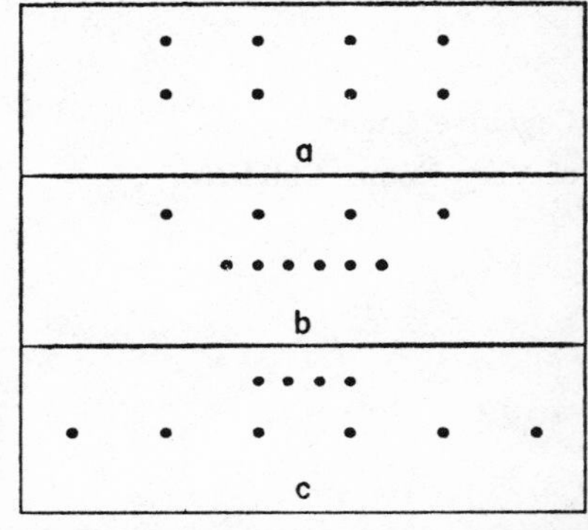


Fig. 1. The length of the rows in (a) was 7 inches (18 cm) for M & M's and 8 inches (20 cm) for clay pellets; in (b) 7 and 3 inches (18 and 8 cm) for M & M's and 8 and 5 inches (20 and 13 cm) for clay pellets. There was a 1⅓-inch (3-cm) space between each of the four clay pellets and a 2-inch (5-cm) space between each of the four M & M's. The clay pellets were ½ inch (1.3 cm) in diameter. The M & M candies were all of the same color.

The valid responses (*3*) are summarized by age in Fig. 2; the ordinate represents the proportion of success in choosing or naming the row which, in fact, had more (that is, the proportion of "conserving" responses) and the abscissa represents increasing age. Two bar graphs are presented, one for choosing which row of clay pellets had "more," (Fig. 2a) and one for taking a row of M & M's (Fig. 2b). Both experiments show a decrease in conserving responses by age, which is at a minimum in the group between 3-8 and 3-11. Thus, as the children get older than 2-6, they get worse, rather than better, at quantity conservation. Even more striking is the fact that the 23 youngest children (under 2-8) show extremely high numbers of conserving responses—100 percent of verbal responses on the quantity of clay pellets and 81 percent for taking rows of M & M's. The decrease with age is strongly significant for the verbal judgments ($P < .001$ by chi-square comparing 2-4 to 2-7 and 4-0 to 4-3 ages for verbal judgments) and nonsignificant for responses to M & M's. At 4-6, the children again show conservation for both kinds of quantity judgment (significance of increase in conservation of clay pellets between 4-0 to 4-3 and 4-4 to 4-7 = $P < .01$; for eating of M & M's, $P < .01$ by chi-square).

Occasionally children responded one way on verbal judgments of which clay row had "more," yet in the case of M & M's they took the other row to eat. This might show some uncertainty in the child's capacity to judge quantity. To strengthen our basic finding that children at 2-6 and 4-6 show more conservation than children of 4-2, we separated those children who showed consistent responses on both M & M's and clay pellets from children with inconsistent responses. Among the children who gave consistent verbal and nonverbal responses, there were more consistent nonconservation responses at age 4-2 than at 2-6 ($P < .02$ by chi-square) or at 4-6 ($P < .03$ by chi-square). Furthermore, if a child gave inconsistent responses, it is more likely that the single conserving response was to the M & M's than to the clay pellets ($P < .01$ by chi-square in favor of M & M conservation) (*4*).

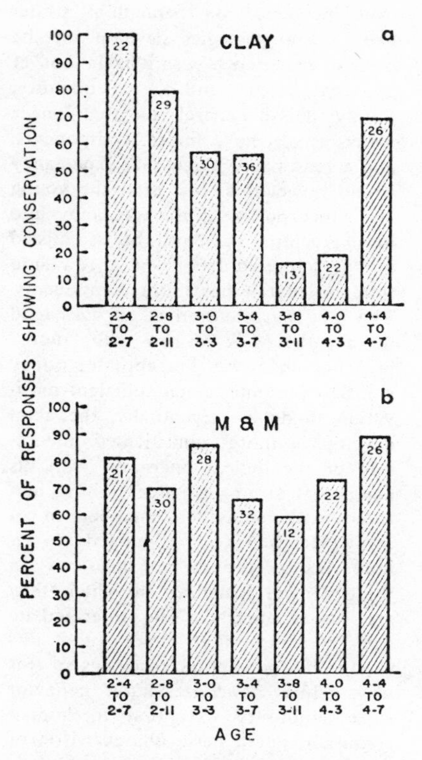


Fig. 2. The proportion by age of responses choosing the row with more members in the situation shown in Fig. 1b. Numbers inside bars indicate total number of subjects of that age.

Our results indicate that the inability to conserve quantity is a temporary phase in the developing child. The child does not gradually acquire quantity conservation during his 4th year; rather, he reacquires it. The fact that the very young child successfully solves the conservation problem shows that he does have the capacities which depend on the logical structure of the cognitive operations. Eventually, he develops an *explicit* understanding of these operations: at age 5 he solves the same problem by counting the pellets in each row. We think that the temporary inability to solve the conservation problem reflects a period of overdependence on perceptual strategies. These strategies develop on the basis of experience with correlations of apparent shapes and actual quantity. Surely, it is a general rule that longer arrays usually have "more" components, and a reasonable perceptual expectancy would reflect this. Just after the young child incorporates this expectancy into his perceptual scheme, he is misled by the apparent length of a row into thinking that it has more components. The fact that children at all ages tend to take the M & M row with "more" indicates that this perceptual strategy can be overcome, given sufficient motivation to do so. Eventually, the child develops a more sophisticated integration of the logical operation with his perceptual strategies which allow him to count the individual members of an array. He then has the capacity to ignore his perceptual expectancies in those critical instances in which they are not confirmed. The intermediate age "nonconserving" child cannot disengage his perceptual strategies in this way. Thus, nonconservation behavior is a temporary exception to human cognition, not a basic characteristic of man's native endowment.

**References and Notes**


1. J. Piaget, *The Child's Conception of Number* (Humanities, New York, 1952); *The Origins of Intelligence in Children* (International Univs. Press, New York, 1952).

2. Subjects were children attending local play groups and private nursery schools in the Greater Boston area as well as some participating in the Harvard Infant Study. Older and younger children were drawn from the same schools and groups whenever possible and were often siblings.
3. Occasionally a child would refuse to respond, or would choose the clay pellets or M & M candies one at a time instead of the whole row. These responses were ignored.
4. We also ascertained that the conservation responses in the young children are not due to a tendency to take and to name short rows. Sixteen children, age 2-4 to 2-9, were presented with an array in which the row with six clay pellets or M & M's is in fact longer (Fig. 1c). In this condition there were 22 conservation responses (picking or naming the long row) and ten nonconservation responses. Out of eight children who responded consistently on M & M's and clay judgments, seven showed consistent conservation responses. This indicates that the young children are attending to the actual quantity in a row. Preliminary analysis indicates that for children below 3 years of age, experimental order of M & M's and clay did not affect the tendency to exhibit conserving responses.

5. Research supported by NIH grant 5-TO1-HD00111-02 to Professor Halle at M.I.T. and by NASA grant NaG 496 and by U.S. Department of Defense, Advanced Research Projects Studies and the Harvard Society of Fellows. We thank J. Epstein, who ran all the experiments in this study. We also thank Professor H.-L. Teuber, H. Koopmans, and Dr. M. Garrett for comments on this manuscript; Dr. T. G. R. Bower for the use of his research space, and D. J. Kagan for providing access to his well-studied group of children. We are also grateful to all those schools that kindly allowed us to test their children.

# Cognitive Capacities of Young Children: A Replication

HARRY BEILIN

Mehler and Bever (*1*) have reported that children below the age of 4 are capable of conserving concepts of quantity. This finding contradicts the reports of Piaget (*2*) and others who place these acquisitions at about age 6 to 7. This age difference in the acquisition of conservation is of theoretical consequence. Mehler and Bever's delineation of a decline in conservation performance from the very youngest age studied (2 years 4 months) and then a rise (with age) implies that these capacities are genetically determined and are a "basic characteristic of man's native endowment" (*1*). The Piaget position, on the other hand, is that these competencies reflect the influence of maturational and experiential determinants under the control of an internal self-regulating mechanism.

In contrast to the usual procedure of testing conservation with a relocation or transformation of objects first identified as equal with respect to a quantitative property, Mehler and Bever used a conservation-of-inequality task based on the inequality of two sets of objects. More importantly, they both added objects to their numerical arrays and relocated them in a single operation. Thus it is not possible to know whether a child's response was due to addition or relocation, or both. It was my prediction that a controlled study which separated these operations would show that the results were due solely to the child's ability to deal with "more" in the additive sense of "more of," or in the relational sense of "more than," rather than with the conservation concept of "more than in the face of a transformation." I now report results of an experiment designed to test the correctness of this prediction.

The concepts measured were as follows. (i) Conservation of equality based upon an initial response of "same" to equal numbers of M & M's (candy-coated chocolate pellets) set in two rows and in one-to-one correspondence (the "before" condition of Fig. 1), followed by a relocation of one row either by expansion or contraction, and a continued response of "same" to the numbers in the two rows (the "after" condition). (ii) Conservation of inequality in which the "before transformation" con-

SCIENCE, 1968, Vol. 162, pp. 920-921. 

dition is one of inequality of both number and location; the "after" condition is still one of inequality, but the beginning and terminal points of the rows are in either one-to-one correspondence or in a different spatial location from the "before" condition. In earlier studies (*3, 4*) a distinction was made between transformational and static conservation. In the latter case no transformation takes place in the stimulus. A conserving subject is required to judge two rows as numerically equal in spite of a lack of alignment between them. In my study both static and transformation-conservation tasks were included in the test. (iii) Relational concept ("more than"): two rows unequal in number and extension had to be judged as unequal in number. (iv) Equality: two rows, equal in both number and extension (that is, in one-to-one correspondence) had to be judged as equal in number. (v) Additive concepts ("more of" or "less of"): one or two rows were presented and M & M's were added to or subtracted from a row.

In each trial a Mommy or Daddy doll accompanied each row. Responses represented a choice between the "same" or "different" and "more" or "same" amounts to eat. Two groups of children were tested in private nursery schools. One group was given the transformation tasks and the other the static tasks. Both groups were administered the same additivity tasks.

The data in Table 1 show different levels of performance. The level of conservation performance for conditions of both equality and inequality is very low for all age groups as represented by the average percentage of correct responses in these trials. Since the probability of chance success by guessing in any static conservation trial is 50 percent and in any transformation trial is 25 percent, response is close to or below chance in all conservation conditions. Not a single child at any age tested was correct in all three conservation-of-equality trials, and only 7 percent in the oldest age group were correct in conservation-of-inequality trials. With a criterion of two out of three correct, the level of correct performance increases, but to no higher than 20 percent in any age group; there is no age trend.

Table 1. Response to conservation, relational, and additive tasks; average percent correct for trials in a series. Transformation and static tasks were administered to two different sample groups. Transformation groups numbered: (1) 7; (2) 16; (3) 21; (4) 16; (5) 15. Static samples numbered: (1) 6; (2) 16; (3) 23; (4) 17; (5) 15. Additivity tasks were the same for both samples; these data are reported for the combined numbers of both groups. Group 1 includes children from 3 years through 3 years 3 months; group 2, 3 years 4 months through 3 years 7 months; group 3, 3 years 8 months through 3 years 11 months; group 4, 4 years through 4 years 3 months; group 5, 4 years 4 months through 4 years 7 months. Figures in brackets represent correct response to the quantity of the array ("same" or "different") prior to the addition, and the quantity after the addition or subtraction. The figures in this category without brackets are for the correct response to the addition or subtraction operation alone. The arrangements (A–H) are shown in Fig. 1.

| Trials | Group | | | | |
|---|---|---|---|---|---|
| | 1 | 2 | 3 | 4 | 5 |
| A | 14 | 15 | 19 | 15 | 9 |
| B | 33 | 44 | 41 | 35 | 30 |
| C | 24 | 33 | 30 | 29 | 38 |
| D | 33 | 47 | 37 | 47 | 47 |
| E | 17 | 63 | 52 | 59 | 67 |
| F | 67 | 81 | 65 | 88 | 87 |
| G | 47 | 65 | 67 | 77 | 82 |
| | [18] | [40] | [42] | [61] | [68] |
| H | 65 | 73 | 78 | 83 | 91 |
| | [26] | [46] | [51] | [61] | [74] |

By contrast, even the youngest children in the sample exhibit a high level of correct performance in the "equality" test, where number and extension of static arrays are equal. This is likewise true where the relational judgment ("more than") is made (*5*).

Although correct responses with respect to conservation of equality and inequality are greater in the static than in the transformation condition, both are at about chance level. This differs from data reported previously (*4, 6*) for equality-of-area judgments in children from kindergarten through fourth

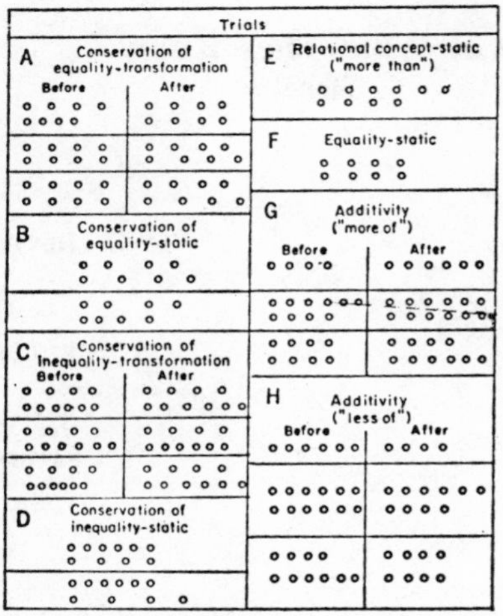

Trials

A Conservation of equality-transformation (Before / After)

B Conservation of equality-static

C Conservation of Inequality-transformation (Before / After)

D Conservation of inequality-static

E Relational concept-static ("more than")

F Equality-static

G Additivity ("more of") (Before / After)

H Additivity ("less of") (Before / After)

Fig. 1. Stimulus arrays for static and transformation trials in conservation, relational, and additive conditions.

grade. Static conservation was consistently more difficult for those children to achieve than transformational conservation. This difference in performance suggests that younger children are unable to correctly utilize the information imparted by the transformation; that is, transformation leads to the incorrect "perceptual" inference that the longer or shorter row is different in number from the standard when it is in fact equal. Older children are more able to use the transformation information because of the possession of an inference-generating mechanism. Younger children apparently lack such a mechanism or, if they have it, are unable to use it; thus performance in both static and transformation conditions is determined by chance factors.

The additivity concepts ("more of" and "less of") are the only ones in the present instance which show an age trend (positive). An appreciable percentage of even the youngest age group respond correctly (7).

Young children, then, within the age range of 3 years to 4 years 7 months display very little, if any, conservation ability. They do have some conceptual capacities ultimately necessary for conservation, but they lack the inference-generating mechanism that makes possible a judgment of equality or inequality in the face of spatial transformation or dislocation. The high level of response of Mehler and Bever's subjects is most likely due to the combination of addition and relocation tasks in the experimental operations. The decline and rise in performance also reported by Mehler and Bever is not confirmed.

### References and Notes


1. J. Mehler and T. G. Bever, *Science* **158**, 141 (1967).
2. J. Piaget, *The Child's Conception of Number* (Routledge and Kegan Paul, London, 1952).
3. H. Beilin, *J. Exp. Child Psychol.* **1**, 208 (1964).
4. ———, *ibid.* **3**, 267 (1966).
5. This result is something of an anomaly since previously I found that in area judgments equality is more difficult to judge than inequality. The difference between the past and present results may be either a function of age (since the present subjects are younger than the kindergarten children of the prior study) or of the different quantitative concepts employed (that is, area as opposed to number) in that the defining characteristics of "same number" are better known to young children than the defining properties of "same area."
6. H. Beilin, in *Studies in Cognitive Development: Essays in Honor of Jean Piaget*, D. Elkind and J. H. Flavell, Eds. (Oxford Univ. Press, New York, in press).
7. The number of responses is somewhat less when the additivity response is contingent upon a correct prior response.


8. Supported in part by PHS research grant HD 00925-07 from the National Institute of Child Health and Human Development. I thank George E. Spontak and Sandra J. Dalton for assistance.

# What Children Do in Spite of What They Know

T. G. Bever

J. Mehler

J. Epstein

In a previous study of cognitive development we found that children of 2 years 6 months can successfully recognize a numerical equality and its transformation into an inequality whereas older children temporarily lose this capacity. We interpreted our results as demonstrating that the capacity to conserve relations between stimuli in the face of transformations is present in the 2-year-old; the older child loses this capacity temporarily due to an overdependence on perceptual generalizations (for example, "if a row looks longer, it has more components in it"). This interpretation conflicts with the position that the ability to conserve numerical relations between stimuli first appears at about 5 to 6 years (*1*).

Beilin's critique of our previous study contains three general points: (i) our study was not a direct test of the child's capacity to conserve; (ii) his experimental evidence indicates that children up to 4 years 8 months do not understand the word "more" as a static relational term but as meaning "more than it had before"; and (iii) his conservation experiments do not find any developmental trend during the 3rd and 4th year.

There can be no conflict regarding the facts of the child's behavior since Beilin did not attempt to replicate our study; he neither studied children under age 3 nor did he present any of his subjects with the experimental problem that we had used. However, since many other psychologists have indicated similar objections to our research, we shall concentrate primarily on the relevant theoretical aspects of Beilin's paper.

When a child discovers a particular set of dimensions that stimuli can have, he must then learn to interrelate those dimensions. For example, the capacity to recognize a property like the length of a row or the number of objects in it does not itself aid the child in making correct judgments about relations between rows. He must first discover general principles for the simultaneous

SCIENCE, 1968, Vol. 162, pp. 921-924. 

combination and transformation of such properties. Piaget (*2*) has suggested that the set of principles required to deal simultaneously with dimensions of a particular class are logically described as a group structure; each group specifies an interrelated set of operations for the combination and transformation of dimensions. The simultaneous presence of all group operations is necessary for the child's cognition to be in a state of equilibrium with respect to those dimensions of his experience.

Piaget interprets the ability to conserve relations between stimuli in the face of superficial transformations as a behavioral sign of the presence of such an equilibrium in the child's thought. For example, if the two stimuli (Table 1) in (1a) are transformed to appear as in (1b), the child can realize that the numerical relation between S1 and S2 is the same in (1b) as in (1a) only if he knows (at least intuitively) that the shape transformation does not involve a change in number from the original relation. Similarly, in (1c) and (1d) a child knows that the numerical relation between S3 and S4 is changed only if he can appreciate the fact that the number transformation between (1c) and (1d) involves addition to one of the rows. Thus, cognitive mastery of the different dimensions of objects requires knowledge of which transformations change a relation and which transformations conserve a relation.

If these considerations are correct, they place several requirements on any experimental demonstration of the presence of the capacity for conservation. First, there must be a set of stimuli which bear an initial relation to each other that the child is capable of understanding. Second, there must be at least one transformation applied to the initial set which changes one dimension of the stimulus. Third, the relation between the stimuli in the transformed set should not be obvious to the child independent of the initial relation [that is, the child must use the relational information presented in

**Table 1. Transformation tasks administered.**

| Sequence | Initial set | | Transformed set |
|---|---|---|---|
| | *Shape transformation* | | |
| S1 | 0 0 0 0 | | 0000 |
| S2 | 0 0 0 0 | | 0 0 0 0 |
| | (a) | → | (b) |
| | *Number transformation* | | |
| S3 | 0 0 0 0 | | 0 0 0 0 0 0 |
| S4 | 0 0 0 0 | | 0 0 0 0 |
| | (c) | → | (d) |
| | *Number and shape transformation* | | |
| S5 | 0 0 0 0 | | 000000 |
| S6 | 0 0 0 0 | | 0 0 0 0 |
| | (e) | → | (f) |

**Table 2. Responses to (b) on equality conservation sequence (1a)–(1b) of Table 1 (*3*). Different subjects were used in paradigms A, B, and C. In paradigm A subjects saw the transformation; in B subjects did not see the transformation; in C subjects were forced to indicate one row as having "more" (did not see the transformation).**

| Age (year and month) | Children (No.) | Percentage response, saying: | | |
|---|---|---|---|---|
| | | Same number | S1 has more | S2 has more |
| | | *Paradigm A* | | |
| 2/0–2/11 | 10 | 80 | 10 | 10 |
| 3/0–3/11 | 16 | 50 | 13 | 38 |
| 4/0–4/11 | 11 | 64 | 9 | 27 |
| | | *Paradigm B* | | |
| 2/0–2/11 | 37 | 48 | 3 | 49 |
| 3/0–3/11 | 34 | 35 | 18 | 47 |
| 4/0–4/11 | 35 | 29 | 0 | 71 |
| | | *Paradigm C* | | |
| 2/0–2/11 | 20 | | 40 | 60 |
| 3/0–3/11 | 8 | | 0 | 100 |

the initial set or in the transformation (or in both) to solve the final problem]. Fourth, the child must have an unambiguous way of spontaneously indicating that he understands the transformed relation.

The sequence (1a)–(1b) fulfills all these conditions for use with older children. They characteristically indicate that there is the same number of objects in each row in set (1b) because there is nothing done in the transformation from set (1a) to change the actual quantity of S1. A surprisingly large number of young children (Table 2A) maintain that the two rows in (1b) have the "same" number of clay balls in them. We felt that the young children might mean that the two rows in (1b) are still individually the same rows as they were in (1a); that is, that identity of the rows was preserved by the young child even though the relation between the rows may not have been conserved. Support for this interpretation is given by the fact that the young children perform less well if they do not observe the transformation from (1a) to (1b) [although they still perform better than older children (Table 2B)]. Thus, for the 2-year-old, the sequence (1a)–(1b) may not meet the fourth requirement on an experimental demonstration of conservation (*3*).

Similarly, a study in which the transformation from (1c) to (1d) was used indicates that the young child performs extremely well (Table 3). However, this too might have been the result of the child's ability to judge the relation in condition (1d) independently of the antecedent condition (1c); that is, in (1d) the relative density of S1 might be an independent perceptual cue for the young child. Thus, the sequence (1c)–(1d) does not meet the third condition above (*4*).

Therefore, to overcome the experimental problems of working with children 2 years old, we combined the shape and number transformations and examined the child's reaction to the transformation of (1e) and (1f) (Table 1). With set (1f) the child was asked which row had "more" balls in it. Although S5 is more dense than S6, it is also shorter; thus it is possible to argue that the third condition is met: there is no obvious perceptual basis for a correct decision in (1f) independent of (1e) and the transformations. Thus, the young child's ability to perform correctly on this problem is a sign of the capacity to conserve. However, we agree that this experimental paradigm is more complex than the usual test of conservation; it was necessary in order to accommodate to the experimental difficulties associated with interviewing 2-year-old children (*5*).

We felt confident that the young child does understand the word "more" as a relational term (so that the fourth condition was met), even though he may not always understand "same" as a quantitative relational term. It is this belief that Beilin questions most strongly. His hypothesis is that our young subjects systematically misunderstood the question about (1f) and were answering that S1 had had "more added" to it, not that it had "more than" S2.

First, linguistic differences are not explanations of cognitive differences but reflections of them (*2*). Second, although it might be true that the young child was using the additive interpretation of "more," there are several empirical considerations which invalidate this possibility. Beilin's data indicate that children do not start to understand the additivity interpretation of the word "more" until age 3 years 4 months. Yet children younger than this respond correctly to condition (1f) whereas the performance of older children is

Table 3. Responses to (d) on sequence (1c)–(1d) of Table 1. Subjects did not observe the transformation.

| Age (year and month) | Children (No.) | Percentage response, saying: | | |
|---|---|---|---|---|
| | | Same number | S3 has more | S4 has more |
| 2/0–2/11 | 13 | 0 | 69 | 31 |
| 3/0–3/11 | 8 | 50 | 38 | 13 |
| 4/0–4/11 | 8 | 13 | 88 | 0 |

Table 4. Performance on (f) in sequence (1e)–(1f) of Table 1. Subjects did not observe the transformation.

| Age | Children (No.) | Percentage correct |
|---|---|---|
| 2/0–2/5 | 14 | 93 |
| 2/6–2/11 | 19 | 37 |
| 3/0–3/5 | 28 | 38 |
| 3/6–3/11 | 30 | 57 |
| 4/0–4/11 | 50 | 50 |

dramatically worse. In addition, we interviewed children from 2 years to 5 years on the same problem as in (1e)–(1f) but these children did not observe us transforming (1e) into (1f). [The stimuli used in (1e) and (1f) were glued on prepared boards and presented in sequence.] Thus the subjects did not observe the activity of our adding more to S5 nor did they observe us compressing it. Despite the lack of additivity cues (or cues which might call attention to S5 as the manipulated row), the results confirm our earlier findings (Table 4).

Beilin scores a child as correct in all his tasks only if the child responds correctly on both the initial and the transformed set of stimuli. According to his own results on static judgments, under 65 percent of children correctly understood the initial relation in the equality paradigm and under 35 percent in the inequality paradigm. Thus, in Beilin's conservation paradigms, less than 50 percent of the children met even the first condition. If most of the children did not understand the relation, how can one assess their failure (or success) at conserving it?

In Beilin's static conservation tests of inequality (in which the child is asked to judge the numerical relation between two rows), children perform extremely poorly. This indicates that the child does not understand the relational term "more" even at age 4 years 4 months to 4 years 7 months. If this were true, how could Beilin (or Piaget) maintain that the child at that age is nonconserving of the equality (or inequality) relations presented in the initial set since he does not understand the question? If Beilin were correct in the view that the child has not even started to interpret "more" as a relational term at age 4 years 7 months, it would be as much a problem for him and Piaget as for us.

There are several specific methodological techniques which may contribute to the extraordinarily low performance of Beilin's subjects at all ages [even on such simple tasks as the equality of the rows in (1a) or the inequality in (1d)]. First, he asked children to make judgments on behalf of dolls; we found that asking children to make judgments on behalf of dolls as opposed to their own behalf often increases fluctuations in the responses (*6*). [However, the same decrease in performance with age is observed in the children who made consistent judgments on which doll has "more" in (1f).] Second, Beilin used a fixed order of experimental paradigms across all children; we have found that the effects of experimental order are large; younger children quickly tire of such experiments (*7*). Finally, we are startled that Beilin did not use Piaget's methodology, which is characteristically adaptable to each particular subject. In particular, the importance of Beilin's data (as well as the true performance of his subjects) would have been significantly enhanced if he had encouraged each child to understand the initial relation of each set, before testing the child's ability to conserve that relation under transformation.

Many structures and functional capacities are present in the cognition of the 2-year-old child. However, his ability to express these capacities is limited because memory and attention span are not well developed. As the child accumulates experience, he develops cognitive heuristics which help him to overcome these basic behavioral limits. Although these cognitive heuristics are generally valid, they fail in critical instances, and eventually the child either rejects the heuristics or learns to use them only when they apply.

We agree with Beilin that these theoretical claims are extremely strong and that a broad base of empirical support is necessary before they are accepted. In particular, our claim that the child of 3 performs less well on cognitive problems, owing to an overdependence on perceptual generalizations, must be explored with tasks other than judging the relative number of small rows of clay balls. We have studied similar decreases in performance with age in the long-term memory of figures, volume inequality, sentence comprehension, discrimination-learning, and other tasks (*8*).

Even more crucial is our hypothesis that the basic cognitive structures are available to the 2-year-old, but that he cannot utilize them efficiently. We certainly agree with the balance of nativism and empiricism in (Beilin's interpretation of) Piaget's view that: "(cognitive) competencies reflect the influence of maturational and experiential determinants under the control of an internal self-regulating mechanism." It remains an empirical question, however, which component functions of human cognitive abilities are relatively autonomous, which emerge with experience as a catalytic agent, and which are learned primarily from experience (*9*).

**References and Notes**


1. J. Mehler and T. Bever, *Science* **158**, 141 (1967).
2. J. Piaget, *The Heinz Werner Lectures* (Clark Univ. Press, Worcester, Mass., 1968); *The Psychology of Intelligence* (Routledge and Kegan Paul, London, 1950).

3. In Table 2, A and B, and Table 3 half the children in each age group were asked: "Do the rows have the same number of balls in them or does one row have more balls in it?" The other children were asked: "Does one of the rows have more balls in it or do the rows have the same number of balls in them?" The questions were force-choiced between "same" or "one row has more," because our work showed that young children tend to say "yes" or "no" to every simple yes/no question. There was an effect of question order: children tended to respond with the last adjective ("same" or "more") in the question. However, this effect was stronger for older children and does not account for the high performance of the young children. As in our previous experiment, the orientation of the sets of stimuli were randomized for each age group in all the experiments reported. All children were pretrained on the concept of a row with five small stuffed animals arranged in a line, as an example.
4. Table 2C indicates that there is no tendency in the 2-year-old child to choose the more dense row as having "more" when the rows are numerically equal, as in (1b). The 3-year-old incorrectly judges the two rows in (1d) as the "same" number much more than the 2-year-old. This is additional evidence that the 3-year-old uses length as the basis for numerical judgments, whereas the 2-year-old does not.
5. We had felt that the basis of our use of the term "conservation" in the absence of a classical test of conservation was clear in our previous paper. We apologize to any reader who was misled by our confusion.

6. We found that asking the young child if it would be "fair" if one doll had S1 in (1b) and another doll had S2 was not satisfactory, since the young children seemed to think that anything was "fair" so long as each doll had at least some balls to play with.
7. In our studies, children below age 4 have some tendency to change their answers when asked the same kind of question more than once; we think that this results from the child's assumption that being asked a second time indicates that his first answer was incorrect. Some of the children in our first study were also asked to choose on behalf of dolls which row in (1f) has "more." Of the children from 2 years to 4 years 6 months who performed on all tasks (observing the transformation), 79 percent took the row of M & M's with more, 62 percent correctly indicated the row with "more," only 39 percent correctly indicated which of two dolls had the row with "more." We interpret this as showing that the more engaged the child is with a perceptual judgment the less likely he is to rely on superficial perceptual generalizations. Making judgments on behalf of dolls does not engage the child's capacity as fully as making a judgment on his own behalf or taking a row of M & M candies to eat.

8. J. Mehler, *Int. J. Psychol.*, in press; T. Bever, J. Mehler, V. Valian, in *The Structure and Psychology of Language*, T. Bever and W. Weksel, Eds. (Holt, Rinehart, and Winston, New York, in press); J. Mehler and T. Bever, *Int. J. Psychol.*, in press; T. Bever, in *Cognition and Language Development*, J. Hayes, Ed. (Prentice-Hall, New York, in press).

9. In response to Beilin's reply to this paper: (i) The (1e) to (1f) transformation is a test of the "capacity" to conserve, not merely a "control condition." (ii) The young child does not have a general strategy of choosing the denser row as having "more" (see footnote (*4*) and Table 2C). (iii) Failures to replicate our findings on the (1a) to (1b) transformation (Table 2, A and B) must be examined for similarity of technique and scoring. (iv) We are indebted to Beilin for pointing out a gap in this report: less than 5 percent of our subjects failed to agree on the initial equality of (1a), (1c), or (1e) (after discussion in some cases), and most of those were over 3 years old. Therefore our data were not significantly "inflated by including children who are incorrect in their initial judgments and correct in the transformation response," while Beilin's data appear to be significantly "deflated" by including such children as "nonconservers." This remains the heart of our critique of Beilin's data analysis: if a child does not understand the initial relation (whether spontaneously or after discussion), how can he be expected to "conserve" that relation under transformation?

10. Supported by Army Research Projects Agency grant SD-187 to Harvard University and Foundation Fund for Research in Psychiatry G67-380. Research was carried out with children whose mothers volunteered their time to us. We are particularly grateful to Jonas Langer and Harry Beilin for stimulating much of the research reported, and to Peter Carey for advice on this manuscript.

---

In Bever, Mehler, and Epstein's defense of the earlier study by Mehler and Bever (*1*), the (1e) to (1f) transformation is no longer used as a test of conservation but at best as a control condition related to such a test. As an attempt to show that a judgment of inequality in the face of contradictory cues must be based upon (still unidentified) nonperceptual processes, it is questionable whether the (1e) to (1f) transformation even meets the requirements of their third condition, since it is possible that the closely packed aggregates of objects may be judged as "more" on perceptual bases alone.

The finding by Bever *et al.* that 60 percent of their sample of 2-year-olds in the forced-choice 2C condition chose the spread-out array as "more" creates a problem in the interpretation of the data of (1f). If 93 percent of the 2-year-olds judge the dense display in (1f) as "more," such a choice must be based on either cognitive or perceptual grounds. Solution in cognitive terms is possible by counting or by using a method of one-to-one correspondence, neither of which is claimed by Bever *et al.* Otherwise, the child is responding to the perceptual arrangements—either the compression of one array, the spread of the other, or the contrast of the two arrays.

Irrespective of the interpretation given to the results of the (1e) to (1f) transformation in this and the earlier study, in the classic conservation case [the (1a) to (1b) transformation] Bever *et al.* obtain results which have not been independently validated in my own and three other studies which cover the entire age range under discussion (*2*). Furthermore, it is difficult to understand the criticism by Bever *et al.* of recording a child's transformation response as correct and relevant only in conjunction with an initially correct equality or inequality judgment, when their third condition requires that "the child use the relational information presented in the initial set and/or the transformation." This also means that the data of Bever *et al.* are inflated by the inclusion of children who are incorrect in their initial judgments and correct in the transformation response. There is no problem, as they imply, created by my initial response data. Between 67 and 87 percent of the subjects were correct in static equality judgments; similarly, the children performed well with additive inequalities, although less well with static relational judgments. The essential point is that very young children have a fairly adequate concept of equality and yet, in spite of this, they fail to conserve that relation. If the child fails to understand the initial relation, however, it is indeterminable whether he can conserve; all such subjects (even 5 percent) would have to be so identified.

My data do not confirm the conservation findings of Bever *et al.*, nor their report of the more basic equality and inequality concepts. I concur in the belief that the differences are probably the result of differences in the test procedure. I find it strange, however, to have to account for using an "experimental" rather than a less specifiable "clinical" method.

While I question the methodological and conceptual bases for the conclusions of Bever *et al.*, I nevertheless feel that they have done a service in exploring one aspect of the little-known cognitive capacities of children between the ages of 2 and 5.

HARRY BEILIN

# Quantification, Conservation, and Nativism

Quantitative evaluations of children aged two to three years are examined.

Jean Piaget

Mehler and Bever's paper on the cognitive capacities of very young children (*1*) presents some new and interesting data on the development of quantitative evaluations from the age of 2½ years onward. Although, unfortunately, these novel results have hardly been subjected to any analysis regarding the possible factors at work, and although they have nothing to do with conservation (whatever the authors may say), they yet are suggestive of a useful complement of information on the development of quantification. In addition, Mehler and Bever's thesis regarding the role of innate structures—like Chomsky's (*2*) which inspired it—provides an effective antidote to the exaggerated simplifications that usually form part of learning theories; but having chosen the other tack, they encounter a series of new problems which it may be instructive to investigate, the better to avoid the Charybdis of empiricist learning as well as the Scylla of rationalist nativism.

The author is professor of psychology at the University of Geneva. This article was prepared with the collaboration of M. Bovet, Professor B. Inhelder, and H. Sinclair, who are members of the staff of the Institut des Sciences de l'Education, University of Geneva.

## Quantitative Evaluations Based on Correspondence, Order, and Crowding

At the level of operatory conservation, children judge two collections to be equal or unequal by looking for a one-to-one correspondence between their elements (even if one collection covers a larger area or is spaced out with greater intervals). At an earlier stage, children judge one collection to be more numerous than the other (or to contain "more" elements, even if they admit that in counting the elements one gets the same number in each) as soon as the line formed is of greater length. How should this length factor be interpreted?

Mehler and Bever analyze this factor briefly but inadequately, since they seem to believe that everything is taken care of once "perception" of length is invoked, as if this perception were sufficient to suppress momentarily an otherwise correct notion of numerical quantity. Evaluation by length is actually based on an ordinal quantification which is already of a conceptual nature, and which is far more complex and general than the experiment on

SCIENCE, 1968, Vol. 162, pp. 976-979. 

number alone would lead us to suppose. Research on the concept of length (of paths, for example) has shown that, at the level of development in question, "longer" means "going further," not because of a dominance of perception, or because of a verbal or semantic confusion, but because the first quantifications that become possible before the synthesis of number (a synthesis of order and inclusion) and that of measure (a synthesis of partition and displacement) are based on an order of the points of arrival. This may be explained by the following. Before the child becomes capable of reversible operations, his thinking proceeds by "functions" in the modern sense of "mappings" (one-way mappings) or of "ordered couples." Psychologically, functions are the expression of action schemes, and every action (particularly an action whereby a certain distance is covered) is a series of ordered movements which will come to an end (at the point of arrival). This concept of "function" explains the dominance of ordinal considerations that underlie quantitative evaluations of and by length between 3 to 4, and 6 to 7, years of age.

But the results obtained by Mehler and Bever seem to show that prior to these purely ordinal evaluations there exists between 2 years, 6 months and 3 years, 2 months an even more primitive mode of quantitative evaluation, which with their display, Fig. 1*b*, leads to 100 percent correct answers. In the light of what we have said about ordinal structures, let us try to understand what kind of factors may be involved in these reactions. In the first place, we should not forget that, as far as space is concerned, children start with topological structures based on proximity, separation, enclosure, and frontiers (interiority or exteriority), before they consider length or even rectilinearity; in a recent work, Laurendeau and Pinard (*3*) have verified by hierarchical analysis the consistency and the anteriority of these topological intuitions as compared with Euclidian metrics.

This being so, it is possible to hypothesize that in the case of Mehler and Bever's (*1*) (Fig. 1) display—six elements crowded on a line 5 inches (13 cm) long, and four elements spread out over 8 inches (20 cm)—the subjects that had not yet reached the stage of evaluation by length (ordinal comparison of points of arrival) used an even more primitive mode of evaluation, which would be a topological evaluation based on a notion which might be called a notion of "heaping" or "crowding." In other words, when a child compares two figures or two rows in a simple topological way (roughly analogous to homeomorphy) he will get the impression that the short row is more "heaped" or more "crowded" than the long one, in the sense that in the former the elements are nearer one to another in relation to the total figure. To verify this hypothesis a number of experiments are necessary (*4*, *5*), and we will discuss some of them below.

Against the concept of "crowding" it can be objected that with reference to Fig. 1*c*, 22 answers out of 32 indicated that the children saw the longer row of six spread out elements as containing "more" than the short row of four crowded elements. But this objection is not decisive, for several reasons. In the first place, a certain number of children (if we understand the authors correctly) still said that there were "more" in the short row of four elements. In the second place, the fact that only 22 out of 32 answers were correct (with only seven subjects out of a total of 16 giving consistent answers) shows that this situation arouses a conflict and is more complex than siuation *b* (Fig. 1*b*). It is easy to understand the origin of this conflict—in Fig. 1*b*, the ratio of the lengths is 8 to 5, that is to say, the long row is only 1.6 times longer than the other, whereas in Fig. 1*c*, the ratio is 25 to 5, that is to say, the long row is five times longer than the other. Subjects at an intermediate stage between evaluation by "crowding" and evaluation by length are obviously more apt to be struck by length in Fig. 1*c* than in Fig. 1*b*, and since *c* is the long row containing six elements (against four in the short row) evaluation by length happens in fact to give the correct answer. However, other experiments are necessary to dissociate these factors. Here are some of our results.

## New Experiments

We interviewed 29 children between the ages of 2 years, 3 months and 3 years, 10 months (*6*), with Mehler and Bever's techniques and also with our technique of presenting two rows of four or six elements in optical correspondence, which are then spread out or crowded together in one of the rows. But, unlike Mehler and Bever, we not only presented unequal collections, but also equal collections where one row had its elements spaced out (length) and the other had its elements close together (heaping or crowding).

Technically the experiments are difficult, since there are perturbing factors which are not mentioned by Mehler and Bever, but which are of importance. (i) Some subjects always consider the row which is nearest to them as containing "a lot" of elements, and the row which is further away as containing "a little" or "not a lot." (ii) Preliminary experiments showed that many very young children do not understand the terms "*plus*" (more) and "*moins*" (less) in any consistent way, whereas "*beaucoup*" (a lot) and "*peu*" (a little) or "*pas beaucoup*" (not a lot) give rise to more consistent answers. We used both types of expressions. (iii) The first meaning attributed to "more" by subjects of up to 3 years, 6 months is that of adding to one collection, and not that of comparing two collections (A > B) without either of them being modified. (iv) Some subjects even say "a lot" for any collection on which the experimenter acts (whether he shoves elements togther, or whether he adds other elements) and "a little" for the collection that remains undisturbed. This is important since in Mehler and Bever's experiment it is always the more numerous row that is manipulated.

Despite these difficulties, the results of our experiments are clear enough except for eight subjects between 2 years, 3 months and 3 years, 0 months, who are totally inconsistent in their answers; that is, they give different answers to the same question asked

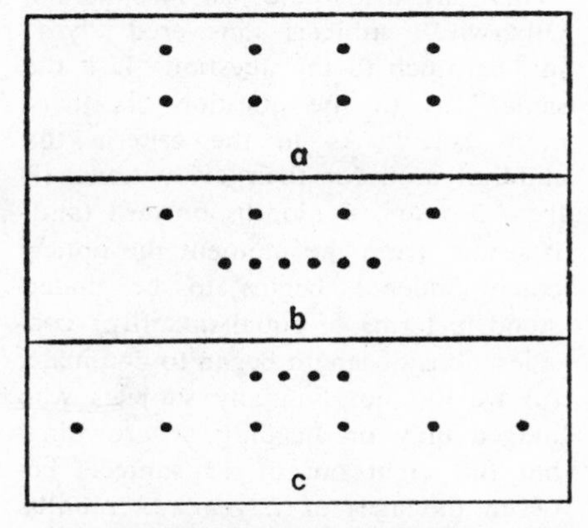


Fig. 1. The length of the rows in (*a*) was 7 inches (18 cm) for M & M's and 8 inches (20 cm) for clay pellets; in (*b*) 7 and 3 inches (18 and 8 cm) for M & M's and 8 and 5 inches (20 and 13 cm) for clay pellets. There was a 1⅓-inch (3-cm) space between each of the four clay pellets and a 2-inch (5-cm) space between each of the four M & M's. The clay pellets were ½ inch (1.3 cm) in diameter. The M & M candies were all of the same color. [Taken from Mehler and Bever (*1*)]

several times in the same situation. We noted the following answers.

1) With rows containing an equal number of elements (four and four, or six and six), where one row is spread out and the other is crowded, 84 answers indicate one of the rows as containing "more" or "a lot" of elements; not one subject said that the rows were equal in number. At this level there can consequently be no question of conservation.

2) With regard to rows with unequal numbers of elements (four against five, six, seven, or eight), we find 28 correct answers ("a lot" for the row with more elements) and 29 incorrect answers (one subject even considered $4 > 8$ because the four elements were widely spread out).

3) With regard to equal rows with optical correspondence (four to four or six to six) the youngest subject who understood and expressed the equality was 3 years, 4 months old (she said, "There are a lot here just like there"). Otherwise, subjects answered "yes" just as much to the question "Is it the same?" as to the question "Is there more here?" As to the criteria the children used for their evaluations, (i) from 3 years, 6 months onward (and, it seems, from the moment the optical correspondence begins to be understood in terms of equal quantity) considerations of length began to dominate; (ii) we did not find any subjects who judged only on heaping or crowding; but (iii) eight out of 15 subjects between the ages of 2 years, 3 months and 3 years, 2 months and one subject of 3 years, 9 months alternated between the crowding criterion and length. In verbal judgments ("a lot" as against "not a lot") as well as when the child is asked to choose a row of candies, four or six crowded elements are sometimes taken to be "more" than four or six spread out elements. Crowding thus **does lead to quantity judgments, and this is more frequent at the earlier age than at the age of 4 to 5, which we studied with Szeminska (*5*).**

## Conservation of Number

Mehler and Bever's experiment has nothing whatever to do with conservation, and I cannot understand why the authors continually talk about conservation, or why they conclude that the answers that coincide with the correct numerical quantities exhibit conservation (*7*). They probably think that since the usual obstacle to number conservation is evaluation by length, it suffices to show that children from 2 years, 6 months to 3 years do not evaluate quantity by length to conclude that they possess the notion of conservation. However, there is no getting away from the need to agree on terminology. We call "conservation" (and this is generally accepted) the invariance of a characteristic despite *transformations* of the object or of a collection of objects possessing this characteristic. Concerning number, a collection of objects "conserves" its number when the shape or disposition of the collection is modified, or when it is partitioned into subsets.

Now, in Mehler and Bever's experiment there never are any transformations of equal collections. A subject of 3 years old who in situation *b*, Fig. 1, says that there are more elements in the short row of six than in the long row of four, may maintain the same judgment if the two rows are given the same length; but conservation of equality is not proven by such conservation of inequality. The former can be shown only if two rows of equal number are presented and one row is then spread out or crowded; or at least, if two rows of unequal length but equal number are presented without modification. In these situations our results were negative (as already mentioned) for subjects between 2 years, 6 months and 3 years, just as they were for subjects from 3 to 4 years of age.

We insist on this problem on conservation because Mehler and Bever curiously end their paper by saying that nonconservation "is not a basic characteristic of man's native endowment," as if I had ever said anything to the contrary. The natural tendency of young children, evidently, is to conserve as long as they are not confronted by facts which they do not expect, and whose inexplicability leads them to change their opinion. We have, for example, described (*8*) the reactions of young children (well before Bruner applied this technique) when the content of a low, wide glass is poured into a tall, narrow glass behind a screen. Before they have seen what actually happens these children expect that there will still be "the same amount to drink," that the quantity of liquid will be conserved, and the level of the liquid will be conserved as well (in fact, the level of the liquid constitutes the measure of its quantity from an ordinal point of view). In these cases we speak about pseudoconservation, since these subjects conserve too much, and therefore incorrectly. Only after having seen that the level goes up in the narrow glass will these subjects deny conservation of quantity and opine that the quantity has increased because the level has changed; yet, to repeat the point, this is not simply due to a perceptual strategy, but to the fact that, in the absence of other means of measurement, an ordinal evaluation by level necessarily leads to this conclusion.

In general, children expect conservation, but since they cannot know beforehand what will be conserved and what will not be conserved, they have to construct new means of quantification in every new sector of experience. The inadequacy of the means of quantification explains nonconservation, and it is worth noting that nonconservation therefore indicates an effort to analyze and to dissociate variables; very young children and severely mentally retarded subjects pay no attention to these variables, whereas the older, normal children pass through a stage of nonconservation as they reorganize relations which they cannot yet grasp in full.

**Role of Innate Structure**

The development of cognition and especially the construction of means of quantification (initial pseudoconservation, followed by nonconservation, and finally by operatory conservation) consitute a coherent whole in which Mehler and Bever's observations will find their place when new facts have clarified the interpretation given to their results. In the meantime, it is necessary to discuss the solution proposed by the authors, that is to say, the hypothesis that an innate kernel furnishes an immediately valid schema of quantitive evaluation, which later deteriorates because of imcomplete performances or misleading perceptual strategies, and which finally brings about a return to the correct, innate ideas.

The explanation of cognitive behavior by means of innate ideas is, in general, a facile and rather lazy solution, which accordingly has always been criticized by empiricists. However, after the excesses of explanation by learning alone, a return to nativism is to be expected, but with the attendant risk of lapsing into its traditional faults, that is, nativism cannot explain the details of the (primarily biological) mechanisms that are at work. What is the way out of this dilemma?

The merit of the solution proposed by Mehler and Bever—and this aspect of their nativism I find particularly pleasing—lies in the fact that, in contrast with all traditions of classical rationalism, they call upon an innate mechanism that is so poor and so fragile that it manifests itself victoriously only between the ages of 2½ and 3 years, after which it fails in its task until new strategies and performances allow the observer to rediscover its traces at the end of early childhood. When nativism presents itself in such a modest way, it is easy to discuss and to weigh its advantages and disadvantages.

In the first place, it is clear that if the "innate ideas" of numerical quantity can be so easily conquered or counteracted by bad "perceptual strategies" at the stage of nonconservation they cannot consist of a real structure with a hereditary, biogenetic programmation; they can be no more than an innate form of functioning. When biologists talk about a specific innate structure, they consider it to be programmed in the genetic information of the DNA, and this programming of ulterior syntheses is sufficiently resistant to conquer the perturbing effects of environment, if the organism survives. The innate ideas of Mehler and Bever remain dependent upon external situations, that is to say, they "function" well or badly according to these situations. If innate "functioning" is what they are talking about, it is easy to agree with them, because, evidently, an innate, intelligent functioning is necessary to arrive at the construction of numbers (it is impossible, for example, to bring about such functioning in the brain of a subject with severe mental defect). I have always maintained that logico-mathemental structures are not derived from language (an empiricist hypothesis) but from the general coordination of actions, with their permanent functional mechanisms of ordering (order of movements), embedding (of a subscheme into a total scheme, for example), establishing correspondences, and equivalences. All these factors intervene in the construction of numerical quantities, and they obviously suppose an innate neurological and organic functioning; as long as only such functioning is involved, without structural hereditary programmation. I accept the necessity of an innate point of departure.

This being so, a second problem immediately arises: What are the mechanisms which are necessary for this innate functioning to proceed toward the completed structure? In other words, is it necessary to suppose a progressive building up of structures which were not initially contained in the functional kernel? On this point Mehler and Bever's arguments seem equivocal: with regard to the psychological problem of number (we are not talking about linguistics), they continuously oscillate between a transformational functionalism and a preformational structuralism. They argue as if the innate kernel consisted nevertheless of some sort of preformed structure, which becomes veiled by bad "perceptual strategies" or by unsuccessful "performances," but which reappears when better circumstances permit.

We would like to ask two further questions. What are the conditions that cause the strategies employed sometimes to counteract, and sometimes to favor, this innate kernel? And once the obstacles have been overcome, is the final structure the same as the structure that existed at the age of 2½ to 3 years, or has it been transformed and enriched, and if so, why? These two questions are closely linked to one another and dominate the problem mentioned earlier: if the final structure is richer than the initial one, a construction must have taken place, and preformation is not the answer; moreover, the intermediate strategies must all have contributed to this construction and cannot be considered as good or bad in function of a (falsely) absolute model, since they constitute the necessary stages for the completion of this construction.

What is lacking in Mehler and Bever's argument is the concept of productive actions and of the operations which stem from these actions. The fundamental characteristic of operations is that they produce novelties (empiricists try to explain this fact by exogenous learning) by means of "reflexive abstraction" from actions at an earlier stage (and it is this endogenous process that presupposes a functional kernel with innate roots). Mehler and Bever only consider, on the one hand, what is innate, and on the other, perceptions and performances. Thus they cut the link between the subject and exterior reality, which leads them to consider the former as sometimes a winner, sometimes a loser. By constrast, the concept of operations explains, and is the only way to explain, how an initial functional kernel yields completed structures, that is, by a series of self-regulations and equilibrations in which even the errors play a functional success-promoting role.

To conclude, Mehler and Bever invoke an innate structure which supposedly accounts for early correct answers (we have interpreted these answers in a different way) and for the final successes but which does not explain why the structure is overpowered so easily during the intermediate stages, or why the final structure is richer than the initial one. I maintain that when these facts are explained, the concept of an "innate structure" becomes superfluous, that an innate functioning is sufficient. I maintain above all, that when the rather Manichaean notion of good and bad structures is replaced by an adequate theory of progressive equilibration starting from self-regulation, the idea of construction will prevail over that of preformation; for, as the great biologist Dobzhansky has said, though predetermination is impossible to disprove, it is on the contrary (and I would add, precisely for that reason) completely useless (9).

**References and Notes**


1. J. Mehler and T. G. Bever, *Science* **158**, 141 (1967).
2. For example, N. Chomsky, *Aspects of the Theory of Syntax* (M.I.T. Press, Cambridge, Mass., 1965).
3. M. Laurendeau and A. Pinard, *Les premières notions spatiales chez l'enfant* (Délachaux et Niestlé, Neuchâtel, in press).

4. In our previous experiments with A. Szeminska (see ref. 5), not all our subjects without conservation between 4 and 5 years of age considered the longer row as containing more elements; some (and these were not the most advanced) considered that there were more elements in the crowded row. Mehler and Bever's results now suggest that such answers show a residue of an earlier stage at which the criterion of quantification is either crowding or sometimes crowding and sometimes length.

5. J. Piaget and A. Szeminska, *La genèse du nombre chez l'enfant* (Délachaux et Niestlé, Neuchâtel, 1941); translation, *The Child's Conception of Number* (Routledge and Kegan Paul, London, 1952).

6. Five subjects from 2 years, 3 months to 2 years, 7 months; ten subjects from 2 years, 8 months to 2 years, 11 months; nine subjects from 3 years 0 month to 3 years, 4 months; and five from 3 years, 5 months to 3 years, 10 months; as well as three subjects from 4 years 0 month, to 4 years, 1 month, whom we have excluded, though reactions were analogous to those of the younger subjects.
7. It may be worth pointing out that misuse of the term "conservation" also occurs in the work of other authors. Bower, in his admirable experiments on newborn babies, seems to have proved (but his results will have to be confirmed by others) that at the end of the first week of life the baby already recognizes an object which has been hidden behind a screen and which is then shown to him again; or at least, that the baby distinguishes this object from another one. However, this only proves that recognition is a very early phenomenon, which I have never denied, it does not tell us whether for the baby the hidden object continues to exist when it is placed behind another object, or whether the object has momentarily ceased to exist, like an image that can disappear and reappear and then be recognized as having been seen already. The hypothesis of conservation would suppose a substantification of reality and an organization of space; recognition by itself does not indicate whether

this organization is present or not, or even whether such organization is possible or not at this age. The hypothesis that the newborn baby's universe consists of tableaux which disappear and reappear is much simpler and just as compatible with very early recognition. With regard to the early "tunnel-effect" this phenomenon has to be .dissociated from a simple oculocephalogyral reflex, a problem for separate discussion elsewhere.

8. J. Piaget and B. Inhelder, *L'Image mentale chez l'enfant* (Presses Universitaires de France, Paris, 1966); and J. S. Bruner, *Amer. Psychol.* 19, 1 (1964); J. S. Bruner *et al.*, *Studies in Cognitive Growth* (Wiley, New York, 1966).
9. Th. Dobzhansky, in *Hundert Jahre Evolutionsforschung*, G. Heberer and F. Schwanitz, Eds. (Fisher, Stuttgart, 1960), p. 32.

# Reply by J. Mehler and T. G. Bever

Our research has been focused on the cognitive capacities of the 2-year-old child. We reported that the 2-year-old performs better than the 4-year-old in judging the relative quantity of rows of clay balls (*1*). (The stimuli are represented in Fig. 1*b* of Piaget's discussion.) Since Piaget developed the theoretical problem as well as the general techniques used, there are many points of agreement between our initial paper and his critique, and some points that remain to be clarified (compare *2* and *3*).

With respect to the experimental issues, Piaget suggests that the young child responds to the relative density or "crowding" in the shorter row, not to its relative numerosity. We have recently used numerically equal rows with one row shorter and denser than the other and with length relations similar to those shown in Fig. 1*b*. We found that there was no tendency for children at any age to choose the denser row as having "more" (*4*). Therefore, the young child appears to make correct quantitative decisions without reference to the relative density of the rows.

Piaget mentions several difficulties he found in replicating our results (*5*). (i) The child tends to choose systematically the row closest to him. However, this effect could not have contributed to our results because in our experiment row orientation was systematically varied. (One-fourth of our subjects, in each age group, saw rows perpendicular to their frontal plane with the shorter line on their right, and one-fourth with the shorter line on the left. One-fourth of the subjects saw the lines parallel to their frontal plan with the shorter line closer to them while the remaining fourth saw the shorter line farther from them.)

(ii) "Preliminary experiments show that many very young children do not understand the term *more*." Our most recent experiments indicate that the young child responds as though he understands the word *more*: he correctly chooses the row with more balls when it is shorter, longer, or the same length as a reference row; conversely he does not consistently choose the longer or denser row when it has the same number of items as a reference row (*4*). Although such correct performance does not necessarily prove correct comprehension, it is a strong sign of it.

This linguistic objection led Piaget to use an experimental procedure that is different from ours; for the relational word *more* [and *same* in our subsequent work (*4*)] Piaget used the absolute terms, *a lot, a little,* and *not a lot.* Although the use of such absolute terms possibly stabilizes the child's behavior (as Piaget indicates), it is likely that, even for a child, a relational problem is very different from an absolute one. Thus, the fact that most of the children tested by Piaget indicate that one of two rows has "a lot" or "a little" cannot be compared directly with our finding that he knows (and says) which row has "more." Furthermore, to compare Piaget's results with ours, only the first response given by his subjects can

---

**Dr. Mehler is on the staff at Centre Nationale de la Recherche Scientifique, Paris. Dr. Bever is at Rockefeller University, New York.**

be used. Throughout, Piaget interviewed his subjects on the same sort of problem several times, and all the responses were considered equivalent. However, we have found that repeated questioning from an adult may lead a young child to believe there was something wrong with his response, and thus he may change it (*4*).

Piaget notes that only the more numerous row was actually manipulated in our original experiment, and he argues that this might account for the results. (iii) Either the young child understands "more" as an additive term and simply chooses the row that he observes being supplemented or (iv) the young child chooses the row that he observes the experimenter manipulate. In a recent experiment, however, we have controlled both possibilities by prior preparation of all rows on cardboard strips. Under these conditions, in which rows are manipulated equally, neither row receiving additional pellets, young children perform extremely well (93 percent choose the correct row as having more), and older children perform markedly less well (*4*).

We agree with Piaget that the term "conservation" should not have been used in our first paper. We used a kind of "*over*conservation" technique because, like Piaget, we observed that quantitative concepts (particularly the concept of equality) are difficult for the young child to verbalize. The "overconservation" technique allowed the child to exhibit judgements of relative quantities in nonverbal responses (pointing to one row, or taking it). Furthermore, we felt that the high level of performance that the 2-year-old achieved on this task (and on later tasks) indicated a fundamental *capacity* to appreciate quantitative relations of the sort that could be studied with the true conservation paradigm. [We have discussed elsewhere the relation between our first experiments and the study of the capacity for conservation and also some true conservation studies with young children (*4*).]

With respect to theoretical issues we take our results to mean that the 2-year-old already has certain basic cognitive capacities; these capacities are subject to the child's general limitations on such expressive functions as attention and memory. To overcome these limits, the child forms (intuitive) perceptual generalizations that extend his capacities beyond the behavioral limits. Since these perceptual generalizations fail in critical cases, the child is ultimately impelled by his experience to integrate them into a system that includes both the basic logical capacities and the perceptual generalizations. This interpretation does not assume a notion of competition between "good" and "bad" strategies, as Piaget suggests. In particular, the perceptual generalizations that the child develops at the end of the third year are not "bad"; on the contrary, they are appropriate consequences of the interaction among the child's basic capacities, his subsidiary skills and experience. Therefore, our interpretation does not "cut the link between the subject and exterior reality." (However, we are not claiming that there is any obvious external reason for the formation of the perceptual generalizations at a particular stage of development, nor is there any automatic empiricist way of accounting for those attributes of stimuli that become the basis for generalizations and those that do not. That is, while the perceptual generalizations represent adaptations to experience, there is nothing in the external world sufficient to explain the particular experiences that the child recognizes, nor why he adapts to them. The organization and motive for these developments must be found in the child himself.)

Our interpretation seems close to Piaget's interpretation that "(young) children expect conservation, but . . . they have to construct new means of quantification. . . . The inadequacy of the means of quantification explains nonconservation . . . very young children *pass through* a stage of nonconservation as they reorganize relations which they cannot yet grasp in full." (Emphasis here is ours.)

Every theory of cognition must include a description of the relation between innate and learned components. Piaget postulates as a basic innate mechanism, the "reflective abstraction process" that extracts the regularities, rules, operations, and coordinations of the child's actions and transfers these to the cognitive domain. Of course, the "reflective abstraction process" entails powerful nativist assumptions, because it must have internal structure, already defined domains of application, and built-in capacity to segment actions and their coordinations. Thus, we must examine further concepts such as "reflective abstraction process" and "actions" before they will have explanatory value. On the one hand, we consider that Piaget's formulation is inadequate, not because of its nativism but rather because of the unjustified emphasis placed upon action as the *only* datum upon which the innate equipment can operate. On the other hand, we cannot conceive of actions without internal guiding principles, which are themselves, crucial components for the genesis of cognitive capacities.

We owe to Piaget our bias toward a functional innateness rather than toward a preformational one. (Indeed, we have never intended to argue exclusively for innate *structure* as opposed to innate *process* which can abstract structure from experience.) Nevertheless cognitive processes (like chemical reactions) are difficult to observe directly—rather we must examine the structure of initial, intermediate, and final functioning and then describe intervening processes to account for the development of the child's performance. Piaget has devoted a great deal of attention to the operations which the child develops by age 7 to 8 and also to the absence of those operations during the preceding years. We are now attempting to expand these investigations by examining the initial strategies and heuristics that the 2-year-old child has as he *starts* this phase of his cognitive development. Whether a particular component of cognition is to be viewed as "innate" or as the result of early learning will be a question for further theoretical and empirical investigations.

**References and Notes**

1. J. Mehler and T. G. Bever, *Science* **158**, 141 (1967).
2. ———, *Int. J. Psychol.*, in press.
3. T. Bever, J. Mehler, V. Valian, in *Structure and Psychology of Language*, T. Bever and W. Weksel, Eds. (Holt, Rinehart and Winston, New York, in press), vol. 2.
4. T. G. Bever, J. Mehler, J. Epstein, *Science* **162**, 921 (1968).
5. The numbers (i), (ii), (iii), and (iv) follow the preceding article by Piaget.
6. Supported by Foundation Funds for Research in Psychiatry, grant G67-380, and by ARPA contract SD-187.

# Conservation of Number in Young Children:

## Recency versus Relational Response Strategies

LINDA S. SIEGEL AND ALVIN G. GOLDSTEIN
*University of Missouri*

According to Piaget (1952), the attainment of conservation of number, which is the ability to recognize that the number of objects in a group remains constant in spite of changes in the spatial arrangement of the objects, represents a significant advance in the intellectual development of the child. Previous investigators (e.g., Dodwell, 1960; Piaget, 1952) have found that children do not show conservation of number until the age of 6 or 7. However, Mehler and Bever (1967), testing the conservation of number of children younger than had previously been studied, reported that children as young as 2 years and 4 months (2–4) had the ability to make correct conservation responses. The present experiment attempts to reconcile these conflicting data.

The standard test of conservation of number involves the transformation of groups of equal numbers of objects into irregular spatial arrangements. Thus, the child must recognize that the number of objects remains the same in spite of the rearrangement of the objects. The technique used by Mehler and Bever (1967) involved both the addition to, and transformation of, a group of objects. This procedure tests the understanding of the relational concept of "more," but not the ability to make conservation responses which involve recognizing identity. The present experiment tested both the understanding of relational concepts and conservation in tasks designed to distinguish between these two abilities.

Since it has recently been reported that young children (4–1 to 5–2) had difficulty in understanding the words "more," "less," and "same" when applied to number (Griffiths, Shantz, & Sigel, 1967), it is important to determine if children can use this relational terminology appropriately when conservation responses are tested. The present experiment added the control of testing the children's understanding of these words.

An alternative explanation for the performance of young children in this conservation task may involve the tendency noted by previous investigators (e.g., Hood, 1962) for young children to choose the last alternative in a series, especially if the situation with which they are confronted involves difficult or confusing questions. The present experiment was a test of this "recency" hypothesis; that is, young children will choose the last alternative presented to them rather than the correct relational one.

The authors wish to thank Barbara Fischer and the staff of Stephens College Childrens School for their cooperation in providing subjects for this study. The authors also wish to thank Sharon Reilly, who assisted in the running of the experiments.

DEVELOPMENTAL PSYCHOLOGY, 1969, Vol. 1, No. 2, pp. 128-130.

## Method

The subjects were 66 children ranging in age from 2–7 to 6–1. The distribution of subjects at each age level was as follows: 2–7 to 3–0, 7; 3–1 to 3–6, 6; 3–7 to 4–0, 8; 4–1 to 4–6, 9; 4–7 to 5–0, 12; 5–1 to 5–6, 16; and 5–7 to 6–1, 8. There were approximately an equal number of males and females within each age group. The children used in this study attended the Stephens College Childrens School and were predominantly middle class and of above average intelligence levels. All the subjects were white and were mostly children of the faculty of Stephens College.

Subjects were individually administered a two part test; Part I was a test of the children's understanding of relational concepts signified by the words more and less, and Part II involved a test of conservation of number. In all tests, the temporal position of the correct response was systematically varied so it was either the first or the last alternative offered to the child. The stimuli used in both parts were pennies.

In Part I the child was presented with two parallel rows of varying numbers of pennies. The test consisted of four questions; the first two required the child to specify which row had more pennies, and the next two questions required judgments of which row had fewer pennies. For a particular question the child was presented with the stimulus configuration and asked by the experimenter, "Which row of pennies has more [less], this one [pointing to the row farther from the child], or this one [pointing to the row closer to the child]?" The first configuration had six and two pennies, the second had two and five, the third had five and one, and the fourth had two and five.

Part II, a test of conservation of number, consisted of a series of three questions asked each child. For Question 1, the child was shown two parallel rows of equal length, each with six pennies, and asked, "Are there the same number of pennies in each row, or does one row have less or more pennies than the other row?" For Question 2, the row of pennies closest to the child was pushed together while the child watched. Then the child was asked the same question as in Question 1. The child's answer to Question 2 determines whether or not he has attained conservation; if he recognizes that both rows are the same, he has conservation, if he thinks that the longer row has more pennies, he has failed to make a conservation response. For Question 3, the altered row was returned to its original position, parallel and equal in length to the other row, and the child was asked again the same question as in Question 1.

To test for the possibility of recency responding, the position of the words more and same was systematically varied for each child such that if more appeared last in Question 1, it appeared first in Question 3. Since the conservation test requires that the child understand identity or sameness, the position of more and same was varied to insure that the child understood the meaning of same and would recognize the identity of the two rows independently of the manner in which the question was asked. For Question 2, half of the subjects had same first and more last, and the other half had the reverse order. This procedure was followed to insure that the choice of a correct conservation response did not depend on the temporal position of the correct alternative.

## Results and Discussion

Figure 1 shows that the mean number of relational responses (correct choice of more and less) and the mean number of recency responses (choice of the last row to which the experimenter pointed) for each age group. A repeated measures analysis of variance for unequal *n*'s revealed a significant interaction between the relational and recency strategies as a function of age ($F = 5.97$, $df = 6/59$, $p < .001$). Clearly, the younger children chose the most recent stimulus and this tendency decreased with increasing age. Only the older children were able to answer the questions about more and less correctly; the younger children responded on the basis of recency. Thus, older children appear to understand relational concepts, while younger children employ a recency strategy in which temporal cues are used.

Clearly, the question of whether or not children have the concept of conservation cannot be assessed unless children recognize sameness. The following were the per-

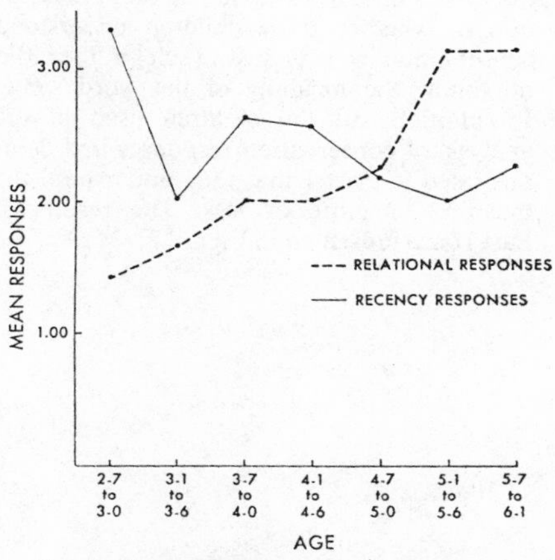


FIG. 1. The mean number of recency and relational responses in Part I.

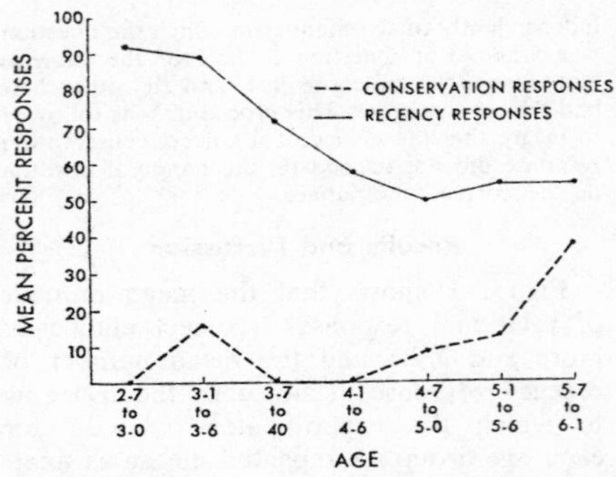


FIG. 2. The mean number of conservation and recency responses in Part II.

centages of children who answered same on Questions 1 and 3 in Part II: 2–7 to 3–0, 0%; 3–1 to 3–6, 16.7%; 3–7 to 4–0, 37.5%; 4–1 to 4–6, 44.4%; 4–7 to 5–0, 66.7%; 5–1 to 5–6, 68.8%; and 5–7 to 6–1, 87.5%. Thus, until the age of 4–7 the majority of children in this sample do not understand the meaning of the word same. Although all the children were tested in Part II, only the children who appeared to understand the concept of sameness were included in the analysis of conservation responses. A total of 31 children were not used in the analysis of conservation responses because they had failed to respond correctly to the questions which tested the understanding of the word same. It was assumed that the question of whether these children understood conservation was unanswerable if they did not know the meaning of the word same. In addition, all the children used in the analysis of conservation responses had demonstrated in Part I that they understood the meaning of more or less. The results of Part II are presented in Figure 2.

The percentage of conservation responses given at each age group is shown in Figure 2. Obviously, not until the age of 5–7 does a sizable percentage of the children show conservation of number and, indeed, many of the older children do not show it. Figure 2 also shows the percentage of responses to each question on which subjects chose the last alternative. The younger children chose the last alternative a large percentage of the time, while the older ones chose it at a chance level.

Thus, it appears that young children do not show conservation of number as previously reported by Mehler and Bever if the understanding of the words more, less, and same is controlled. Instead, young children tend to respond on the basis of positional preferences for the last alternative. The data support Piaget's assumption that conservation of number is not characteristic of the thought processes of very young children.

## REFERENCES


DODWELL, P. C. Children's understanding of number and related concepts. *Canadian Journal of Psychology,* 1966, **14,** 191–205.

GRIFFITHS, J. A., SHANTZ, C. A., & SIGEL, I. E. A methodological problem in conservation studies: The use of relational terms. *Child Development,* 1967, **38,** 841–848.

HOOD, H. B. An experimental study of Piaget's theory of the development of number in children. *British Journal of Psychology,* 1962, **53**, 273–286.

MEHLER, J., & BEVER, T. G. Cognitive capacity of very young children. *Science,* 1967, **153,** 141–142.

PIAGET, J. *The child's conception of number.* New York: Humanities, 1952.

# "CONSERVATION" BELOW AGE THREE: FACT OR ARTIFACT?[1]

THOMAS M. ACHENBACH
*Yale University*

Mehler and Bever (1967) reported that 100% of children aged 2 yr. 4 mo. (2:4) to 2 yr. 7 mo. (2:7) correctly indicated that a row of six clay pellets 5 in. long contained more than a row of four pellets 8 in. long, but correct responses dropped below 20% at ages 3:8 to 4:3. When told to take the row of M & Ms they wished to eat, a majority 2:4 to 4:7 took a shorter row containing six M & Ms rather than a longer row of four M & Ms. These findings were interpreted to mean that nonconservation of quantity was a temporary phase reflecting an overdependence on a perceptual strategy, but the consistent majority choosing the six M & Ms indicated that the perceptual strategy could be overcome with sufficient motivation.

Piaget (1968) and Beilen (1968) rejected the term "conservation" for the finding because it involved two unequal rows rather than two containing an equal number of objects. While Mehler and Bever (1968) acknowledged that their usage of the term "conservation" was unorthodox, they contended that their "overconservation" technique allowed *S* to indicate relative quantities without verbal responses and that the 2-yr.-olds revealed a capacity to appreciate quantitative relations like those studied with the conservation paradigm. The experiments carried out by Piaget and Beilen supported their criticisms, but did not replicate the Mehler-Bever procedures.

The disagreements concerning the significance of the Mehler and Bever (1968) findings for Piaget's theory may not be easily resolved, but it is difficult to ignore the evidence for the ability of young children to make correct choices from perceptual arrays which fool older children. Their position that allowing nonverbal responses is preferable to depending upon verbalizations is supported by

[1] Supported by National Institute of Child Health and Human Development Grant HD-MH-03008. The author is grateful to Andrea Danzig and Gail Ellinghaus for their help in carrying out the study.

Proceedings 77th Annual Convention of the American Psychological Association, 1969, pp. 275-276.

Griffiths, Shantz, and Sigel's (1967) finding that the term "same" is difficult for young children to use. However, in experiments which avoided complex verbal responses, Braine and Shanks (1965) found no evidence of conservation between ages 2:7 and 3:5, though their procedures differed from Mehler and Bever's and cannot be said to disprove the Mehler-Bever conclusions.

Rothenberg and Courtney (1968) did replicate the Mehler-Bever procedures, except that only horizontal orientations of the rows of M & Ms and clay were placed before *S*, whereas Mehler and Bever (1968) later reported that horizontal and vertical orientations as well as nearness of the longer row were systematically varied. The Rothenberg-Courtney procedure may also have differed from the original one in that the longer row was placed in the same position (i.e., nearer or farther from *S*) both for M & Ms and clay for a given *S*, while Mehler and Bever did not indicate whether the proximity of the longer row was counterbalanced for the two tasks within *S*.

Rothenberg and Courtney found a significant tendency to take the closer row. This may have accounted for the extremely low level of correct responses (17%) by *S*s 3:0 to 3:7 in a study by Ayabe, Gotts, and Hardy (1968) where the six-element row was always farther away. Moreover, as in the Ayabe et al. study, *S*s receiving first the task in which they were told to eat the M & Ms chose the row containing six elements more often than *S*s receiving this task second. No *S*s below 2:8 were tested, but the trend for the remaining ages was like Mehler and Bever's only in that the percentage of correct responses was highest (75% compared to their 81%) in the 2:8 to 2:11 group. The *S*s aged 3:8 to 4:3 gave over 50% correct responses compared to the less than 20% correct found by Mehler and Bever. No age groups reached the 90% correct found by Mehler and Bever for M & Ms in the 3:0 to 3:3 and 4:4 to 4:7 groups.

In view of the order and position factors revealed in the Rothenberg-Courtney (1968) and Ayabe et al. (1968) studies, the primary question to be asked of the Mehler-Bever findings is not whether they demonstrate conservation above zero, but whether, when the error factors are controlled, they demonstrate correct responses significantly different from the chance level of 50% for the binary choice offered *S*s. This question cannot be answered from the original report because of a lack of detailed specification of what constituted "valid" responses, what shaping may have accompanied the training procedure and *E*'s reaction to invalid responses, and what proportion of *S*s receiving each of the two orientations and locations of the rows were included in the results.

## METHOD

The Mehler-Bever procedures (1967) were replicated

with the two rows of objects placed perpendicular to *S*'s frontal plane. Although both rows were directly in front of *S*, four orders were used which within each *S* counterbalanced right-left location for the four- and six-element rows and within each age group counterbalanced the order of tasks (M & Ms and clay) and the task for which the six-element row appeared in right or left location. A task then followed in which conservation was violated by pouring 1½ qt. of Kool-Aid (tasted by *S*) from a large pitcher into a 1-pt. pitcher partially emptied by a hidden drain. Expressions of surprise to this violation of conservation correlated with Binet MA in normals and retardates higher than many minimally verbal conservation tasks in a previous study (Achenbach, 1969).

A fourth task employed the M & M procedure with two 250-ml. beakers, each containing 20 mints. The *E* emptied one beaker into a 100-ml. cylinder, causing the mints to rise higher than in the beaker, and four mints were added to the remaining beaker. The *S* then chose the "glass" (beaker of 24 or cylinder of 20 mints) he wanted to have. Half the *S*s saw two cylinders instead of two beakers first, with order counterbalanced within age group.

The *E* recorded *S*'s answer to whether the amounts in the rows and beakers or cylinders were initially equal and any surprise when the Kool-Aid fit. An observer (*O*) independently made similar judgments and recorded everything said. Seventy-four *S*s aged 2:4 to 5:9 were tested in nursery school or their homes. Fathers of most were graduate students or professionals.

## RESULTS

Table 1 presents the percentage of *S*s giving correct responses to the M & Ms, clay, and mints. The *S*s are grouped by pairs of 4-mo. intervals that showed similar levels of performance in the Mehler-Bever (1967) study,

**TABLE 1**

**Percentage of "Conserving" Responses**

| Age | M & Ms | | Clay | | Mints | |
|---|---|---|---|---|---|---|
| | *n* | % | *n* | % | *n* | % |
| 2:4-2:11 | 26 | 42 | 24 | 46 | 25 | 56 |
| 3:0-3:7 | 14 | 71 | 14 | 21* | 14 | 79* |
| 3:8-4:3 | 10 | 80 | 10 | 60 | 10 | 60 |
| 4:4-4:11 | 16 | 56 | 16 | 50 | 16 | 31 |
| 5:0-5:9 | 6 | 67 | 6 | 83 | 6 | 100** |

*$p$ = .06 by binomial test.
**$p$ = .03 by binomial test.

plus a group above the highest ages in their study. Breakdowns into the 4-mo. intervals did not alter the pattern. At 2:4-2:7, where Mehler and Bever found 100%

correct, only 6 of the 12 scorable responses to the clay were correct. Dropping one *S* who believed the initial rows to be unequal changed the proportion to 5/11. Of the 14 scorable responses to the M & Ms, 7 were correct. Dropping one *S* who did not agree to the initial equality changed this to 7/13 (54%) compared to the 81% reported by Mehler and Bever. At 2:8-2:11, the proportions correct were 5/12 for clay and 4/12 for M & Ms. Omitting one *S* who missed the equality changed the M & Ms to 3/11.

By binomial test, the proportions of correct and incorrect responses differed significantly only for the mints at ages 5:0-5:9 (6/6 correct, $p = .03$). The occurrence of 3/14 correct to the clay and 11/14 correct to the mints in the 3:0-3:7 group each had a $p = .06$. The $n$ in the oldest group is too small to be conclusive, but it is above the range tested by Mehler and Bever (1967). No trend like theirs exists for the younger groups. Of the *S*s who on both Mehler-Bever tasks consistently chose either the four- or six-element row, 5/12 were correct at 2:4-2:11, 2/6 at 3:0-3:7, 6/8 at 3:8-4:3, 6/9 at 4:4-4:11, and 3/3 at 5:0-5:9. None of these proportions approached statistical significance.

The *E* and *O* reached 88% agreement in scoring surprise reactions, compared to 99.5% on the other tasks. The *S*s who *E* and *O* agreed showed surprise were aged 3:7, 3:10, 4:5, 4:6, 5:1, and 5:9. Awareness of a violation of conservation thus seemed nonexistent at the younger ages and infrequent even through 5:9.

## CONCLUSIONS

The reduction of order and position effects in the Mehler-Bever procedures appears to decrease "conserving" responses below age 3. Those that remain are no more than would be expected from random responding to a binary choice.

## REFERENCES


Achenbach, T. Conservation of illusion-distorted identity: Its relation to CA and MA in normals and retardates. *Child Development,* 1969, **40**, in press.

Ayabe, H., Gotts, E., & Hardy, R. "Conservation" responses in very young children. Unpublished manuscript, University of Indiana, 1968.

Beilen, H. Cognitive capacities of young children: A replication. *Science,* 1968, **162**, 920-921.

Braine, M., & Shanks, B. The development of conservation of size. *Journal of Verbal Learning and Verbal Behavior,* 1965, **4**, 227-242.

Griffiths, J., Shantz, C., & Sigel, I. A methodological problem in conservation studies: The use of relational terms. *Child Development,* 1967, **38**, 841-848.

Mehler, J., & Bever, T. Cognitive capacity of very young children. *Science,* 1967, **158**, 141-142.

Mehler, J., & Bever, T. Reply by J. Mehler and T. G. Bever. *Science,* 1968, **162**, 979-981.

Piaget, J. Quantification, conservation, and nativism. *Science,* 1968, **162**, 976-979.

Rothenberg, B., & Courtney, R. Conservation of number in very young children: A replication of and comparison with Mehler and Bever's study. *Journal of Psychology,* 1968, **70**, 205-212.

# THE ACQUISITION OF CONSERVATION OF SUBSTANCE AND WEIGHT IN CHILDREN

## I. *Introduction*

JAN SMEDSLUND

This series of articles will be concerned with the following specific problem: What processes are involved in children's acquisition of conservation of substance and weight? These phenomena are defined as follows. A subject has conservation of substance when he thinks the amount of substance in an object must necessarily remain unchanged during changes in its form, as long as nothing is added or taken away. Similarly, a subject has conservation of weight when he thinks the weight of an object must necessarily remain unchanged during changes in its form, as long as nothing is added or taken away.

The classical test for the study of conservation of substance and weight employs pieces of plasticine. The child is presented with two equal balls of plasticine and is told that they are equally heavy. Then one of the balls is changed into a sausage or something else, and in the test of conservation of substance the following standard question is asked: 'Do you think there is more plasticine in the ball, or the same amount in both, or more in the sausage?' The corresponding question in the test of conservation of weight is: 'Which is heavier, the ball or the sausage, or do they weigh the same?' After the child has answered the question he is asked: 'Why do you think so?'

Children with conservation of substance answer that the objects contain the same amount of plasticine because they contained the same amount in the beginning; because only the shape is changed; or because nothing has been added or taken away. Children with conservation of weight answer that the objects weigh the same, and use the same arguments as in the case of conservation of substance. Children who do not have a principle of conservation usually rely on perceptual features of the objects: The sausage contains more because it is longer; the ball weighs more because it is thicker and rounder, because it looks a little bigger, etc.

### TRANSITION AGES

Several earlier studies have established the generality of the developmental transition from non-conservation to conservation in the domains of substance and weight. The classical study of Piaget & Inhelder (1941) first drew attention to these phenomena. These writers did not report the exact number and ages of their subjects, but stated that conservation of

SCANDINAVIAN JOURNAL OF PSYCHOLOGY, 1961, Vol. 2, pp. 11-20.

substance is reached on the average around 7–8 years, and conservation of weight around 9–10 years. Furthermore, their data seemed to indicate that conservation of substance and weight are invariably acquired in this order, i.e. subjects with conservation of weight always have conservation of substance but not vice versa.

The generality of this sequence seemed to be confirmed in parallel studies of children's interpretations of the melting of sugar in water and of the swelling of popcorn on a hot plate. In each situation they observed some children who asserted conservation of substance and denied conservation of weight, but they observed no children who asserted conservation of weight but denied conservation of substance. This early study was conducted by means of Piaget's *méthode clinique*, which consists of flexible and intuitively directed conversation and play. This method has proved very fruitful in the initial steps of research, but has the drawback that it cannot be exactly replicated, and it allows for unknown degrees of subjectivity in the procedure and interpretations.

A study by Inhelder (1944) verified the substance–weight sequence and indicated that these tests, together with those of conservation of volume and transitivity of weight, may have considerable diagnostic utility in practical application. The general developmental level of feeble-minded children and adults was reported as being clearly reflected in the test-responses.

A large scale standardization by Vinh-Bang (in preparation) has provided reliable and exact information on the transition ages in the population of Geneva. Nearly 1500 children between 4 and 12 years of age were given a battery of some thirty objective tests, including conservation of substance and conservation of weight. The 50 per cent level for the acquisition of conservation of substance is at 7½ years, and the corresponding level for conservation of weight is at 8 years. See also Vinh-Bang (1959). The study of Lovell (1960) in England gave approximately the same results. On the other hand, Smedslund (1959) found somewhat earlier transition ages in a group of children (sons and daughters of delegates to the international committees and organizations) from a socio-economically superior milieu in Geneva.

The studies of conservation of number by Slater (1958) in England and by Hyde (1959) with European and non-European subjects in Aden further support the hypothesis that the rate of development of concepts of conservation is influenced by environment.

## POSSIBLE INTERPRETATIONS

Historically, the diverging interpretations of the phenomena of cognitive development may be traced to the conflict between the classical philosophical schools of *empiricism* and *rationalism*. Briefly stated, the former assumes that everything that is in the mind comes from experience. The latter asserts that there are certain structures and categories which impose themselves by necessity upon the human mind and which exist independently of any experience. In contemporary psychology one may discern at least four major interpretations of the type of developmental phenomena to be studied here (and combinations of them).

### *Nativism*

According to this point of view, the human nervous system is organized in such a way that the intrinsic validity of the inference of conservation is immediately recognized at the moment when the child has acquired a knowledge of the empirical elements involved. This line of thought assumes that even very small children are always logical *within those limited areas where they have sufficient knowledge*. Development is seen as a process where appropriate inferential behavior is immediately applied to every new domain of experience.

This continues the old empiricist tradition and assumes that the child acquires the concepts of conservation as a function of repeated external reinforcements. According to this point of view, the subjective validity and necessity of the inference of conservation derives from an *empirical law*. The children discover empirically that as long as nothing is added or taken away, objects maintain the same amount of substance and the same weight, irrespective of changes of shape.

Alternatively, learning theorists may interpret the developmental transition as resulting from *social* reinforcements. The sanctions from adults and older children may gradually lead to the 'correct' behavior relative to physical substance and weight. The training in the rules of language may contribute in various ways to the same outcome.

### *Maturation theory*

This theory asserts that logical structure may not be present from the beginning in children's behavior, but that it develops as a function of nervous maturation and independently of experience. No amount of experience can bring about a given type of inferential behavior in a child who is not mature enough, and once he has reached a sufficient degree of nervous maturation his experiences are immediately integrated into a logical framework. Small children may be "illogical", but there is nothing one can do about it, just wait for nature to take its course.

### *Equilibration theory*

This is the position of Piaget and his co-workers (Piaget, 1950; 1957), who assert that logical structure is not originally present in the child's thinking, but that it develops as a function of an internal process, equilibration, which is heavily dependent on *activity* and *experience*. This point of view differs radically from that of learning theory, since practice is not assumed to act through external reinforcements, but by a process of mutual influence of the child's activities on each other. Logical inferences are not derived from any properties of the external world, but from the placing into relationship (*mise-en-relation*) of the subject's own activities. The process of equilibration is not identical with maturation, since it is highly influenced by practice which brings out latent contradictions and gaps in mental structure, and thereby initiates a process of inner reorganization. The theory is somewhat similar to Festinger's theory of cognitive dissonance (1957) and Heider's theory of balance (1958), but is more general.

These are, briefly, the four main theories of the mechanisms of cognitive development. Needless to say, many psychologists may choose intermediate positions, e.g. by postulating some kind of *interaction* of learning and maturation.

Nativism and learning theory represent opposite positions with respect to the role of experience, but they share the idea that children's thinking is essentially similar to that of adults. Both theories assume that in situations with insufficient knowledge adults will behave like children, and that in situations with sufficient knowledge children will behave like adults.

## CRITICAL DISCUSSION

The well-established findings of Piaget and his collaborators in a variety of fields seem to have excluded *nativism* as a serious possibility. (For a summary of many of these findings see Piaget, 1950, pp. 129–147.) Children below a certain age do not, for example, have notions of conservation, and they seem to acquire these notions at a relatively late stage of their development. Young children show amazingly 'illogical' behavior even in situations where they seem to be in possession of all the relevant knowledge necessary for a correct conclusion. A child may know that nothing has been added to or taken away from a piece of clay, and still assert that the amount of clay and the weight has increased or diminished when the form is changed from ball to sausage. Even when every possible precaution is taken to ensure that the child has grasped the essential elements of the situation, one may observe the same type of perception-bound, 'irrational' behavior.

We must conclude that the available evidence is clearly against the theory that logical structure follows automatically when the elements of a situation have been understood.

It is most tempting to apply some variant of *learning theory* to the developmental process. However, this application encounters a number of obstacles, some of which stem from the fact that it is so difficult to imagine how conservation can be established by external reinforcements in the normal life of children.

Let us begin with conservation of substance. According to Piaget & Inhelder (1941) this notion is established before conservation of weight and volume, i.e. before there exists any unequivocal empirical criterion of conservation. The subject cannot *observe* the conservation of substance during changes in form. On the contrary, his perceptual schemata lead him to suppose that the amount changes, and he has to fight to overcome the impact of how things 'look'. 'It *looks* as if there were more in the ball, but I *know* it can't be.' Thus, the child acquires conservation of substance by learning to *ignore* the appearance of things and his own direct experience.

In the experiment of melting sugar in water (Piaget & Inhelder, 1941), some children with conservation of substance asserted that the melted sugar was still there, even though they thought that the glass with the sugar would weigh exactly the same as the other glass with pure water, and that the water level would be the same in the two glasses. In this case, the child ignores the visual disappearance of substance, and asserts conservation without relying on a single empirical support. Even the taste is supposed to disappear after some time. It is difficult to imagine by what means children in normal conditions could be led by their observations to assume exact conservation of substance.

There are at least three possible auxiliary hypotheses, which depart more or less from a strict learning theory interpretation, but which nevertheless attribute a crucial role to external reinforcement.

1. The subject may have learned empirically that objects become larger when something is added to them and smaller when something is taken away. This may be generalized in some complex way to the class of situations where nothing is added or taken away and where consequently no change is assumed.

The difficulty with this explanation is that even very young children understand that nothing has been taken away or added in the conservation test, and still think that the amount of substance has increased or decreased. They do not appear to regard the absence of adding and taking away as a relevant argument for conservation, and this is really the crucial problem. Why does this argument suddenly become relevant and lead to the idea that conservation is logically necessary?

2. It may be thought that the discovery of *empirical reversibility*, i.e. the fact that one may return to the point of departure after a deformation, would be sufficient to induce conservation. More generally, the set of expectancies associated with other possible deformations remain unchanged by any given deformation, and by some complex mechanism this might lead to the notion of conservation.

A large amount of evidence shows that empirical reversibility cannot explain the acquisition of conservation. Even very young children know practically always that one may return to the starting point; the sausage can be remade into a ball that contains exactly as much plasticine as the unchanged standard. Even so, the sausage is seen as containing *more* or *less* plasticine than the standard! Finally, it should be noted that in the experiment with the melting of sugar, children assert conservation of substance even though the melting process is not empirically reversible in their field of experience.

3. One may assume that the lack of conservation of substance stems from a *difficulty of recall*, and that this can be improved upon by a process of 'learning to learn'. Perhaps the small child is unable to recall the initial state of equality, after just one presentation? This hypothesis is clearly contradicted by the available evidence, since the children, with few exceptions, do remember the initial state. However, they do not feel that the initial state of equality is relevant for the judgment of the state after the deformation, and learning theory probably cannot easily provide an explanation of how this is changed.

The preceding considerations are equally valid for conservation of weight. In this case, however, learning theory might seem to be in a somewhat better position, since weight is a directly observable factor. Perhaps children learn directly that weight does not change with changes in form? Again the answer seems to be negative. It is well known that the direct kinesthetic–tactile impression of weight is highly unreliable and extremely sensitive to irrelevant visual stimuli. We have repeatedly observed how children *confirm* their idea of non-conservation by weighing the objects in their hands. 'Yes, I can feel that the sausage is heavier than the ball'; 'the ball is much heavier now', etc. Again, we must conclude that the children acquire conservation *against* the perceptual appearance of things.

It has been suggested that children learn conservation of weight by means of scales. The answer to this is that children relatively seldom play with scales. Furthermore, the scales designed for children and available in the nurseries are technically rather primitive and do not easily lend themselves to any test of the principle of conservation.

A direct learning interpretation of the acquisition of conservation of weight also fails to explain why conservation of substance seems regularly to precede it genetically, although conservation of substance has no unambiguous observable referent.

Learning theorists may also try to explain the transition from non-conservation to conservation as a result of accumulated direct and indirect *social reinforcements*. We are aware of no evidence pointing to any direct training in these matters in the homes, and the sequential development of the various notions does not have any obvious connection with the teaching program in nurseries and schools. On the other hand, as mentioned above, several recent studies have shown an effect of children's socio-economic and cultural background on the speed of acquisition of the various concepts of conservation. This is in accordance both with a learning theory interpretation and an equilibration theory interpretation. The former would attribute the acceleration to a higher frequency of direct and/or indirect reinforcements, whereas the latter would assume that certain environments more frequently than others confront the child with complex intellectual problems, thus forcing him to organize his thinking.

Altogether, we may conclude that, despite apparent difficulties, one cannot discard the possibility of a learning theory interpretation of the acquisition of notions of conservation. Among recent authors on this subject, Apostel (1959) apparently believes in this possibility, whereas Berlyne (1960) introduces so many new assumptions into the Hullian framework that it becomes almost indistinguishable from the equilibration theory.

The *maturation theory* is in some ways a relatively plausible one. It takes account of the general observations of pre-logical behavior and of the absence of evidence for direct learning. The great difficulty from this point of view is (*a*) to explain the *time lag* between the occurrence of the various notions of conservation (Piaget, 1950; Vinh-Bang, 1959), and (*b*) to explain the accelerating *v.* retarding effects of the various environments. These two types of observations show that the maturation hypothesis is invalid as a general explanation, and that maturation can at most be a necessary condition for certain other processes to occur. The main problem is to discover the nature of these other processes.

Most of the arguments so far presented are not only *against* the three other interpretations, but also *for* the equilibration theory. The following tentative conclusions may be drawn from the preceding discussion; that the existing evidence seems to exclude nativism as a possible interpretation, and that maturation can at most be a contributing factor in providing the necessary neurological conditions for the acquisition of the successively more complex cognitive levels. The respective validities of learning theory and equilibration theory remain undetermined, although many findings seem to point against the former. In what follows, we will focus on the problem of how experience influences cognitive development, and on the question of learning *v.* equilibration. A brief review of some relevant earlier studies will conclude this introductory paper.

## RELEVANT PREVIOUS STUDIES

The direct predecessor of the present investigations was a study by Smedslund (1959). It was designed to show the effects of direct external reinforcement on the acquisition of conservation and transitivity of weight.

The experiment on conservation learning included three groups of subjects between 5;10 and 7;1, who consistently asserted non-conservation. Group A ($N = 8$) went through a series of 30 empirical controls on a pair of scales, permitting direct observation that objects do not change weight during deformation. Group B ($N = 8$) likewise had 30 controls on the scales, but 11 of the items of deformation were exchanged for items of addition and subtraction.

It was thought that if the learning theory interpretation were true, group A should learn more and faster than group B, since A had only direct reinforcements of the response category to be learned. On the other hand, equilibration theory would lead one to expect more improvement in group B, since this involved practice on the operations of addition and subtraction, whose combination is assumed to lie beneath the concept of conservation. ('Nothing is added and nothing is taken away.') Finally, there was a group C ($N = 5$) which did not take part in any practice sessions, and which functioned as a control.

There was a considerable amount of learning in both the experimental groups and no significant difference between them, although group A had slightly better results. Taken at their face value these results seemed to indicate that a concept of conservation of weight may be acquired as a function of external reinforcements. Furthermore, the slight advantage of group A over group B was in the direction of confirming the learning theory interpretation and went against the equilibration theory.

However, there are at least two alternative interpretations of the findings which, if true, would radically change the conclusions.

1. It is quite possible that what occurred was a simple response learning leading to a *pseudoconcept* without the quality of insight and necessity that accompanies the genuine concept. The genuine concept of conservation is inaccessible to experimental extinction, whereas the

outcome of simple response learning would presumably be easy to extinguish. In article III of this series the outcome of an experimental test of this possibility will be reported.

2. The possibility of an easy response learning in group B (the majority of the items involved simple deformations which were identical to those in group A), may have inhibited any tendency to active cognitive reorganization induced by the small number of addition/subtraction items; cf. the discussion of Greco's experiments below. A more crucial test would be to compare a condition with only addition/subtraction items with a condition with only deformation items. The outcome of such an experiment is described in article II of this series.

The experiment of Wohlwill (1959) on the acquisition of conservation of number is highly relevant for our purpose. A subject has conservation of number when he thinks that the number of objects in a collection must necessarily remain unchanged during changes in the spatial arrangement of the collection, as long as nothing is added or taken away.

Wohlwill posed the problem of whether conservation of number develops from the operations of adding and subtracting by means of some inferential process, or whether it results from direct reinforcement. He decided to check this by comparing the outcome of direct external reinforcement of conservation with the outcome of reinforcement of the operations of adding and subtracting.

The results show a not quite significant but highly suggestive superiority of the group trained on additions and subtractions as compared with the group trained directly on conservation over deformations. Since ordinary S-R learning principles would lead one to expect more learning in the latter group, this experiment represents a very suggestive strengthening of the equilibration theory. Wohlwill's data are at variance with our own, reported above, and this provided further encouragement to repeat our experiment with a more clearcut design involving only addition/subtraction items *v.* only deformation items.

The study of Greco (1959*a*) concerns the learning to understand successive spatial rotations. The materials were a cardboard tube and a wooden rod to which were fastened a black, a white, and a red bead, in that order. The rod with the beads is moved into the tube until it is completely hidden and the child is asked: 'Which color comes out first at the other end?' This simple question is answered correctly by most children at the age of 5–6 years. The tube with the rod inside is then rotated slowly and horizontally 180 degrees, once or twice, and the question of which color comes out is again asked. Greco was interested in whether young children could learn to understand the meaning of the successive rotations of the tube. To the adult the rotations form a kind of logical grouping. The rotations may be combined with each other to deduce the effect, and the outcome is considered as *logically necessary*. If red is expected to come out in the direct order, then black must come out after one rotation and red again after two rotations.

Greco's design involved two main experimental groups, D and S. The subjects in group D learned one rotation and two rotations separately to perfection, before they were presented with a mixed set of items containing both one and two rotations. The subjects in group S were mainly trained on the mixed set of items. The subjects in both groups learned to anticipate correctly the outcome of both one and two rotations. After a period of between one and three months a post-test was given to test the stability of the achievements. Furthermore, the *generalization* to *n* rotations was studied and the *transfer* to an analogous situation (a rotating disk with red and black placed in diametrically opposite positions). The data show a striking difference between the two groups. The children in group D had forgotten practically everything they had learned, whereas the children in group S had retained almost everything. The children in S also showed a considerable, but not complete generalization to *n* rotations and some transfer to an analogous situation.

Greco's conclusion is as follows. In this situation it is possible for most pre-school children to learn behavior that is seemingly equivalent to the performance of older children. However, this learning seems to proceed in two ways which lead to quite different results. The subjects in group D seemed to have learned the outcome of one and two rotations separately as empirical laws and with no understanding of their 'necessary' character. The subjects in group S never had a possibility to learn in this way; directly confronted with the more complex mixed set of items, they were probably forced into an intense 'structuring activity'. Apparently this led them to understand that two rotations represent the outcome of one rotation and another rotation.

These findings seem to strengthen the hypothesis that situations which permit simple response learning are detrimental to the occurrence of more profound cognitive reorganizations. Unfortunately, the two experimental conditions differed in several other respects, such as standardized *v.* clinical procedure and massed *v.* distributed practice. This makes the interpretation very uncertain.

The experiment of Morf (1959) concerned the acquisition of certain operations of class-inclusion. In a typical test the subject is presented with a collection of wooden beads, most of which are brown and a few are white. The subject is led to acknowledge explicitly that all the beads are made of wood and that most of them are brown and only a few are white. Finally, the following question is asked: 'Can you tell me whether there are more brown beads or more beads made of wood?' The typical answer of the 5–6 year old is: 'There are more brown beads because there are only two or three white ones.'

No amount of reformulation or rearrangement of the materials seems to bring these children to understand the correct answer. Morf wanted to find out whether it was possible for children to acquire the operations of class inclusion as a function of some kind of training or practice.

Very briefly, the findings were as follows: With a method of various empirical controls and with several concrete materials the outcome was completely negative as far as the correct answer was concerned. The outcome of a method of free play was likewise negative. A third technique tried to make the relations between the total class and the subclasses directly visible, but again there was no real learning. Finally, some success was obtained with a technique involving exercise of the operations of *logical multiplication.*

The children were trained in seeing objects as being simultaneously members of two or more classes, and this induced learning in 7 of 30 subjects. These results, as far as they go, are more in accordance with equilibration theory than with ordinary learning theories.

Churchill (1958) in a study of the acquisition of conservation of number, apparently succeeded in inducing conservation to a considerable extent, but the exact procedure is not given in the summary that has been available.

## TENTATIVE GENERALIZATIONS

The preceding experiments are mostly very complex and exploratory and have served to raise questions rather than answer them. Nevertheless, they permit us to formulate certain tentative generalizations, which may act as a frame of reference for further research.

1. The possibility of inducing a cognitive reorganization depends on the subject's already available schemata. If he has a structure which already approaches the given notion, the probability of the desired reorganization is high, whereas if he is still far from the notion, the chances are small that he will change sufficiently during a limited series of experimental sessions. Greco (1959*b*) was able to show that children of the same age as those in the experiment with the rotating tube were unable to learn an exactly analogous but purely empirical and arbitrary problem. The probable reason was that the subjects in the former experiment already had a beginning 'intuition' about the rotations, whereas the subjects in the latter experiment had to start from scratch. The studies of children's learning at different age levels by Greco (1959*b*), Goustard (1959), and Matalon (1959) all demonstrate directly how the ability to profit from experience depends on the initial developmental level.

2. Situations which permit immediate and simple response learning with empirical control are unlikely to lead to any profound cognitive reorganization. This is exemplified by Greco's group D and by our own groups A and B. For evidence supporting this interpretation see article III of this series.

3. Situations stressing empirical control, which do not permit simple response learning, may or may not induce a cognitive reorganization, which probably depends on the conditions mentioned under 1. Morf's groups with empirical control and our own experiment on learning of transitivity of weight (Smedslund, 1959) gave completely negative results. Correct inferences of transitivity and class-inclusion involve different stimuli and different responses in each new situation, and thus would be expected to yield little learning on the basis of current learning theories. These situations would also be expected to yield little improvement on the basis of equilibration theory, since they emphasize the empirical outcomes instead of the activities of the subject. Positive results were found in Greco's group S.

4. Direct exercise of the relevant operations is likely to induce cognitive change to the extent that the conditions mentioned under 1 are favorable. This is exemplified by Morf's group, trained on the multiplication of classes, and by Wohlwill's addition/subtraction group.

These are only vague statements with little predictive value. In the subsequent articles attempts will be made to determine the exact conditions for the acquisition of conservation of substance and weight and to construct a more specific theory.

This project has been supported by the Norwegian Research Council for Science and the Humanities.

REFERENCES

Apostel, L. (1959). Logique et apprentissage. *Études d'Épistémol. génét.*, *8*, 1–138.

Berlyne, D. (1960). Les équivalences psychologiques et les notions quantitatives. *Études d'Épistémol. génét.*, *12*, 1–76.

Churchill, E. M. (1958). The number concepts of the young child. Leeds Univer. Res. and Stud., No. *17*, 34–49 and No. *18*, 28–46.

Festinger, L. (1957). *A Theory of Cognitive Dissonance.* New York: Row, Petersen & Co.

Goustard, M. (1959). Étude psychogénétique de la résolution d'un problème (Labyrinthe en T). *Études d'Épistémol. génét.*, *10*, 83–112.

Greco, P. (1959*a*). L'apprentissage dans une situation à structure opératoire concrète: Les inversions successives de l'ordre lineaire par des rotations de 180°. *Études d'Épistémol. génét.*, 7, 68–182.

Greco, P. (1959*b*). Induction, déduction et apprentissage. *Études d'Épistémol. génét.*, *10*, 3–59.

Heider, F. (1958). *The Psychology of Interpersonal Relations.* New York: Wiley.

Hyde, D. M. (1959). An investigation of Piaget's theories of the development of the concept of number. Unpublished Ph.D. thesis, London Univ.

INHELDER, B. (1944) *Le diagnostic du raisonnement chez les débiles mentaux.* Neuchâtel: Delachaux & Niestlé.

LOVELL, K. (1960). A study of the concept of conservation of substance in the junior school child. *Brit. J. educ. Psychol.*, *30*, 109–118.

MATALON, B. (1959). Apprentissages en situations aléatoires et systematiques. *Études d'Épistémol. génét.*, *10*, 61–91.

MORF, A. (1959). Apprentissage d'une structure logique concrète (inclusion). Effets et limites. *Études d'Épistémol. génét.*, 9, 15–83.

PIAGET, J. (1950). *The Psychology of Intelligence.* London: Routledge & Kegan Paul.

PIAGET, J. (1957). Logique et équilibre dans les comportements du sujet. *Études d'Épistémol. génét.*, *2*, 27–117.

PIAGET, J., and INHELDER, B. (1941). *Le développement des quantités chez l'enfant.* Neuchâtel & Paris: Delachaux & Niestlé.

SLATER, G. W. (1958). A study of the influence which environment plays in determining the rate at which a child attains Piaget's 'operational' level in his early number concepts. Unpublished dissertation, Birmingham University.

SMEDSLUND, J. (1959). Apprentissage des notions de la conservation et de la transitivité du poids. *Études d'Épistémol. génét.*, 9, 85–124.

VINH-BANG (1959). Évolution des conduites et apprentissage. *Études d'Épistémol. génét.*, 9, 3–13.

VINH-BANG (in preparation). Elaboration d'une échelle de développement du raisonnement. Institut des Sciences de l'Éducation, Genève.

WOHLWILL, J. (1959). Un essai d'apprentissage dans le domaine de la conservation du nombre. *Études d'Épistémol. génét.*, 9, 125–135.

# TRAINING AND THE ACQUISITION OF THE CONSERVATION OF LENGTH IN CHILDREN

FRANK B. MURRAY

More surprising than the phenomenon of nonconservation, itself, is the finding in conservation training studies that even though the training methods seem "sound and reasonable and well suited to the educative job at hand, . . . most of them have had remarkably little success in producing cognitive change" (Flavell, 1963, p. 378). The evidence from training studies of the conservation of number, substance, weight, and length indicates that the child apparently cannot be taught the concept in question unless he has developed the particular cognitive structure in question, and the development of this structure does not seem significantly altered by external reinforcement or manipulation.

Smedslund (1961) proposed that a state of cognitive conflict was the precursor of the cognitive reorganization that was required to support conservation. He created the conflict by changing the shape of a clay ball to make it appear larger when a piece was taken away to make it actually lighter. In the training of length conservation, Smedslund (1963), using this method of juxtaposing competing forces, has had only mild success. The cognitive conflict technique used in the present study made the same stick appear longer and sometimes shorter than an equal length stick.

The technique was based primarily on the notion that the cognitive operations that support conservation are reversible, e.g., the operation that made the equal

Proceedings of the 75th Annual Convention of the American Psychological Association, 1967, pp. 297-298.

length sticks unequal can be undone by the inverse operation. To conserve any property the child presumably needs the rule that allows him to get from the original state to the transformed state and back again. The reversibility procedure produced a conflict between the original and transformed states that could be resolved by allowing *S* to perform the actions that connected the two states.

## Method

*Subjects*. The mean age for each grade was 5.76 yr., 6.71 yr., and 7.79 yr., kindergarten through second grade, respectively. The mean IQ from the SRA Primary Mental Abilities Test was 112.4 and 112.5 for the first and second grades; no test results for the kindergarten were available. There were in all 31 kindergartners, 42 first, and 46 second graders. All testing was done individually.

*Materials*. The materials for the length conservation test were: (*a*) ten round white sticks, two of which were the same length, four were unequally longer and the rest, shorter, (*b*) a black rectangular composition board on which were glued three cardboard figures—the arrows and feathers of the Muller-Lyer figure in horizontal position.

*Procedure*. The *E* took the two equal sticks that *S* had selected from those mentioned above and placed them uprightly side by side to enable *S* to reconfirm their equality, before *E* slowly placed them in the Muller-Lyer configuration to make their lengths appear unequal. One-half the *S*s in each grade had the "feathered figure" on the left and the rest had it on the right. *S*s were asked:

Does this stick (*E* pointed to the stick in the "feathered" configuration) look longer than this stick (*E* pointed to the arrowed stick), does it look the same length as this stick, or does it look shorter than this stick?

If *S* answered that the sticks looked the same length, i.e., he failed to see the illusion, he was discarded from the experiment.

The *S*s were asked a second question:

If the sticks were standing up the way they were before would this stick (*E* pointed to the stick in the feathered configuration) be longer than this stick (*E* pointed to the other stick), would it be the same length as this stick, or would it be shorter than this stick?

To nullify any leading influence the order of the alternatives (longer, shorter, the same length as) might have on the *S*s response, the order of the alternatives was varied randomly among the *S*s for both questions.

One week from the session in which the above procedures were administered, and after completing the procedures described in Murray (1967) *S*s who were scored as nonconservers on the Muller-Lyer problem were again given that length conservation test. All *S*s who could still be scored as nonconservers were randomly divided within each grade into a control group and an experimental group that would receive training in length conservation.

The control group *S*s met individually with *E* and were given the following tests: (*a*) the length conservation test on the Muller-Lyer described above, (*b*) a length conservation test in which the sticks were held by the experimenter in the form of the Oppel inverted *T* illusion, and (*c*) a size or area conservation problem in which two equal ring segments were held by *E* in the pattern of the Jastrow illusion.

In the inverted *T* problem, *S*s were asked (*a*) if the vertical stick looked longer, etc., than the horizontal one (*E* pointed to both sticks), and (*b*) if it was really longer, etc. In the Jastrow figure, *S*s were asked similar questions about the apparent and real size differences between the bottom and top ring segments.

Before the experimental group was subjected to the three conservation tests given to the control group, they were trained in the following manner: (*a*) the sticks in the Muller-Lyer figure were placed by the experimenter before the *S*s as before, but *S* was allowed to pick them up to confirm their equality and himself replace them in the distorting figure, (*b*) *S* was permitted to pick up and replace the sticks two more times, (*c*) *S* was directed to try switching the sticks, that is, replacing the one from the feathered configuration in the place of the one from the arrowed configuration and vice versa, and (*d*) *S* was permitted to switch the sticks two more times.

## Results

Each *S* was scored as having conserved length only if (*a*) he saw the Muller-Lyer illusion; that is, said the feathered stick looked longer, and (*b*) despite seeing the illusion maintained that the sticks were the same length. If *S* maintained that the sticks were unequal in length, he was scored, of course, as a nonconserver.

A median test was applied to the scores, and indicated a significant difference in conservation for the group above the median age (6.91 yr.) and for the group below it ($\chi^2 = 14.4$, $p < .001$).

On the Muller-Lyer length conservation task (Table 1) there were by the Fisher Test a significantly greater number of conservers from the training group than the control group ($p < .01$). On the test of length conservation transfer to the Oppel inverted *T* task, there were also by the Fisher Test a significantly greater number of conservers in the training group than the control group ($p < .01$), but on the Jastrow size or area conservation test the difference in conservers between the training and control groups was insignificant ($p > .10$). The significance levels are two-tailed and conservative since a greater number of conservers was predicted in the group that had training.

**TABLE 1**

**Number of Conservers (C) and Nonconservers (NC) in Length Conservation and Transfer of Length Conservation Tasks Between Training and Control Groups**

| Groups | Muller-Lyer Task* | | Transfer Tasks | | | |
|---|---|---|---|---|---|---|
| | | | Oppel T* | | Jastrow** | |
| | C | NC | C | NC | C | NC |
| Experimental N = 15 | 14 | 1 | 11 | 4 | 7 | 8 |
| Control N = 14 | 0 | 14 | 1 | 13 | 0 | 14 |

* $p < .01$.
** $p > .10$

## Discussion

As a result of reversibility and cognitive conflict training, nonconservers acquired conservation in the Muller-Lyer task they were trained on, and in the Oppel inverted *T* task on which they were not trained. Training did not seem to be effective in producing transfer to the area or size conservation task. It would seem that the conservations are acquired for each concept separately, although it could be, as Smedslund has shown, that conservation that is laboratory acquired may not have as much depth or generality as conservation that is "naturally" acquired.

Some reasons for the effectiveness of the training procedure can be speculated on. The success may result in part from the use of nonconservers whose age (median age 6.16 yr.) was close to the age that length conservation would begin to occur "naturally." Since forgetting the equality is not a significant factor in nonconservation, the child may lack an awareness of the possibility of return to the original situation. The child considers the two states to be static and separate, because the rules or action relating them are absent. Inhelder (1965) cites evidence to show that young preoperational children were unaware, for example, of the successive forms an arc would take in being straightened, while those that conserved could represent the intermediate stages of the transformation from arc to straight line. It could be argued that the present training procedure, by allowing the *S* to actively manipulate the sticks from one state to the other, facilitated *S*'s awareness of the relationship between the equal and unequal appearing states.

## REFERENCES


Flavell, J. *The developmental psychology Jean Piaget.* New York: Van Nostrand, 1963.

Inhelder, B. Operational thought and symbolic imagery. In Paul Mussen (Ed.) European Research in Cognitive Development. *Monograph of the Society of Research in Child Development,* 1965, *35,* 4–18.

Murray, F. Some factors related to the conservation of illusion-distorted length by primary school children. AERA Paper Abstracts 1967, 193–194.

Murray, F. Conservation of illusion-distorted length and illusion strength. *Psychonomic Science,* 1967, *7,* 65–66.

Smedslund, J. The acquisition of conservation of substance and weight in children. *Scandinavian Journal of Psychology,* 1961, *2,* 71–160.

Smedslund, J. Patterns of experience and the acquisition of conservation of length in children. *Scandinavian Journal of Psychology,* 1963, *4,* 257–264.

# Acquisition of Conservation through Social Interaction

FRANK B. MURRAY[1]
*College of Education, University of Delaware*

That so many reasonable attempts to train nonconservers in conservation have been surprising failures raises the question of how children normally acquire conserved concepts. In the *Language and Thought of the Child*, Piaget suggested originally that a necessary condition for the movement from the stage of preoperational or egocentric thought to more mature stages of thought was the occurrence of repeated communication conflicts between children. These conflicts would require the young child to attend to another child's point of view and perspective, and the ability to maintain a perspective of another or to take another's role appears to be related to operational modes of thought (Flavell, 1967) and to the opportunities for social interaction (Neale, 1966). Since nonconservation is the salient mode of preoperational thought, one would expect that an effective conservation training procedure would be one in which the child was confronted with opposing points of view. This expectation was investigated in an experiment and a replication experiment in which the child's point of view was brought into conflict with other children's points of view. Specifically it was expected that the young child's ability to give conservation judgments, and to support those judgments with adequate reasons, would improve after he had been subjected to the contrary arguments and viewpoints of other children.

## Method

### *Subjects*

In Experiment I, there were 57 white children, 28 boys and 29 girls, whose mean age was 6.70 years ($SD$ = .72 years) from kindergarten and first grades of a suburban Minneapolis elementary school. In Experiment II, there were 51 white children, 28 boys and 23 girls, with a mean age of 6.74 ($SD$ = .31 years) from the first grade of a suburban parochial elementary school in Wilmington, Delaware. The data were collected by female experimenters in a vacant classroom in the child's school during the months of November and December.

### *Procedure*

In the first of three sessions of both experiments, all subjects were given Form A of the Concept Assessment Kit (Goldschmid & Bentler, 1968), which provided a standardized and individual testing procedure for six conservation problems (two-dimensional space, number, substance, continuous quantity, weight, and discontinuous quantity). Two points were given for each correct problem, one point for a correct judgment and one point for an explanation that noted reversibility, compensation, or invariant quantity. In Experiments I and II, one noncon-

[1] The assistance of Anne Matthews at the University of Minnesota and Virginia Flynn at the University of Delaware and the cooperation of the children and staff at the Bloomington Elementary School and the St. Mary Magdalan Elementary School is greatly appreciated.

DEVELOPMENTAL PSYCHOLOGY, 1972, Vol. 6, No. 1, pp. 1-6.

server (subjects with scores from 0–4 on Form A) was grouped with two conservers (subjects with scores from 10–12 on Form A).

In a second session of both experiments, each group of three subjects was given the same problems from Form A of the Concept Assessment Kit. In each group, subjects were told that they could not receive a score until all of them agreed on the answer to each problem. Subjects were given 5 minutes to solve each problem. The experimenter started with the lowest scorers on Form A, and asked each child in a group to answer a problem, and when there was disagreement between children, they were directed to discuss the problem, and explain to each other why they had said what they had. Subjects were allowed to manipulate the conservation stimuli, but the experimenter gave no information or reinforcement for correct or incorrect answers.

One week later in the critical third session each subject was tested alone, as in the first session. Conservation problems from Form B, Form C, and lastly Form A of the Concept Assessment Kit were presented. Form B consisted of parallel problems on the same six concepts as Form A, but different conservation stimuli or different conservation transformations were used. Form C tested the conservation of two new concepts, length and area, with three area and three length conservation problems. As on Form A, each problem on Forms B and C, was scored one point for the correct judgment and a second point for the appropriate explanation of that judgment. Thus the maximum score on any form was 12.

### Results

Scores between 0 and 6 were taken to indicate nonconservation on that form, and scores between 7 and 12 were taken to indicate conservation. This somewhat arbitrary division preserved all the data and required that all children labeled as conservers give at least one acceptable reason for their conservation judgments. Since less than 9% of the children earned scores of 5, 6, 7, or 8 on any form, the dichotomy and labeling of the subjects was not inappropriate. The effect of the conflict situation on the nonconservers was evident in both experiments from the significant numbers of nonconservers on Pretest Form A who conserved on Posttest Form A, Posttest Form B, and Posttest Form C. In both experiments, the shifts from nonconservation to conservation were all significant at the .001 level by the McNemar test between Pretest Form A and Posttest Form A, between Pretest Form A and Posttest Form B, and between Pretest Form A and Posttest Form C (Table 1).

The effects of the conflict situation upon the nonconservers was also evident in both experiments in the comparison of their mean scores on the pretest with those on the posttests, which are presented in Table 2. The difference between the mean score of these subjects on Pretest Form A and the mean scores of subjects on Posttests Forms A, B, and C were all significant at the .001 level by the $t$ test (Experiment I, $t = 14.79$, $t = 11.57$, and $t = 7.99$, respectively; Experiment II, $t = 6.74$, $t = 7.32$, and $t = 7.51$, respectively).

Of special interest are 11 firm nonconservers in Experiment II who had scores of zero on Pretest Form A. Their mean scores on Posttests Form A, Form B, and Form C are presented in Table 2, and by the $t$ test these differences between the pretest mean and posttest means were significant at the .01 level. The remaining 15 nonconservers in Experiment II (scores between 1 and 6) had a mean score of 2.80 on Pretest Form A. The mean scores of these subjects on Posttests Forms A, B, and C are also presented in Table 2, and the differences between the pretest mean and posttest means were all significant at the .001 level by the $t$ test ($t = 7.11$, $t = 6.98$, and $t = 11.09$, respectively). Gains in conservation from pre-

TABLE 1

NUMBERS OF CONSERVERS (Cs) AND NONCONSERVERS (NCs) WHO SHIFTED OR WERE CONSISTENT IN EXPERIMENTS I AND II BETWEEN PRETEST FORM A AND POSTTESTS FORMS A, B, AND C, AND THE CHI-SQUARE FOR EACH COMPARISON

| Pretest | Posttest | | | | | |
|---|---|---|---|---|---|---|
| Form A | Form A | | Form B | | Form C | |
| | Cs | NCs | Cs | NCs | Cs | NCs |
| Exp. I ($N = 57$) | | | | | | |
| Cs | 40 | 0 | 40 | 0 | 38 | 2 |
| NCs | 16 | 1 | 15 | 2 | 14 | 3 |
| $\chi^2$ | 14.06** | | 13.06** | | 7.56* | |
| Exp. II ($N = 51$) | | | | | | |
| Cs | 25 | 0 | 25 | 0 | 24 | 1 |
| Ns | 18 | 8 | 19 | 7 | 21 | 5 |
| $\chi^2$ | 16.06** | | 17.05** | | 16.40** | |

* $p < .01$.
** $p < .001$.

TABLE 2

MEAN SCORES AND STANDARD DEVIATIONS FOR PRETEST A AND POSTTESTS A, B, AND C FOR CONSERVERS (Cs) AND NONCONSERVERS (NCs) ON PRETEST A IN EXPERIMENTS I AND II, AND FOR NONCONSERVERS WHO SCORED ZERO OR MORE THAN ZERO ON PRETEST A IN EXPERIMENT II

| Experiment | Test | | | | | | | |
|---|---|---|---|---|---|---|---|---|
| | Pretest A | | Posttest A | | Posttest B | | Posttest C | |
| | *M* | *SD* | *M* | *SD* | *M* | *SD* | *M* | *SD* |
| Exp. I | | | | | | | | |
| Cs | 10.77 | 1.3 | 11.90* | .4 | 11.55* | .8 | 11.40 | 1.9 |
| NCs | 2.35 | 1.9 | 11.41* | 1.4 | 10.18* | 1.9 | 8.82* | 2.6 |
| Exp. II | | | | | | | | |
| Cs | 10.37 | 1.8 | 11.91* | .4 | 11.87* | .4 | 11.08 | 1.9 |
| NCs | 1.61 | 1.8 | 8.08* | 4.4 | 8.38* | 4.2 | 8.19* | 3.9 |
| NCs who scored 0 | .00 | .0 | 6.00* | 4.9 | 7.09* | 5.1 | 5.73* | 4.7 |
| NCs who did not score 0 | 2.80 | 1.6 | 9.60* | 3.2 | 9.33* | 3.1 | 10.00* | 1.8 |

* Compared to Pretest A, $p < .01$.

TABLE 3

COMPARISON OF MEAN SCORES OF EXPERIMENTAL SUBJECTS ON PRETEST A AND POSTTESTS A, B, AND C WITH MEAN SCORES OF STANDARDIZED SAMPLE ON FORMS A, B, AND C

| Group | Test | | | | | | | |
|---|---|---|---|---|---|---|---|---|
| | Pretest Form A | | Posttest Form A | | Posttest Form B | | Posttest Form C | |
| | Girls | Boys | Girls | Boys | Girls | Boys | Girls | Boys |
| Standarized | 7.15* | 5.15* | 7.15** | 5.15** | 7.37** | 7.64** | 6.82** | 5.03** |
| Experimental | 7.72* | 6.77* | 10.52** | 11.25** | 10.48** | 10.66** | 10.38** | 10.03** |

* $p > .05$.
** $p < .01$.

test to posttest were compared for those subjects ($N = 11$) who had exhibited no conservation on the pretest and those ($N = 15$) who had exhibited some conservation on it. None of the contrasts was significant (Form A, $t = .54$, $p > .05$; Form B, $t = .24$, $p > .05$; Form C, $t = .89$, $p > .05$).

Another indicator of the effect of the conflict situation upon children's ability to conserve was found in the comparison of their performance on the pretest and posttests with the performance of an appropriate control group on Forms A, B, and C. Since the norms for the standardized sample are separated by sex for the Concept Assessment Kit, the appropriate boy and girl mean scores from the norms are presented in Table 3 for Forms A, B, and C along with the boy and girl mean scores from the experimental subjects for Pretest Form A and Posttests Forms A, B, and C. As they should be, the differences between the norm mean scores on Form A and experimental mean scores on Pretest Form A were insignificant by the $t$ test (girls, $t = .48$, $p > .05$; boys, $t = .97$, $p > .05$). However, all other differences between the norm mean scores on Forms A, B, and C and experimental mean scores on Posttests Form A, B, and C were significant at the .01 level (Form A: girls, $t = 3.06$, $p < .01$; boys, $t = 5.00$, $p < .01$; Form B: girls, $t = 2.66$, $p < .01$; boys, $t = 2.29$, $p < .01$; Form C: girls, $t = 4.24$, $p < .001$; boys, $t = 6.02$, $p < .001$).

Not only did the social conflict situation influence the nonconservers' performance on the posttests, it influenced as well the performance of the conservers. The mean scores of the conservers in both experiments on Pretest Form A and Posttests Form A, Form B, and Form C are presented in Table 2. The differences between these mean scores were significant between Pretest Form A and Posttest Form A, between Pretest Form A and Posttest Form B, but not between Pretest Form A and Posttest Form C (Experiment I: $t = 5.17$, $p < .001$; $t = 3.15$, $p < .01$; $t = 1.70$, $p > .05$, respectively; Experiment II: $t = 3.99$, $p < .001$; $t = 3.88$, $p < .001$; $t = 1.29$, $p > .05$, respectively).

In Experiment II, some of the first graders had attended kindergarten where it might be expected that the opportunities for social interaction and conflict would be greater than it would be for those children who had not attended kindergarten. This expectation was not supported by any significant difference in mean performance on Pretest Form A between those who had (6.06) and those who had not (5.81) attended kindergarten ($t = .18$, $p > .05$).

In both experiments there were no significant differences in the proportions of conservers and nonconservers on Pretest Form A between boys and girls (Experiment I, $\chi^2 = .53$, $p > .25$; Experiment II, $\chi^2 = .49$, $p > .25$). However there were the usual differences in these proportions between older and younger children in Experiment I, but not in Experiment II. In Experiment I, there were significantly fewer conservers and more nonconservers in the group below 6.66 years (median age) than in the group above it ($\chi^2 = 6.06$, $p < .02$); in Experiment II, there were insignificant differences in these proportions between the group above and below the sample's median age of 6.50 years ($\chi^2 = .94$, $p > .25$).

Although the principal findings of Experiment I were replicated in Experiment II, there were significant differences in the proportions of conservers and nonconservers in Experiment I and conservers and nonconservers in Experiment II on Pretest A ($\chi^2 = 4.18$, $p < .05$). The mean score for subjects in Experiment I was 8.16 and the mean score for subjects in Experiment II was 5.85 on Pretest Form A, and the difference in these means was significant ($t = 2.67$, $p < .02$).

## Discussion

The issue of whether or not conservation development can be accelerated is complicated in the research literature by theoretical doubts of its possibility, conflicting empirical results, and ambiguity in the criterion of conservation. Theoretically, conservation is taken to be one of many symptoms of concrete operational thought, and in a sense the manipulation of responses which indicate conservation is as trivial as any exercise that manipulates the symptom and not the disease. Although the acceleration of conservation responses without an attending presence of other aspects of operational thought may be an empty accomplishment in developmental theory, it is not one in education. The conservation response, regardless of its theoretical status, is an important behavior in itself for educational psychology. Procedures, like the present social conflict procedure, that induce or facilitate conservation behavior, and also have classroom applications constitute an important part of the psychology of curriculum and instruction.

The data indicate that social conflict or interaction is an important mediator of cognitive growth. Virtually all the children made significant gains in conservation performance after the social conflict situation. Since there were no significant differences in conservation performance between the children in the standardized sample and the children in both experiments on Pretest A, the standardized sample can serve as a control group. Performance on Posttests A, B, C was significantly higher than that of the standardized children on these tests, and indicates that the training effect cannot be attributed to retesting or maturation effects, although the effect may have been due to modeling and not the communication interaction (Waghorn & Sullivan, 1970), or to the efficacy of Lancastrian or peer instruction (Rothenberg & Orost, 1969). In general, conservation training studies have been most successful with nonconservers who were close to the threshold of conservation. However, there were no significant differences in the gains in conservation between those nonconservers who exhibited no conservation on the pretest and those who exhibited some conservation on the pretest. In fact, of 15 children from Experiments I and II who scored 0 on the pretest, 8 had scores of 11 or 12 on the posttests. It should be noted that these gains include the more demanding conservation criterion of an appropriate explanation for the conservation judgment. It should also be noted that there was considerable transfer to different forms of the same concepts and to different concepts.

Brison (1966) was able to induce some form of conservation in one-half of a group of nonconservers with a combination social training procedure and conflict-reversibility instruction. Since there was no deliberate instruction in the present experiments, the data emphasize the effectiveness of social interaction even in the absence of any systematic instructional effort. It was the case that the children often resorted to reversibility explanations to persuade their lagging colleagues, and that in the social situations nonconservers acquiesced and generally gave conservation responses after the third problem ($M = 2.76$) on Form A and generally (80%) did not give a nonconserving response after they had once given a conserving one.

It is not clear what the nonconservers learned in the social situation that sustained them in the individual situation. It probably was not a set to say, "the same," since all forms contained items in which the stimuli were unequal before the conservation transformation. The reversibility explanation for the conservation judgment, although strictly speaking incorrect (Murray & Johnson, 1969), and the invariant quantity explanation ("Your did not add or substract anything"; "they were the same before, and you didn't change the weight, etc.") could be used as rules that would lead to the correct response on all forms if the child had grasped the initial relationship (equal or unequal) between the stimuli before they were transformed. If these rules or algorithms were acquired, and the children's reasons indicate that in some sense they were, they would account for the very high level of performance on the transfer tasks, Forms B and C.

Smedslund (1966) in a review of the research on the many conditions that have been found to be inconsistently related to the acquisition of operational thought concluded that "the occurrence of communication conflicts is a necessary condition for intellectual decentration" and recommended that the key interaction needed for the growth of intelligence was not so much between the individual and the physical environment as it was between the individual and those about him. The present data support his hypothesis and emphasize, as Piaget has (Sigel, 1969), the educational role of social interaction in the transition from egocentrism to operational thought.

## REFERENCES

Brison, D. W. Acceleration of conservation of substance. *Journal of Genetic Psychology*, 1966, **109**, 311–322.

Flavell, J. Role-taking and communication skills in children. In W. Hartup & N. Smothergill (Eds.), *The young child*. Washington, D. C.: National Association for the Education of Young

Children, 1967.
GOLDSCHMID, M., & BENTLER, P. *Concept assessment kit-conservation manual.* San Diego: Educational and Industrial Testing Service, 1968.
MURRAY, F. B., & JOHNSON, P. E. Reversibility in the nonconservation of weight. *Psychonomic Science,* 1969, **16,** 285-287.
NEALE, J. M. Egocentrism in institutionalized and non-institutionalized children. *Child Development,* 1966, **37,** 97–101.
ROTHENBERG, B. B., & OROST, J. H. The training of conservation of number in young children. *Child Development,* 1969, **40,** 707–726.
SIGEL, I. E. The Piagetian system and the world of education. In D. Elkind & J. H. Flavell (Eds.), *Studies in cognitive development. Essays in honor of Jean Piaget.* New York: Oxford University Press, 1969.
SMEDSLUND, J. Les origines sociales de la centration. In F. Bresson & M. de Montmalin (Eds.), *Psychologie et épistémologie génétiques.* Paris: Dunod, 1966.
WAGHORN, L., & SULLIVAN, E. The exploration of transition rules in conservation of quantity (substance) using film mediated modeling. *Acta Psychologica,* 1970, **32,** 65–80.

# SKILL AND CONSERVATION:

## A STUDY OF POTTERY-MAKING CHILDREN[1]

DOUGLASS PRICE-WILLIAMS, WILLIAM GORDON
AND MANUEL RAMIREZ III
*Rice University*

A series of conservation tests of the Piaget type was given to Mexican children in two separate locations. The concepts investigated were those of number, liquid, substance, weight, and volume. Application of the tests followed the classic procedure of previous investigations, but translated into Spanish. An experimental group was composed of children who had grown up in pottery-making families. A control group was composed of children of matching age, years of schooling, and socioeconomic class, but whose families engaged in skills other than pottery making. The two locations were the town of Tlaquepaque, Jalisco, and the village of San Marcos, Jalisco. In the Tlaquepaque sample, there were 12 children in both the experimental and control group, all boys, composed of 3 children in each of the four age groups with an age range of 6–9 years. In the San Marcos sample there were 16 children in each of the two groups, 4 from each year group of 6 through 9.

The guiding principle behind the choice of selecting children versed in pottery making was that of the role of experience and specifically manipulation in the attainment of conservation. It was predicted that experience in pottery making should promote for these children earlier conservation in at least the concept of substance (in which clay is the experimental medium), while the question of transfer to other concepts of number, liquid, weight, and volume was left open.

Conservation was judged present if all answers were correct on all trials. In the Tlaquepaque sample, Fischer's exact probability test was used for each of the five conservation tests. Nonsignificant results were found on the four tasks of number, liquid, weight, and volume, but were found to be significant for substance ($p < .05$), in the direction of the pottery group. On all five tasks the potters' sons conserved more frequently than the other group, but not significantly. Overall, there was a one-third more conservation in the pottery group. Analysis of reasons given by the children in both samples, in equality or inequality, supported the direction of the quantitative results. The results of the San Marcos sample were more dramatic. Out of a possible 80 total, composed of five tests for 16 children, 77 of the sample showed conservation in the pottery group, while there were 10 only in the nonpottery group. The reasons given in either group supported the quantitative results.

This study suggests that the role of skills in cognitive growth may be a very important factor. Manipulation may be a prior and necessary prerequisite in the attainment of conservation, but a skill embodies a set of operations with a recognizable end—making cups from clay for example. The authors chose pottery making as the variable to be investigated for the study of conservation, but the craft of weaving may be another skill by means of which a child's appreciation of coordinate systems and one-to-one relationships could be tested.

[1] The study was funded by the Advanced Research Projects Agency under ARPA Order No. 738, monitored by the Office of Naval Research, Group Psychology Branch, under Contract No. N00014–67–A–0145–0001, NR 177–909.

DEVELOPMENTAL PSYCHOLOGY, 1969, Vol. 1, No. 6, p. 769.

# STIMULUS MODE AND THE CONSERVATION OF WEIGHT AND NUMBER[1]

FRANK B. MURRAY
*University of Delaware*

Highly insignificant differences in the proportions of conservers and nonconservers on three conservation of weight problems were found between four groups of second graders ($N = 80$) in which the stimuli were presented as (*a*) concrete objects, (*b*) photographs of the objects, (*c*) line drawings of the objects, or (*d*) verbal descriptions. This finding was found also with 33 kindergarten and first-grade subjects on three conservation of number tasks who received all four stimulus modes. However, significant differences in those proportions were found between older and younger subjects in both studies, and between higher and lower socioeconomic groups of subjects in the conservation of weight study. It was concluded that even the most obvious recommendations from Piaget's theory of cognitive development for instruction are empirically uncertain.

The recommendations from Piaget's theory of cognitive development for instruction, as Cronbach (1964) has noted, are not clear. At least two somewhat contradictory recommendations from the theory are consistent with it. One recommendation is that instruction should "match" (Hunt, 1961) in some artful way the level of cognitive development the child has attained. Bruner's (1961) often quoted maxim that any subject can be taught with integrity to a child at any age explicitly provided for a match between the child's cognitive structure and the character of the instructional effort. In the early grades, for example, instruction and curriculum would recognize and push the limitations of preoperational and highly egocentric thought, and would not presuppose or demand, for example, hypothetical and inferential thought, or awareness of proportionality. The theory predicted that not until early adolescence would cognitive structure have developed to assimilate less concrete and more logically complex forms of information. Moreover, instruction in concepts before the prerequisite schemata have developed could result in serious "misacquisitions" (Flavell, 1963, p. 365) often indicated by a superficial verbal fluency such as "counting" without number conservation.

The second recommendation requires that instruction not match the level of the child's intellectual development at first, but rather that it begin at the most primitive and basic levels of cognitive development and move quickly through the stages of the pupil's intellectual history. This recommendation has been made by Piaget's colleague, Hans Aebli, and is reminiscent of Werner's orthogenic and microgenic principles applied to the learning act in which the acquisition of a subject matter would recapitulate the stages in the development of the intellect. Since the principal concept in Piaget's theory is that mental operations are the result of the gradual transformation of overt actions, Aebli has suggested that instruction

might begin by having the child operate directly on physical entities, then on pictorial representations of these entities, then have him proceed to cognitive anticipation and retrospections of opera-

[1] This work was supported in part by a grant to the MINNEMAST Center at the University of Minnesota from the National Science Foundation (GE-3), and in part by grants to the University of Minnesota Center for Research in Human Learning from the National Science Foundation (GS-1761), the National Institute of Child Health and Human Development (HD-01136-04) and from the Graduate School of the University of Minnesota. The assistance of Dorothy Highland and Susan Nummedal was greatly appreciated. A shorter version of this research was presented at the annual meeting of the American Psychological Association in Washington, D. C., September 1969.

JOURNAL OF EDUCATIONAL PSYCHOLOGY, 1970, Vol. 61, pp. 287-291.

tions not actually performed at the moment, and so on, until the originally external actions can take place internally and in complete autonomy from the environment [Flavell, 1963, pp. 368–369].

In the present study, an aspect of this second recommendation was investigated. If the conservation stimuli were of different degrees of abstractness, one might expect that the acquisition of conservation behavior would be facilitated, or be more likely to occur, when the stimuli were more concrete than abstract. This expectation was investigated in an experiment on the conservation of weight (Experiment I) and an experiment of the conservation of number (Experiment II).

## Experiment I: Conservation of Weight

Four groups of second graders were presented with three conservation of weight problems in which clay balls and the conservation transformations were either shown, demonstrated, and described (Group 1), or shown in photographs and described (Group 2), or shown in line drawings and described (Group 3), or simply verbally described (Group 4). The descriptions in each mode were the same, except that in the fourth mode the description was introduced by the expression, "Imagine that."

### *Method*

*Subjects.* A random sample of 80 white second graders (mean age = 8.25 years, range 7.50–9.25 years) was drawn from four Minneapolis schools of three grossly different socioeconomic levels where the second grade unit from the Minnesota Mathematics and Science Teaching Project on weight had been completed. Subjects were randomly assigned to the four groups (concrete objects, photographs, drawings, and verbal descriptions) with the restriction that each group have 20 members and equal numbers of boys and girls.

*Materials.* The materials for each of the four treatment groups were respectively: (*a*) one green clay ball (6 centimeters in diameter) and two red clay balls (3½ centimeters and 8½ centimeters in diameter, respectively), (*b*) six black and white glossy prints (3½ × 3½ inches), one for the initial and one for the transformed stage of each of the three conservation problems, (*c*) green line drawings (11 × 14 inches) of each situation that was photographed, and (*d*) no objects or transformations shown, but verbally described.

*Problems.* Each subject in the four groups received in random order all three conservation problems, although between each group the style of stimulus presentation differed. For each problem, subjects were presented essentially with the green clay ball (or its more abstract counterpart) and after it was transformed (or the transformation described) the subject was asked if the transformed clay ball (or its counterpart) weighed the same as it had before the transformation, or if it weighed less than it had before, or if it weighed more than it had before. The order of the alternative parts of each question (same, more, less) was randomized for each subject. The transformations of the three problems (Problems 1, 2, and 3) were respectively: (1) a shape transformation in which the clay ball was rolled into a sausage, (2) a transformation in which the ball was divided into three pieces, and (3) a complicated transformation in which the green clay ball was placed first next to a larger red clay ball and then next to a small red clay ball and it was asked if the green clay ball weighed more, etc. when it was the larger of the two or when it was the smaller of the two.

### *Results*

Conservers on any problem were those who answered that the ball's weight was unchanged by the transformation, and nonconservers, of course, were those who answered that the ball's weight had changed. Seventy-three percent of the subjects conserved Problem 1, 72% conserved Problem 2, and only 26% conserved Problem 3; for each of the four groups, the problems were of unequal difficulty. (Cochran's $Q = 10.2$, $p < .01$; $12.1$, $p < .01$; $11.4$, $p < .01$; $14.0$, $p < .001$ for Groups 1–4, respectively). No significant differences in the proportions of conservers and nonconservers were found between the four groups on Problem 1 ($\chi^2 = 3.87$, $p > .20$), Problem 2 ($\chi^2 = 4.26$, $p > .20$), and Problem 3 ($\chi^2 = .84$, $p > .80$), or between the four groups when the criterion for conservation was that the subject answer at least two of the three problems correctly ($\chi^2 = 1.32$, $p > .70$).

To interpret this finding of the insensitivity of performance on the three conservation problems to differences in stimulus abstractness it is important to show that the performance was sensitive to the the usual independent conservation variables, such as age. By the same two-thirds correct criterion of conservation, there were significantly more conservers (34)

TABLE 1

NUMBER OF CONSERVERS (TWO-THIRDS CORRECT RESPONSES) AND NONCONSERVERS OF OBJECT, PHOTO, DRAWING, VERBAL STIMULUS MODES IN EXPERIMENTS I AND II

| Condition | Stimulus mode | | | |
|---|---|---|---|---|
| | Object | Photograph | Drawing | Verbal |
| Experiment I | | | | |
| Conservers | 12 | 15 | 13 | 12 |
| Nonconservers | 8 | 5 | 7 | 8 |
| Experiment II | | | | |
| Conservers | 22 | 21 | 20 | 20 |
| Nonconservers | 11 | 12 | 13 | 13 |

Note.—For Experiment I, $N = 80$; 20 in each group; for Experiment II, $N = 33$.

and fewer nonconservers (18) in the group above the sample's median age of 8.25 years than in the group below it in which there were 5 conservers and 23 nonconservers ($\chi^2 = 14.61$, $p < .001$). There were again no significant differences in the proportion of conservers and nonconservers between the four groups within the older group of subjects (Fisher test, $p > .05$) and within the younger group of subjects ($\chi^2 = .62$, $p > .80$). Within each school this no difference finding was also found.

When subjects from generally high-, middle-, and low-socioeconomic-level schools were matched for age, significant differences (Fisher test, $p < .05$) in the proportion of conservers and nonconservers were found between the middle (15 conservers and 8 nonconservers) and low groups (7 conservers and 13 nonconservers), but not between middle and high groups ($\chi^2 = .003$ $p > .90$). Sex and conservation were not related in the sample ($\chi^2 = 1.37$, $p > .10$).

## EXPERIMENT II: CONSERVATION OF NUMBER

In this experiment each subject received three conservation of number problems in not just one mode as in Experiment I, but in all four modes so that the effect of the concrete-abstract dimension could be measured within subjects rather than between them.

### *Method*

*Subjects.* All 33 subjects were participants in a summer school program administered by the Minnesota Mathematics and Science Teaching Project of the University of Minnesota. The mean age of subjects was 6.24 years; 15 subjects were to enter first grade and 18 were to enter second grade in the fall.

*Problems and procedure.* The three conservation of number problems were: (1) an identity conservation problem (Elkind, 1967) with one 3-inch horizontal row of three 1-inch things; (2) an identity problem with one 6-inch horizontal row of six 1-inch things, and (3) an equivalence conservation problem (Elkind, 1967) with two 6-inch horizontal rows, one evenly above the other, of six 1-inch objects. In the conservation transformation of each problem, the experimenter spread out evenly to the right the objects so that in Problem 1 the row was 6 inches long; in Problem 2 the row was 12 inches long; and in Problem 3 the bottom row was 12 inches long and even with a shorter row above it at the left extremity. As in Experiment I, subjects received the problems in random order for each of the four modes (objects, color photographs, black line drawings, and verbal descriptions).

Subjects were asked after each transformation, or its description, if there were the same number or a different number of things in the transformed row than before, and if they said there was a different number, they were asked if there were more or less things in that row. The order of the alternative parts of each question was randomized for each problem. In the equivalence problem, all subjects were asked if the two rows had the same number of objects before the transformation of the bottom row.

For each subject the three problems were presented in the four modes—(1) object, (2) photograph, (3) drawing, (4) verbal description—in one of four counterbalanced orders (1,2,3,4,; 2,4,1,3,; 3,1,4,2,; 4,3,2,1). Subjects were randomly assigned to each of these orders. There were also four differently shaped objects. (Playskool beads) which were randomly assigned to each mode of presentation so that each subject used the same shaped objects in the three problems of one mode, but used a different shape in each.

In sum, each subject received 12 problems—three conservation of number problems in the four modes of presentation described in Experiment I.

### *Results*

Conservers on each problem were those subjects who said that the number of objects remained the same after the transformation; nonconservers were those who did not. The proportions of subjects who conserved on at least two of the three problems in each mode and those who did not are also presented in Table 1, and the differences in those proportions are insignificant by the Cochran $Q$ Test ($Q = .89$, $p > .80$). Between the four modes the differences in the proportions of conservers and nonconservers were insignificant as well as by the Cochran $Q$ Test for Problem 1 ($Q = 1.83$, $p > .50$), for Problem 2 ($Q = 2.89$, $p > .30$), and for Problem 3 ($Q = 2.56$, $p > .30$). These findings were equally true for those subjects about to enter the first grade, and those about to enter the second grade (first grade: $Q = .25$, $p > .90$; $Q = 4.37$, $p > .20$; $Q = 3.24$, $p > .30$ and second grade: $Q = 4.67$, $p > .10$; $Q = .67$, $p > .80$; $Q = .75$, $p > .80$ for Problems 1, 2, 3, respectively.)

As in Experiment I, it is important to show that conservation was significantly related to the traditional age variable. In this study, there were 8 conservers (two-thirds criterion, or 8 out of 12 problems correct) and 12 nonconservers among the subjects under 7 years, and 10 conservers and only 3 nonconservers among the 7-year-olds (Fisher test, $p < .05$). However, the differences in the proportions of conservers and nonconservers between the three problems were insignificant by the Cochran $Q$ Test for each mode, (object: $Q = .13$, $p > .90$; photograph: $Q = 5.57$, $p > .05$; drawing: $Q = 1.29$, $p > .50$; verbal: $Q = .87$, $p > .50$). As in Experiment I, sex was unrelated to conservation.

Analysis of the differences in the proportions of conservation and nonconservation between the four counterbalanced orders, and between the overall sequences of modes for all subjects indicated that these differences were not significant.

## Discussion

In view of the concept formation and verbal learning literature on concrete-abstract variables as well as the variety of task and stimulus parameters that have now been shown to be related to the transition from nonconservation to conservation, it is surprising that conservation of weight and conservation of number were found to be so strongly insensitive to the concrete-abstract stimulus dimension and yet at the same time sensitive to the traditional conservation variables. Considering the number of nonconservers in Experiments I and II, particularly in the younger group where more than half the subjects were nonconservers and where the no difference finding was strong ($p > .80$), the results are all the more suprising since it is in this group that one would expect the concrete-abstract variable to have its maximum effect.

An argument could be made that the expected facilitation from the concrete mode was balanced by facilitation from the other conditions in which the transformation was simply described and therefore not as seductive as if it had been performed. Although their results are not supported by the present data, Shantz and Smock (1966) found, for example, more distance conservation with drawings than with objects ($p < .12$). The expected difficulty of the verbal condition, moreover, may have been mitigated by the lack of a perceptual confrontation that was most strongly present in the concrete condition. The importance of the perceptual confrontation in conservation has been emphasized by Frank (1966), but its importance has been challenged recently by Silverman and Marsh (1969). The matter of whether the transformation need actually be performed or only imagined by the subject is not clear in the literature. For example, Elkind (1961) found that as much conservation and nonconservation occurred when children predicted the outcome of a transformation before it was performed as when they judged the situation after it was performed. However, Smedslund (1963) and Pratoomraj and Johnson (1966) found more conservation when the outcome was anticipated or predicted than when the situation was judged after the transformation was actually performed. The present data, nevertheless, indicate that a transformation is as seductive when it is simply described and imagined by the subject as when it is actually performed.

Contrary to Elkind's (1967) expectation and Hooper's (1969) conclusions, no significant differences in conservation were found in the present data between identity and equivalence conservation problems in any of the four modes of presentation. Moreover, a close analysis of Hooper's (1969) findings indicates that the differences in the number of subjects conserving between the identity and equivalence conditions were quite small, and that the only significant difference between the conditions was found for subjects who were younger than the subjects of the present study, and not for subjects who were the same age or older than those of the present study.

Besides differing in the identity-equivalence task variable, the problems differed in the number of objects to be conserved, and the finding of no difference in conservation between those problems that differed in the number of objects to be conserved was found by Zimiles (1966) also.

The present data indicate that the concrete-abstract dimension is not a major dimension in the conservation assessment situation, although it very well may be that training procedures based on that dimension would be effective. In this regard, one of the four orders of mode presentation in Experiment II [namely, (1) object, (2) photograph, (3) drawing, and (4) verbal] can be viewed as an appropriate training sequence for the second recommendation discussed earlier. Of the nine subjects who received the modes in this order, there were by the two-thirds criterion 5, 4, 6, and 6 conservers, respectively, with each mode. The numbers are too small to interpret and afford only the loosest speculation, but such speculation should note that the number of conservers when the modes were presented in the opposite order were 2, 3, 4, and 4, respectively, for the eight subjects who received the modes in this order, namely, 4, 3, 2, 1. Further research with larger samples might make the interpretation of this apparent improvement with two opposite training orders more obvious.

Although teachers may have been correctly admonished since Pestalozzi, Montessori, Dewey, and now Piaget to begin instruction with the concrete form of the thing to be learned, the theoretical and empirical support for the admonition is not clear.

## REFERENCES


Bruner, J. S. *The process of education.* Cambridge, Mass.: Harvard University Press, 1961.

Cronbach, L. Learning research and curriculum development. In E. Ripple and V. N. Rockcastle (Eds.) *Piaget rediscovered: A report of the conference on cognitive studies and curriculum development.* Cited by J. S. Bruner, *On the conservation of liquids.* 1964, 73–77. Ithaca, N. Y.: Cornell University, School of Education.

Elkind, D. Children's discovery of the conservation of mass, weight, and volume: Piaget replication study II. *Journal of Genetic Psychology,* 1961, **87**, 219–227.

Elkind, D. Piaget's conservation problem. *Child Development,* 1967, **38**, 15–27.

Flavell, J. *The developmental psychology of Jean Piaget.* New York: Von Nostrand, 1963.

Frank, F., R. Oliver, & P. Greenfield. In, J. S. Bruner (Eds.), *Studies in cognitive growth.* New York: Wiley, 1966.

Hooper, F. Piaget's conservation tasks: The logical and developmental priority of identity conservation. Paper presented at the meeting of the Society for Research in Child Development, Santa Monica, March 1969.

Hunt, J. McV. *Intelligence and experience.* New York: Ronald Press, 1961.

Pratoomraj, S., & Johnson, R. Kinds of questions and types of conservation tasks as related to children's conservation responses. *Child Development,* 1966, **37**, 343–353.

Shantz, C., & Smock, C. Development of distance conservation and the spatial coordinate system. *Child Development,* 1966, **37**, 943–948.

Silverman, I., & Marsh, K. On the production of images within the conservation experiment. Paper presented at the meeting of the Society for Research in Child Development, Santa Monica, March 1969.

Smedslund, J. Patterns of experience and the acquisition of conservation of length. *Scandinavian Journal of Psychology,* 1963, **4**, 257–264.

Zimiles, H. The development of conservation and differentiation of number. *Monographs of the Society for Research in Child Development,* 1966, **31**(6, Whole No. 108).

# Comments on the INRC Group

J. A. Easley, Jr.

*University of Illinois, Urbana, Illinois*

A matter of concern to me and several others has been how we can apply Professor Piaget's theory, because application seems to require deduction of new consequences from the theory. If the theory is not clearly formulated in our minds, if we cannot translate the theory into terms that we understand, we cannot carry out deductive reasoning from the theory. So I think that precise formulation is an important goal. I understand that some important work is going on in this direction, but I have been able to keep up only to a very small extent.

I have tried to work out the connection between the INRC group and the snail problem to see how this abstract group applies to a particular problem. I would like to be able to deduce some consequences of the acquisition of the INRC structure, a structure characterizing the stage of formal operations, which I can test in the classroom. In fact, I have a very immediate motive for doing so. I have seen children solve problems very much like the snail problem at a very young age. The question is, can children solve the snail problem by the age of seven or eight (which seems much too young for formal operations), after a period of instruction? Is this acceleration to the formal level, or is this something else that is not properly called formal? Because we think there is an apparent conflict, the question of deduction arises.

Now, very briefly, as I understand from the literature, the INRC group is a set of four operations or transformations applied to logical formulas rather than to physical objects. As I understand it, one could take any logical formula and could transform it according to each of these transformations. The first one is identity (I); if I start with $p \vee q$, then I write the formula, $p \vee q$. The second one is negation (N); if I start with $p \vee q$, I get either the negation of that, $\sim (p \vee q)$, or I write it this way: $\sim p \wedge \sim q$, which can be shown equivalent by truth tables. The third transformation (R) is a little more unusual. This is the negation of both the $p$ and the $q$, $\sim p \vee \sim q$. That is, I write the negation of each of the propositional variables and I keep the operator. In the last one (C), I copy the variables but I change the operator giving me $p \wedge q$. Now, if these are correct illustrations of the application of these transformations, one can set up the

JOURNAL OF RESEARCH IN SCIENCE TEACHING, 1964, Vol. 2, pp. 233-235.

group multiplication table INRC, and fill it in by composition, that is, by applying each operator to the result obtained from any one of the operators and finding which operator gives the result equivalent to the two successive transformations. This leads to one of the two *four-groups* of mathematics, so these logical transformations provide a sort of definition of the INRC group. They tell me what the structure of the INRC group is.

| | I | N | R | C |
|---|---|---|---|---|
| I | I | N | R | C |
| N | N | I | C | R |
| R | R | C | I | N |
| C | C | R | N | I |

Now the question is, how does this structure apply to the problem of the snail? The snail has two possible motions of translation, which I will represent as S, going to the right, and ⁻S going to the left. The board similarly has two motions B and ⁻B, and the question is how do the INRC operations relate to this problem? In particular, Professor Piaget gave a formula for this problem which considerably puzzled me: IN = RC = 0.

One has to reinterpret somewhat the meanings of the four operations (INRC) as they apply to the four translations. Instead of using logical formulas we will use 'S', '⁻S', 'B', and '⁻B' for the snail-board operations, but interpreting these symbols as statements. 'S' means the snail moves to the right. '⁻S' means the snail moves to the left. 'B' means the board moves to the right, and '⁻B' means the board moves to the left. Now the identity transformation (I) leaves them unchanged. The negation (N) reverses the direction of motion. R reverses the directions and interchanges the objects, for example, R transforms 'B' to '⁻S' and '⁻B' to 'S'. C is most conveniently interpreted by composition of N and R. I won't go through the demonstration, but the INRC table above shows that to apply C, you first transform a statement by N and then you transform the result by R. Here is the result:

| | S | ⁻S | B | ⁻B |
|---|---|---|---|---|
| I | S | ⁻S | B | ⁻B |
| N | ⁻S | S | ⁻B | B |
| R | ⁻B | B | ⁻S | S |
| C | B | ⁻B | S | ⁻S |

If this is the correct application of this set of four operations to these snail-board statements, then from this we can derive a table predicting the results of combinations of any pair of them. Consider 'X' to be a statement describing any one of the snail-board translations. We can add these snail-board translations, so we agree to write X + N(X) = 0. This means, for example, move the snail to the right, then move him to the left, and the result is the equivalent of doing nothing. We can also write, X + IN(X) = 0, since the identity (I) does not change anything. Also, you get the same result by adding X + RC(X). For instance, you can take ⁻S + RC(⁻S) = ⁻S + R(⁻B) = ⁻S + S = 0. Both sums are 0, so the equations 'IN = RC = 0' now begin to make sense.

From the above table, you can in this fashion derive the table of results of any combinations of two different translations you may wish to present. For example, you may ask a child what happens if the snail moves to the right and the board moves to the left, etc. You can put each of these four translations against the others. The resulting table, which I will not take time

| | S | ⁻S | B | ⁻B |
|---|---|---|---|---|
| S | | 0 | + | 0 |
| ⁻S | 0 | | 0 | - |
| B | + | 0 | | 0 |
| ⁻B | 0 | - | 0 | |

to explain, presents the answers to all possible questions—the combinatorial analysis, presumably, which for Piaget is the mark of thought at the formal stage.

My resulting question is: To infer that the child possesses an INRC cognitive structure, is it sufficient that the child answer all of these questions correctly? If the child answers all these questions correctly, is the child then at the level of formal operations? It seems to me that quite young children, after instruction or work with examples of relative motion, can answer these questions correctly.